WORD
MEANINGS
in the
New Testament

5

WORD MEANINGS
in the
New Testament

volume 5
PHILIPPIANS—PHILEMON

by
Ralph Earle, Th.D.

BAKER BOOK HOUSE
Grand Rapids, Michigan

Contents

Preface

The generous reception given to volume 3 of *Word Meanings* (on Romans) has been encouraging. Herewith we present volume 5, covering the Books of Philippians, Colossians, 1 and 2 Thessalonians, 1 and 2 Timothy, Titus, and Philemon. Volume 4, which will contain 1 and 2 Corinthians, Galatians, and Ephesians, will be next in line in the series. These three volumes will cover all of Paul's Epistles, which comprise 13 of the 27 books of the New Testament.

The completed project calls for volume 6 to cover Hebrews—Revelation. Volume 1 is planned for the three Synoptic Gospels and volume 2 for John and Acts.

It should be emphasized that this work is written primarily for preachers and studious laymen, not scholars. For this reason all Greek words are transliterated, and the discussion is at a practical rather than technical level. The author, who has been teaching the Greek New Testament for 44 years, is eager to share with his fellow preachers of the Word some of the riches that lie in the Greek text.

Several good English versions of the New Testament have appeared in recent years. But no translation can possibly bring out the varied nuances of the Greek. That is why word studies are important for anyone who would adequately understand and expound the Word of God. May the present work contribute toward that end.

—RALPH EARLE

Abbreviations and Acknowledgments

(For additional abbreviations, see vol. 3.)

Abbott	T. K. Abbott, *A Critical and Exegetical Commentary on the Epistles to the Ephesians and to the Colossians.* "International Critical Commentary" (Edinburgh: T. & T. Clark, 1897).
AG	W. F. Arndt and F. W. Gingrich, *A Greek-English Lexicon of the New Testament and Other Early Christian Literature* (Chicago: University of Chicago Press, 1957).
Bernard	J. H. Bernard, *The Pastoral Epistles.* "Cambridge Greek Testament" (Cambridge: University Press, 1899).
CGT	Cambridge Greek Testament
DNTT	*The New International Dictionary of New Testament Theology,* ed. Colin Brown (Grand Rapids, Mich.: Zondervan Publishing House, 1975), vol. 1.
Eadie	John Eadie, *Commentary on the Epistle to the Colossians* (Reprint ed., Grand Rapids, Mich.: Zondervan Publishing House, 1957).
Ellicott	on Philippians, Colossians, Philemon: Charles J. Ellicott, *Commentary on St. Paul's Epistles to the Philippians, Colossians, and to Philemon* (Andover, Mass.: Warren F. Draper, 1890). on 1 & 2 Timothy, Titus: Charles J. Ellicott, *Commentary on the Pastoral Epistles* (Andover, Mass.: Warren F. Draper, 1890).
ERV	English Revised Version.

Frame	James E. Frame, *A Critical and Exegetical Commentary on the Epistles of St. Paul to the Thessalonians.* "International Critical Commentary" (Edinburgh: T. & T. Clark, 1912).
ICC	*International Critical Commentary*
Lightfoot	on Philippians: J. B. Lightfoot, *Saint Paul's Epistle to the Philippians* (Reprint ed., Grand Rapids, Mich.: Zondervan Publishing House, 1953). on Colossians, Philemon: J. B. Lightfoot, *Saint Paul's Epistle to the Colossians and to Philemon* (Reprint ed., Grand Rapids, Mich.: Zondervan Publishing House, n.d.). on Thessalonians: J. B. Lightfoot, *Notes on the Epistles of St. Paul* (Reprint ed., Grand Rapids, Mich.: Zondervan Publishing House, 1957).
Lock (ICC)	Walter Lock, *A Critical and Exegetical Commentary on the Pastoral Epistles.* ICC (Edinburgh: T. & T. Clark, 1924).
Meyer	H. A. W. Meyer, *Critical and Exegetical Handbook to the Epistles to the Philippians and Colossians, and to Philemon* (New York: Funk & Wagnalls, 1885).
Milligan	George Milligan, *St. Paul's Epistles to the Thessalonians* (Reprint ed., Grand Rapids, Mich.: Wm. B. Eerdmans Publishing Co., 1952).
NIV	*New International Version* (NT, 1973).
NT	New Testament
NTW	William Barclay, *A New Testament Wordbook* (London: SCM Press, 1955).
OT	Old Testament
Simpson	E. K. Simpson, *The Pastoral Epistles* (Grand Rapids, Mich.: Wm. B. Eerdmans Publishing Co., 1954).
TCNT	*Twentieth Century New Testament* (New York: Fleming H. Revell Co., 1904, rev. ed.).

Vincent (ICC)   Marvin Vincent, *A Critical and Exegetical Com-
                 mentary on the Epistles to the Philippians and
                 to Philemon.* ICC (Edinburgh: T. & T. Clark,
                 1897).

WM   Ralph Earle, *Word Meanings in the New Testa-
                 ment.* Vol. 3 (Kansas City: Beacon Hill Press of
                 Kansas City, 1974).

PHILIPPIANS

꧁ঔৣ꧂

Bishops (1:1)

The Greek word for "bishop" is *episcopos* (cf. *episco-pal*). It occurs five times in the NT. In Acts 20:28 it is translated "overseers." In 1 Pet. 2:25 it refers to Christ, "the Shepherd and Bishop of your souls." It is found twice in the Pastorals (1 Tim. 3:2; Titus 1:7) and is correctly translated "bishop." ("Office of a bishop" in 1 Tim. 3:1 is another word, *episcopē*.) Critics have sometimes insisted that the technical use of *episcopos* for "bishop" in the Pastoral Epistles reflects a later development in church organization and so demands a second-century date for these letters. But the same usage here in Philippians (written about A.D. 61) undercuts that argument.

The word *episcopos* comes from *scopos*, "a watcher." So it means "a superintendent, guardian, overseer" (A-S). Thayer notes that it has this same comprehensive sense in Homer's *Iliad* and *Odyssey* and in classical Greek writers from that time on (p. 243). The large *Lexicon* of Liddell-Scott-Jones (1940) gives as the first meaning of *episcopos* "one who watches over," and lists numerous examples of this use (p. 657). "This was the name given in Athens to the men sent into subdued states to conduct their affairs" (Cremer, p. 527). The word was used 14 times in the Septuagint in the sense of "overseer," or "inspector." Deissmann notes that in Rhodes, *episcopos* was "a technical term for the holder of a *religious* office" (in the temple of Apollo), as well as being used in the plural for "communal officials" (BS, pp. 230-31).

Lightfoot mentions its use at Athens, and adds: "The title however is not confined to Attic usage; it is the designation for instance of the inspectors whose business it was to report to the Indian kings . . . ; of the commissioner appointed by Mithridates to settle affairs in Ephesus . . . ; of magistrates who regulated the sale of provisions under the Romans . . . ; and of certain officers in Rhodes whose functions are unknown" (p. 95).

Beyer writes: "In Greek *episcopos* is first used . . . with a free understanding of the 'onlooker' as 'watcher,' 'protector,' 'patron.'" Then it came to be used "as a title to denote various offices" (TDNT, 2:609). He notes that protective care is "the heart of the activity which men pursue as episcopoi" (TDNT, 2:610). This is its classical usage.

By the end of the second century we read of diocesan bishops. Early in the second century Ignatius indicates that in each church there was one bishop, a group of presbyters, and a group of deacons. But in Paul's Epistles (here and in the Pastorals) "bishop" and "presbyter" seem to be used synonymously. Lightfoot observes: "It is a fact now generally recognized by the theologians of all shade of opinion, that in the language of the New Testament the same officer in the Church is called indifferently 'bishop' *(episcopos)* and 'elder' or 'presbyter' *(presbyteros)*" (p. 95). In TDNT, Coenen thinks it "probable that the terms *presbyteros* and *episcopos* (bishop) are interchangeable" (1:199).

Deacons (1:1)

The word *diaconos* occurs no less than 30 times in the NT. But it has the technical meaning of "deacon" only 3 times—here and in 1 Tim. 3:8, 12. Elsewhere in the KJV it is translated "minister" 20 times and "servant" 7 times. But since "minister" usually carries an ecclesiastical connotation today, it would be better rendered simply as "servant" (except in the 3 passages noted above).

Thayer defines the word thus: "one who executes the commands of another, especially of a master; a servant, attendant, minister"; it was also used for "a waiter, one who serves food and drink" (p. 138).

In pre-Christian inscriptions the term was already employed for an *"attendant* or *official* in a temple or religious guild" (LSJ, p. 398). From this it was an easy transition to the church "deacon."

Moulton and Milligan cite approvingly Hort's rendering of this passage: "with them that have oversight, and them that do service" (VGT, p. 245). But it seems better to take "bishops and deacons" as referring to the titles of officers in the church.

Prayer or Request? (1:4)

"Always in every prayer of mine for you all making request with joy." But "prayer" and "request" are the same word in Greek, *deēsis*. The word literally means "a wanting, need," and so "an asking, entreaty, supplication" (A-S, p. 99). Probably the two occurrences of the term should be rendered consistently: "always in every prayer of mine for you all making my prayer with joy"

(RSV)—an excellent literal translation of the Greek (cf. NASB, NIV).

Fellowship or Partnership? (1:5)

Paul thanks God for the "fellowship" of the Philippians in proclaiming the gospel. The word is *koinōnia*. It is translated "fellowship" in Gal. 2:9; Eph. 3:9; and 3 times in this Epistle (1:5; 2:1; 3:10), as well as 4 times in 1 John (1:3 [twice], 6, 7). Altogether it occurs 20 times in the NT.

H. A. A. Kennedy notes that the reference here is to "their common participation with Paul in spreading the Gospel" (EGT, 3:418). So it would seem better to translate the term as "partnership" (RSV, NIV).

Perform or Complete? (1:6)

Paul expresses his confidence that the One who had begun a good work in his readers would "perform" it until the day of Jesus Christ. The Greek verb is *epiteleō* from *epi,* "upon," and *telos,* "end." So it clearly means "to complete, accomplish, execute" (A-S, p. 175). Occurring 11 times in the NT, it is translated 7 different ways in KJV. The best rendering here is "bring it to completion" (RSV, NEB, Berk.).

I or You? (1:7)

A good example of the perplexing ambiguity sometimes found in the Greek NT is furnished by this verse. The second clause reads, "because I have you in my heart" (KJV, ASV). But the margin of the ASV has "ye have me in your heart." Which is correct?

The problem arises because of the difference in Greek and English idiom and the presence of two accusatives with the infinitive *echein.* Very literally the Greek reads: "On account of the to have me in the heart you." A. T. Robertson writes: "One accusative is the object of the infinitive *echein,* the other is the accusative of general reference. There is no way to decide which is the idea meant except to say that love begets love" (WP, 4:436). That is, the pastor's love for his people will beget in their hearts a love for him. This seems to be the most natural way to take Paul's statement: He holds the Philippian Christians in his heart (cf. RSV). The majority of the translators have taken it this way. Exceptions are: "you have me in your hearts" (Ballantine) and "you hold me in such affection" (NEB). We prefer "I have you in my heart" (NIV).

Bowels or Affection? (1:8)

This verse provides one of the best examples of the fact that a literal translation may actually be an incorrect translation. Paul says that he longs after the Philippians in the "bowels" of Jesus Christ.

The Greek word is *splanchnon,* which means "bowels" or "inward parts." It is used literally of these physical organs in Acts 1:18. But elsewhere in the NT (10 times) it is employed metaphorically. The Greeks thought of the bowels as the center of affection. But we use the term "heart" for that. So the translation "bowels" here is actually misleading. Not only does it convey entirely the wrong idea, but it is apt to start the mind off on a sidetrack of unpleasant thought that will divert the attention away from the true meaning of the passage. Therefore any well-informed person reading the Bible in public will change the word "bowels" to something else like "tender mercies" (ERV, ASV) or "affection" (RSV, NASB, NIV). In Acts 1:18, where the word is used literally, "bowels" could be changed to "inward parts."

It is interesting to note that in Luke 1:78 the King James translators rendered what is literally "bowels of mercy of our God" as "tender mercy of our God." Evidently they balked at speaking of the bowels of God! But is "bowels of Jesus Christ" in our present passage any better? In 2 Cor. 7:15 they rightly used "inward affection" for *splanchnon*.

Judgment or Discernment? (1:9)

The last word translates a Greek term found only here in the NT—*aisthēsis*. Thayer defines it as: "perception . . . cognition, discernment" (p. 17). The last of these terms is perhaps the best rendering here (so ASV, RSV, NASB), or "insight" (NIV). Arndt and Gingrich suggest, *"become rich in every* (moral) *experience"* (p. 24).

Approve the Excellent (1:10)

This phrase is translated much the same way in KJV, ERV, ASV, RSV, and NASB. Phillips suggests: "recognize the highest and best." *The Berkeley Version* has "distinguish differences." Weymouth comes perhaps closest to the Greek when he renders it "testing things that differ." One of the most striking translations is that of Moffatt: "enabling you to have a sense of what is vital" (cf. Goodspeed). This is one of the many passages in the NT where a comparison of different translations and versions can add much richness to one's study and preaching. "Discern what is best" (NIV) puts it very simply.

Sincere (1:10)

The Greek word is *heilikrines,* found only here and 2 Pet. 3:1, where it is translated "pure." Its basic meaning

is "unmixed." Buechsel writes: *"Heilikrines* derives from
heile (halea, hēlios), meaning 'warmth or light of the sun,"
and *krinō,* so that the full sense is 'tested by the light of
the sun,' 'completely pure'" (TDNT, 2:397). He goes on to
say that the word always denotes "moral purity" (p. 398).
C. B. Williams translates the whole phrase: "Be men of
transparent character and blameless life"—a very meaningful wording. After considering this possibility, however,
Trench writes: "It is not so much the clear, the transparent, as the purged, the winnowed, the unmingled" (p. 319).

In either case, the idea of purity or sincerity is dominant. Barclay favors combining the two figures of suggested etymologies. He writes: "The Christian purity is a
purity which is sifted until the last admixture of evil is
gone, a purity which has nothing to conceal and whose
inmost thoughts and desires will stand the full glare of the
light of day" (NTW, p. 33).

Furtherance or Progress? (1:12)

The word is *prokopē.* It literally means "a striking
forward." First indicating progress on a journey, it came to
be used metaphorically for progress in any realm. The best
translation is "progress" (ASV, NASB)—here and in the
other two places where the word occurs (v. 25; 1 Tim. 4:15)
—or "advance" (NIV).

Palace or Praetorian Guard? (1:13)

Paul tells the Philippians that his "bonds in Christ"
—that is, his imprisonment in the cause of Christ—have
become well known in the whole "palace." The Greek
word is *praitōrion.* Elsewhere in the NT it is found once
each in Matthew, Mark, and Acts, and four times in John.
It is translated "common hall" in Matt. 27:27, and "Prae-

torium" in Mark 15:16. In John and in Acts 23:35 it is
rendered "judgment hall" (once "hall of judgment"). In
each of these cases it refers to the governor's palace. But
what does it mean in Philippians?

The first use of *praitōrion* (which comes from the Latin) was for the headquarters in a Roman camp, the
tent of the commander in chief. Then it was used (as in the
Gospels and Acts) for the palace in which the governor of
a province resided. In the third place it referred to the
camp of Praetorian soldiers (Thayer, p. 534).

The most thorough treatment of this term is in the
commentary by Lightfoot. He calls attention to the fact
that the Greek fathers interpreted the word here as referring to the imperial palace at Rome. But he affirms: "Not
a single instance of this usage has been produced. . . . the
imperial residence on the Palatine is not once so called"
(p. 100).

Lightfoot declares that a second interpretation—the
Praetorian barracks attached to the palace—"is equally
destitute of authority" (p. 101). The same can be said for a
third suggestion, that it refers to the great camp of the
Praetorian soldiers. He concludes: "All attempts to give a
local sense to 'praetorium' thus fail for want of evidence"
(*ibid.*).

What, then, does it mean? "Praetorium signifies not a
place, but a body of men"; it most frequently "denotes
the praetorian regiments, the imperial guards" (pp. 101-2).

This fits best with the phrase which follows. In KJV
this reads: "and in all other *places.*" It will be noted that
"places" is in italics, indicating that it is not in the original. The Greek simply says "to [or 'in'] all the remaining."
This can mean remaining people or places. Probably the
best translation is still that of the ASV (1901): "throughout the whole praetorian guard, and to all the rest," or
"throughout the whole palace guard and to everyone else"

(NIV). Arndt and Gingrich say: "If the letter was written from Rome, the words *en holō tō praitōriō* are best taken to mean *in the whole praetorian* (or *imperial*) *guard*" (p. 704).

Vincent calls attention to the fact that Paul was probably chained at all times to a member of the imperial guard, since he was an imperial prisoner. He adds: "His contact with the different members of the corps in succession, explains the statement that his bonds had become manifest throughout the praetorian guard" (3:420).

In Acts 23:35 the word clearly refers to the palace of Herod at Caesarea. In the Gospels it means the governor's official residence at Jerusalem. But there is still a dispute as to whether that was the palace of Herod the Great or the Tower of Antonia.

Many or Most? (1:14)

Paul rejoices that "many" of the brethren have been emboldened by his imprisonment to speak the word of God fearlessly. The Greek for "many" is *pleionas*. This is the comparative degree of the adjective for "many." So it would literally mean "more." But since in the NT the comparative is usually used for the superlative, the proper rendering is "most." That is what is found in "most" recent translations.

Contention or Ambition? (1:16-17)

The careful reader will note that these verses are in reverse order in the revised versions, as compared with KJV. As in all such cases, the more recent translations follow the better Greek text of the earliest manuscripts, while KJV is based on later manuscripts.

In verse 16 (17 in the better text) Paul declares that some of his contemporaries were preaching Christ "of contention." The Greek word is *eritheias* (genitive case). It means "ambition, self-seeking, rivalry" (A-S, p. 179). Cremer notes that the general meaning of the term is "self-ishness, self-willedness" (p. 263). Thayer gives: "a courting distinction, a desire to put one's self forward, a partisan and factious spirit . . . partisanship, factiousness" (p. 249).

Arndt and Gingrich state that before NT times the word is found only in Aristotle, "where it denotes a self-seeking pursuit of political office by unfair means" (p. 309). The KJV rendering "contention" is based on the older theory that *eritheia* comes from *eris,* which is correctly translated "strife" in verse 15. But this view is rejected by scholars today. The true meaning is "selfishness, selfish ambition" *(ibid.)*.

The term is now commonly held to be derived from a verb meaning to work for hire. H. A. A. Kennedy says: "Now that which degraded the hired worker, in the estimation of antiquity, was his labouring wholly for his own interests, while it was a sign of the noble to devote himself to the common weal" (EGT, 3:425). Moulton and Milligan write: "The meaning of 'selfish' rather than 'factious' ambition perhaps suits best all the New Testament occurrences of *eritheia"* (VGT, p. 254). A good translation, then, would be, "out of selfish ambition" (NASB, NIV).

Sincerely (1:16, KJV)

The Greek word is *hagnos,* which means "purely." A. T. Robertson points out the true meaning: "'Not purely,' that is with mixed and impure motives" (WP, 4:439).

Pretence (1:18)

The Greek word is *prophasis.* According to Abbott-Smith it comes from *prophēmi,* "speak forth"—"the ostensible presentation often untrue" (WP, 4:439). It "is the 'ostensible reason' for which a thing is done, and generally points to a false reason as opposed to the true" (VGT, p. 555). Occurring seven times in the NT, it is translated four different ways in the KJV.

Salvation or Deliverance? (1:19)

Paul asserts his faith that whatever happens will turn out for his "salvation." But was he not already "saved"?

The Greek word is *sotēria*. Its classical meaning was "deliverance, preservation" (LSJ, p. 1751). Moulton and Milligan state that this word "is common in the papyri in the general sense of 'bodily health,' 'well-being,' 'safety'" (VGT, p. 622).

Foerster says that the verb *sōzō* and the noun *sotēria* "mean first 'to save' and 'salvation' in the sense of an acutely dynamic act in which gods or men snatch others by force from serious peril" (TDNT, 7:966). He also notes that these words sometimes have more the idea of preservation from danger.

Arndt and Gingrich note that in Philo and Josephus (both first century) the term is used "generally of preservation in danger, deliverance from impending death" (p. 808). The latter meaning fits Paul's case perfectly. He was hoping to be freed safely from his imprisonment, instead of being executed (cf. 2:24). Rather obviously, then, the correct rendering here is "deliverance" (RSV, NEB, NASB, NIV). Phillips seems to miss the point entirely when he translates it: "for the good of my own soul."

Bountiful Supply (1:19)

The Greek word for "supply" is *epichorēgia*. It comes from *chorēgos*, "chorus-leader." The verb *epichorēgeō* first meant to furnish a chorus at one's own expense, then simply to supply. So the noun is normally translated "provision" (NASB), "supply," or "support" (AG). It is a late and rare word, found in only one inscription (from A.D. 79). Vincent says: "The word implies *bountiful* supply" (3:423). This seems to be the best translation (so Weymouth, C. B. Williams). Regarding the following phrase, "of the Spirit of Jesus Christ," Vincent comments: "Either the supply furnished by the Spirit, or the supply which is the Spirit. It is better to take it as including both" *(ibid.).*

Earnest Expectation (1:20)

This is one word in the Greek, *apokaradokian,* found only here and in Rom. 8:19. Vincent defines it thus: "From *apo away, kara the head, dokein to watch.* A watching with the head erect or outstretched" (3:22). Lightfoot comments: "The idea of eagerness conveyed by the simple word *karadokein* is further intensified by the preposition which implies abstraction, absorption" (p. 91). The term may be translated either "earnest expectation" (KJV, ASV, NASB) or "eager expectation" (Weymouth, C. B. Williams, RSV).

Boldness or Courage? (1:20)

Paul hopes that with "all boldness" he may magnify Christ. The Greek for "boldness" is *parrēsia* (see comments on Eph. 3:12). Arndt and Gingrich give as its meaning: "1. *outspokenness, frankness, plainness* of speech, that conceals nothing and passes over nothing. . . . 2. 'Openness' sometimes develops into *openness to the public,* before whom speaking and actions take place. . . . 3.

courage, confidence, boldness, fearlessness, especially in
the presence of persons of high rank" (pp. 635-36).

Weymouth adopts the first of these definitions. He
renders the phrase "by my perfect freedom of speech."
Arndt and Gingrich prefer the second. But most recent
translators adopt the third—"unfailing courage" (TCNT,
Goodspeed), "fearless courage" (Moffatt), "full courage"
(RSV). The context seems to favor "sufficient courage"
(NIV).

Magnified or Honored? (1:20)

The Greek verb is *megalynō,* from *megas,* "great." It
means "to make great" or "to declare great." "Magnified"
is a good translation. So also is "honored" (TCNT, C. B.
Williams, RSV). The same idea is expressed in "do honour" (Moffatt) and "honor" (Phillips). Weymouth has
"glorified" ("exalted," NIV). A good paraphrase is: "The
greatness of Christ will shine out clearly in my person"
(NEB).

Fruit from Labor (1:22)

This verse seems a bit ambiguous. Perhaps the meaning is best expressed by C. B. Williams: "But if to keep on
living here means fruit from my labor, I cannot tell which
to choose" (cf. NIV).

Wot? (1:22)

This archaic word occurs no less than 10 times in the
KJV. In every case it renders a Hebrew or Greek term
meaning "know." This history of the word goes back to
around A.D. 1300. It had definitely become obsolete by the
beginning of the twentieth century. Retained in ERV

(1881), it was changed to "know" in ASV (1901). In fact, "wot" does not occur in the latter version. Many recent translations use "tell" here—"I cannot tell." Closely related to "wot" is "wit," used three times in KJV in the sense of "know." The past tense of "wot" is "wist." This occurs 14 times in KJV.

Hard-pressed (1:23)

Paul says that he is "in a strait betwixt two." The Greek literally says, "I am held together *(synechomai)* out of the two" *(ek tōn duo)*. The verb means "to hem in, press on every side" (A-S, p. 428). Thayer says that the thought here is: "I am hard pressed on both sides, my mind is impelled or disturbed from each side" (p. 604). Lightfoot suggests: *"I am hemmed in on both sides,* I am prevented from inclining one way or the other." He adds: "The *duo* are the two horns of the dilemma, stated in verses 21, 22" (p. 93). The best translation is, "I am hard pressed between the two" (RSV), or "I am hard pressed from both directions" (NASB).

Stand By (1:25)

Paul is convinced that for him to "abide in the flesh" is more necessary for the Philippian Christians (v. 24). So he declares: "I shall abide and continue with you."

These two verbs in the Greek are from the same root—*menō* and *paramenō*. The prefix of the second is a preposition meaning "beside." In order to bring out the connection of the two words in the original, the TCNT has, "I shall stay, and stay near you all." C. B. Williams renders it, "stay on and stay by." Lightfoot offers, "bide and abide" (p. 94). The second verb may be translated "stand by" (Phillips, NEB). H. A. A. Kennedy writes: *"Para-*

menō (which is best attested) has in later Greek the special sense of 'remaining alive'" (EGT, 3:429). So Moffatt has, "remain alive and serve."

Coming (1:26)

Parousia occurs 24 times in the NT. In all but 6 of these instances it is used for the second coming of Christ. Literally it means "presence" (see Phil. 2:12). But it was also employed in the sense of "arrival." Here "coming . . . again" means "return" (Moffatt). The literal meaning is reflected by "my being with you again" (Weymouth, NIV).

Conversation (1:27)

Paul admonishes his readers: "Only let your conversation be as it becometh the gospel of Christ." "Let your conversation be" is all one word in the Greek, *politeuesthe*. This verb occurs (in NT) only here and Acts 23:1, where it is correctly translated, "I have lived."

The word comes from *politēs*, "citizen" (Luke 15:15; 19:14; Acts 21:39). This, in turn, is from *polis*, "city," just as our English word "citizen" comes from "city." The reason for this derivation goes back to the Greek city-states. One was not a citizen of a country, as today, but a citizen of a city.

The verb *politeuō*, used here, literally means "to be a citizen, live as a citizen" (A-S, p. 371). Thayer develops the usage of the word further, as follows: *"to behave as a citizen; to avail one's self of or recognize the laws;* so from Thucydides down; in Hellenistic writings *to conduct oneself as pledged to some law of life"* (p. 528). Here it may mean "Discharge your obligations."

Vincent says, "The exhortation contemplates the Philippians as members of the Christian *commonwealth,"*

and adds: "The figure would be naturally suggested to
Paul by his residence in Rome, and would appeal to the
Philippians as a Roman colony, which was a reproduction
of the parent commonwealth on a smaller scale" (3:426).
A. T. Robertson comments: "The Authorized Version
missed the figure completely by the word 'conversation'
which did refer to conduct and not mere talk as now, but
did not preserve the figure of citizenship" (WP, 4:441).
The correct translation is, "Conduct yourselves in a man-
ner worthy of the gospel of the Christ" (NASB, NIV).
Lightfoot paraphrases the first part of verse 27 as follows:
"But under all circumstances do your duty as good citizens
of a heavenly kingdom; act worthily of the Gospel of
Christ" (p. 105).

Striving or Contending? (1:27)

Paul hopes he may hear that the Philippian believers
are "with one mind [literally, 'one soul'] striving together
for the faith of the Gospel." The verb is *synathleō*, found
only in this Epistle (cf. 4:3). It is a compound of *syn*
("with" or "together") and *athleō* ("to be an athlete, contend in games"). The simple verb is found only in 2 Tim.
2:5.

Thayer defines the compound as meaning *"to strive
at the same time with* another" (p. 600). The whole
phrase may be translated, "joined in conflict for the faith
of the Gospel" (Berk.). A good rendering is, "contending
as one man for the faith of the gospel" (NIV).

Terrified or Intimidated? (1:28)

Paul also hopes to hear of his readers that they are "in
nothing terrified by your adversaries." The strong word

"terrified" has been changed to "affrighted" (ASV) or "frightened" (RSV, C. B. Williams, NIV).

The verb is *ptyromai* (only here in NT). It means "to be startled, frightened" (A-S, p. 392). Arndt and Gingrich translate the phrase here, "in no way intimidated by your opponents" (p. 735). *The Berkeley Version* adopted this meaning—"not for a moment intimidated by the antagonists." Typical paraphrases are "not caring two straws for your enemies" (Phillips) and "meeting your opponents without so much as a tremor" (NEB).

Perdition or Destruction? (1:28)

The Greek word is *apōleia*. It means "destruction, waste, loss, perishing" (A-S, p. 56). In the NT it has the particular sense of "the destruction which consists in the loss of eternal life" (Thayer, p. 71). Of its use in Rev. 17:8, Oepke says: "What is meant here is not a simple extinction of existence, but an everlasting state of torment and death" (TDNT, 1:397). The best translation here is "destruction" (Goodspeed, Weymouth, C. B. Williams, RSV, NASB).

Conflict or Contest? (1:30)

The Greek word for "conflict" is *agōn*. This comes from the verb *agō*, which means "lead" or "bring." So the noun means: "1. *a place of assembly* (in Homer); specifically the place in which the Greeks assembled to celebrate solemn games (as the Pythian, the Olympian); hence 2. *a contest*, of athletes, runners, charioteers. In a figurative sense . . . any struggle with dangers, annoyances, obstacles, standing in the way of faith, holiness, and a desire to spread the gospel" (Thayer, p. 10). The rendering "contest" (NEB) points best to the athletic background of the term.

Ethelbert Stauffer has a good summary of the main emphasis of this paragraph (vv. 27-30) on the Christian's contest. We must "stand firm in one spirit, contending as one man" (v. 27). The victory over our adversaries is assured (v. 28). Faith in Christ costs suffering (v. 29). Stauffer concludes of Paul: "He thinks of the conflicts and sufferings of the Christian life itself as a life which in its totality stands under the sign of the cross and in this sign carries the cause of Christ to victory" (TDNT, 1:139).

Consolation or Encouragement? (2:1)

The Greek word is *paraklēsis*. It comes from *para-kaleō*, "call to one's side." So the noun literally means "a calling to one's aid," then "exhortation" or "encouragement," and finally "consolation" or "comfort." Abbott-Smith lists this passage under the second of these three sets of meanings, as do also Thayer and Arndt and Gingrich.

The word occurs 29 times in the NT. In the KJV it is translated "consolation" 14 times, "exhortation" 8 times, "comfort" 6 times, and "intreaty" once. It appears that the best rendering here may be "encouragement" (RSV, Phillips, NASB, NIV). Arndt and Gingrich and ASV both prefer "exhortation," as does H. A. A. Kennedy (EGT, 3:432).

Comfort (2:1)

In contrast to the fairly frequent occurrence of *para-klēsis,* the Greek word *paramythion* ("comfort") is found only here. Thayer gives only one meaning, "persuasive address" (cf. Berk., "persuasive appeal"), although he notes (p. 485) that in the classics it was used in the sense of "consolation" (NEB, NASB). Abbott-Smith has "an exhortation, persuasion, encouragement." Arndt and Gingrich would translate the phrase here, "if there is any solace afforded by love" (p. 626).

Lightfoot says about this word: "*'incentive,'* encouragement, not 'comfort,' as the word more commonly means" (p. 107). Kennedy comments: "Almost equivalent to *paraklēsis,* but having a suggestion of tenderness involved" (EGT, 3:432). Vine agrees with this. Of the closely related word *paramythia* he writes: "primarily a speaking closely to anyone, (*para,* near, *mythos,* speech), hence denotes consolation, comfort, with a greater degree of tenderness than *paraklēsis*" (1:207).

In his excellent article in the *TDNT,* Staehlin notes that these similar terms have "the favourable sense of a friendly relation" and that "it is almost impossible to separate the elements of petition, admonition and consolation." He says also that the basic sense "can develop along two main lines: with reference to what ought to be done, 'to admonish to something,' and with reference to what has happened, 'to console about something'" (5:817).

Staehlin affirms that both *paraklēsis* and *paramythion* "are characterized by the twofoldness of admonition and comfort" and adds: "In the NT . . . admonition becomes genuine comfort and *vice versa,* so that it is hard to distinguish between the two. . . . The unity of admonition and consolation is rooted in the Gospel itself, which is both gift and task" (5:821). He also notes: "All thoughts of comfort in the NT are in some way orientated to Christ" (5:823). That is the case here.

There is still something to be said for the rendering "incentive" (Moffatt, Goodspeed, RSV). Weymouth and Charles B. Williams have, "if there is any persuasive power in love." Wand translates: "of the persuasive influence of love." But the NIV returns to the traditional "comfort."

Fellowship (2:1)

This is the famous word *koinōnia,* which has become well known in church circles today. It is a favorite term with Paul. He uses it 14 out of the 20 times it occurs in the NT. John also has it 4 times in his First Epistle.

The noun comes from the adjective *koinos,* "common." So its basic idea is that of sharing something in common. Thayer notes that its first meaning is "the share which one has in anything, participation" (p. 352). This is brought out by Weymouth's rendering, "any common sharing of the Spirit" (cf. C. B. Williams: "any common share in the Spirit"). The NIV and NASB have "fellowship."

Bowels or Affection? (2:1)

The Greek word is *splangchnon,* which literally means "bowels." But this physical sense is found only once in the NT (Acts 1:18). The other 10 times it occurs it is used metaphorically and should be rendered "heart" or "affection" (or some similar expression). Abbott-Smith says: "The characteristic LXX and NT reference of the word to the feelings of kindness, benevolence and pity, is found in papyri" (p. 414). The correct translation here is "affection" (RSV, NEB, NASB) or "tenderness" (NIV).

Mercies or Compassion? (2:1)

The Greek word *oiktirmos,* like the previous term *splangchnon,* primarily refers to "the viscera, which were thought to be the seat of compassion" (Thayer, p. 442).

Both words are usually in the plural in the NT and OT (LXX). For a comparison of the two, Lightfoot says: "By *splangchna* is signified the abode of tender feelings, by *oiktirmoi* the manifestation of these in compassionate yearnings and actions" (p. 108).

Oiktirmos occurs only five times in the NT. In the KJV it is regularly translated "mercies" (once, "mercy"). Probably a preferable rendering is "compassion" (NEB, NASB, NIV), or "sympathy" (RSV, Phillips). Actually "compassion" (from the Latin) and "sympathy" (from the Greek) both have exactly the same literal meaning—a "suffering with." Real sympathy or compassion demands that we become involved.

One Accord—One Mind (2:2)

Paul desires that the Philippians shall be "of one accord, of one mind." The first expression is one word in Greek, *sympsychos* (found only here in NT). Literally it means "together-souled," and so "harmonious, united in spirit" (AG, p. 789).

The second expression is an entirely different construction. Literally it reads: "thinking the one thing." Obviously it is a bit difficult to put these two together. Charles B. Williams has: "your hearts beating in unison, your minds set on one purpose." *The Berkeley Version* reads: "your fellowship of feeling and your harmonious thinking." The NASB has: "united in spirit, intent on one purpose." The NIV reads: "being one in spirit and purpose." That is about as well as can be done with the passage. Strangely, Phillips reverses these: "as though you had only one mind and one spirit between you." The similarity of meaning of these two expressions leads Lightfoot to make this cogent observation: "The redundancy of expression is a measure of the Apostle's earnestness" (p. 108).

Strife or Rivalry? (2:3)

The Greek word is *eritheia*. It means "ambition, self-seeking, rivalry" (A-S, p. 179). The best translation would seem to be either "rivalry" (Phillips, NEB), "selfishness" (RSV, NASB), or "selfish ambition" (NIV).

Vainglory or Empty Conceit? (2:3)

Paul also warns against being motivated by *kenodoxia* (only here in NT). Arndt and Gingrich say it means "vanity, conceit, excessive ambition" (p. 428). For this passage they suggest "empty conceit," the rendering which was chosen for NASB. The prefix *kenos* means "empty," while *doxa* means "opinion." The idea, then, is of one having an empty, or groundless, opinion of himself.

True Humility (2:3)

"Lowliness of mind" is a compound word in Greek, *tapeinophrosynē*. It has already been discussed at length in connection with Eph. 4:2. After noting that in pagan writers it meant "grovelling" or "abject," Lightfoot says: "It was one great result of the life of Christ (on which St. Paul dwells here) to raise 'humility' to its proper level; and if not fresh coined for this purpose, the word *tapeinophrosynē* now first became current through the influence of Christian ethics" (p. 109). Arndt and Gingrich list only two occurrences of the term, one in Epictetus and one in Josephus (both in a bad sense). These are later than Paul.

The Mind of Christ (2:5)

"Let this mind be in you" has the same Greek verb

that is found twice in verse 2, where it reads "be likemind-ed" and "of one mind." The latter of these is a participial construction.

The verb is *phroneō,* which means "think" or "have in mind." Literally the passage reads: "Think this in you [plural]—or among you—which also in Christ Jesus." Obviously this needs some amplification to make sense in English. Arndt and Gingrich suggest the following transla-tion: "Have the same thought among yourselves as you have in your communion with Christ Jesus" (p. 874). The NEB gives a good paraphrase: "Let your bearing towards one another arise out of your life in Christ Jesus." Phillips puts it a bit more briefly: "Let Christ Jesus be your exam-ple as to what your attitude should be" (cf. NIV). Probably the most meaningful rendering is that given by Lightfoot: "Reflect in your own minds the mind of Christ Jesus" (p. 110).

Robbery or Prize? (2:6)

The second clause reads, "Thought it not robbery to be equal with God." The ASV has, "Counted not the being on an equality with God a thing to be grasped." The RSV and NIV read almost exactly the same.

"A thing to be grasped" is all one word in Greek, *hapargmos.* Most modern expositors are agreed that it does not have the active meaning, "the act of seizing" or "robbery," but rather the passive meaning, "a thing seized" or "a prize." For instance, Lightfoot paraphrases the passage: *"Though* He pre-existed in the form of God, *yet* He did not look upon equality with God as a prize which must not slip from His grasp" (p. 111). Ellicott favors this interpretation: *"He did not deem the being on an equality with God a thing to be seized on,* a state to be exclusively (so to speak) clutched at, and retained as a prize" (p. 56). Marvin Vincent (ICC) says that the correct meaning is "thing seized" (p. 58). Thayer gives for this passage the sense: "A thing to be seized upon or to be held fast, retained" (p. 74). Probably a good translation for the whole phrase is that given here by Vincent: "Counted it not a prize to be on an equality with God." Somewhat smoother would be this wording: "He did not consider being equal with God a prize to be retained."

The Kenosis (2:7)

Paul goes on to say that Christ "made himself of no reputation." The verb here is simply *ekenōsen*—literally, "he emptied." That is why this is called the "kenosis" passage. It describes the self-emptying of the Son of God. The correct translation is: "He emptied himself." Of what? All orthodox theologians are agreed that it does not mean that He emptied himself of His divine nature. Rather, it was His heavenly glory—"The glory which I had with thee before the world was" (John 17:5).

Oepke writes: "What is meant is that the heavenly Christ did not selfishly exploit His divine form and mode of being, but by His own decision emptied himself of it or laid it by, taking the form of a servant by becoming man. . . . The essence remains, the mode of being changes" (TDNT, 3:661).

Vincent (ICC) issues a salutary note of warning at this point. He says of the verb employed here: "Not used or intended here in a metaphysical sense to define the limitations of Christ's incarnate state, but as a strong and graphic expression of the completeness of his self-renunciation. It includes all the details of humiliation which follow, and is defined by these" (p. 59).

Form and Fashion (2:6-8)

The former word (vv. 6-7) is *morphē* in the Greek, the latter (v. 8) *schēma*. Regarding the first word Trench writes: "The *morphē* then, it may be assumed, is of the essence of a thing" (p. 265). Concerning the latter he comments: "The *schēma* here signifying his whole outward presentation" (p. 263).

Lightfoot emphasizes the idea that *morphē* means "what He *is* in Himself"—truly God become truly servant —but *schēma* indicates "what He *appeared* in the eyes of men" (p. 112). Of the latter Vincent (ICC) writes: *"Schēma* is the outward *fashion* which appeals to the senses" (p. 60). The former word refers to the inner being, the latter to the outer appearance. Christ not only *appeared* to be a servant in His incarnation; He *was one.* There was no playacting here. But manifesting himself to men as a man, He yet humbled himself further to the ignominious death on the Cross.

Highly Exalted (2:9)

Because Christ humbled himself to become obedient to a shameful, but sacrificial, death on the Cross, God has "highly exalted him, and given him a name which is above every name." This refers to His ascension and glorification.

The verb translated "highly exalted" is *hyperypsoō*. It is not found in classical Greek and occurs only here in the NT—though it is used in the Septuagint several times. Abbott-Smith defines it thus: "To exalt beyond measure, exalt to the highest place" (p. 459). Similarly Arndt and Gingrich say that it means to "raise to the loftiest height" (p. 849). Vincent (ICC) writes: "Paul is fond of *hyper* in compounds, and the compounds with *hyper* are nearly all in his writings . . . Its force here is not 'more than before,' nor 'above his previous state of humiliation,' but 'in superlative measure'" (p. 61).

Given or Graced? (2:9)

The Greek verb translated "given" is *charizomai*. It comes from the noun *charis* which means "grace." So the verb signifies. "1. *to show favour or kindness* . . . 2. *to give freely,* bestow . . . 3. In late Gk. . . . *to grant forgiveness,* forgive freely" (A-S, p. 479).

The verb occurs 23 times in the NT. About half the time it means "give," and the other half "forgive." In both cases the emphasis is on the idea of doing it freely or graciously.

The KJV rendering here is correct and probably adequate, and is followed in most modern translations. But because of the derivation from *charis,* one is tempted to favor the wording of *The Berkeley Version:* "God . . . has graced him with a name that surpasses every name."

A Name or the Name? (2:9)

The best Greek text has "the name." The definite article is omitted in the late, medieval manuscripts, which formed the basis of the KJV. The ASV (1901) has "the name." Weymouth (1902) reads: "God . . . has conferred on Him the Name which is supreme above every other name." That expresses it well. "Name" signifies "title and dignity" (Lightfoot, p. 113).

At or In? (2:10)

The tenth verse says, "That at the name of Jesus every knee should bow." The preposition "at" is *en,* which properly means "in." That gives a very different sense here and is obviously more fitting. It is not a matter of bowing at the mention of the name of Jesus.

What does it mean to bow "in the name of Jesus"? Vincent (ICC) writes: "Paul follows the Hebrew usage, in which the name is used for everything which the name covers, so that the name is equivalent to the person himself" (p. 62). To bow in the name of Jesus is to recognize Him as Lord, exalted at the right hand of the Father.

Things or Persons? (2:10)

The KJV specifies what knees will bow by saying: "of *things* in heaven, and *things* in earth, and *things* under the earth." It will be noticed that the word *things* in all three instances is italicized, indicating that it is not in the original.

In the Greek there are simply three adjectives. The first is *epouranios,* which means *"in* or *of heaven, heavenly"* (A-S, p. 177). In the oldest Greek writer, Homer, it is used of the gods. The second adjective is *epigeios,* "of the earth, earthly." The third is *katachthonios,* "subterranean, under the earth." It is used in classical Greek for the infernal gods.

These three adjectives are in the genitive plural ("of ——s"). Unfortunately, in the Greek of most adjectives the same form is used for the masculine and neuter in genitive and dative cases. (The feminine is a different form usually.) Hence it is impossible to tell whether the masculine or the neuter is meant, except as the context may indicate. In English we put a noun with the adjective to make the matter specific. But the Greek has the habit of using an adjective, usually with the definite article, as a substantive. For instance, the key phrase of Ephesians, "in heavenly *places,"* is in the Greek simply "in the heavenlies."

In the case of the Ephesian phrase it seems clear that the adjective must be neuter. But the matter is not so evident in the passage before us; so the commentators differ in their interpretation. For instance, Lightfoot thinks the reference is to "all creation, all things whatsoever and wheresoever they be. The whole universe, whether animate or inanimate, bends the knee in homage and raises its voice in praise." He goes on to say, "It would seem therefore that the adjectives here are neuter" (p. 115).

Vincent (ICC) considers Lightfoot's arguments for the neuter to be a case of "over-subtilising." He interprets the language as indicating: "The whole body of created intelligent beings in all departments of the universe" (p. 62). He and Abbott-Smith agree in interpreting the third adjective as referring to "the departed in Hades." It seems that this is about as definite as we can be.

Looking at the modern translations, we find that Weymouth has: "Of beings in the highest heavens, of those on the earth, and of those in the underworld." Similarly, Charles B. Williams reads: "So that in the name of Jesus everyone should kneel, in heaven, on earth, and in the underworld." Likewise Goodspeed has "everyone." John Wesley (1755) had "of those in heaven, and those on earth, and those under the earth," taking the adjectives as masculine. In spite of the fact that ERV (1881) and the ASV (1901) followed the KJV in using "things," most modern translators have preferred the masculine form. The RSV, NEB, and NIV avoid the issue by simply saying, "every knee should bow, in heaven." That is perhaps the safest way to treat the passage. However, the use of "tongue" in verse 11 seems definitely to favor the reference in verse 10 as being to persons rather than "things."

Presence and Absence (2:12)

In the Greek there is a play on words. "Presence" is *parousia,* which literally means "being beside," while "absence" is *apousia,* "being away from." The Philippian Christians were to be as faithful in Paul's absence as when he was with them.

Work Out (2:12)

Paul said: "Work out your own salvation." The verb is *katergazesthe.* It means "work on to the finish," or "carry out to the goal." While Christ purchased our salvation and offers it to us as a free gift, yet there is a part that we must do if the salvation is to be completed in our case.

A. T. Robertson, the great Baptist Greek scholar, makes an excellent observation on the relation between these two ideas. He says of Paul: "He exhorts as if he were an Arminian in addressing men. He prays as if he were a Calvinist in addressing God and feels no inconsistency in the two attitudes. Paul makes no attempt to reconcile divine sovereignty and human free agency, but boldly proclaims both" (WP, 4:446). We should pray as if all depended on God and "work to the end" as if all depended on us.

Fear (2:12)

It is with fear *(phobos)* that we are to "work out"—or "make sure of"—our salvation. Vincent says of this fear: "Not slavish terror, but wholesome, serious caution" (3:437). He gives this excellent quotation from the old Scottish preacher, Wardlaw: "This fear is self-distrust; it is tenderness of conscience; it is vigilance against temptation; it is the fear which inspiration opposes to high-mindedness in the admonition 'be not high-minded

but fear.' It is taking heed lest we fall; it is a constant
apprehension of the deceitfulness of the heart, and of the
insidiousness and power of inward corruption [in the un-
sanctified]. It is the caution and circumspection which
timidly shrinks from whatever would offend and dishonor
God and the Saviour" *(ibid.)*.

The Divine Energizer (2:13)

As we "work out" our own salvation, we find that God
"worketh in" us. The verb is *energeō,* which means "energize." We do not have to depend on our own strength, but
let the all-powerful One energize us.

The Willing and the Working (2:13)

"To will and to do" is literally "the willing and the
working." As we submit to let Him, God wills and works
in us in accordance with "his good pleasure." Augustine
expressed it this way: "We will, but God works the will in
us. We work, therefore, but God works the working in us"
(quoted in Vincent, 3:438). In this verse "do" is the same
verb as the "worketh in" of the previous verse. The point
is that our energy comes from Him.

Good Pleasure (2:13)

Only as we let God work in us can we fulfill His "good
pleasure." This is one word in Greek, *eudokia.* It means
"good pleasure, good-will, satisfaction, approval" (A-S,
p. 185). Cremer says that *eudokia* denotes *"a free will* (will-
ingness, pleasure), *whose intent is something good*—benevolence, gracious purpose." Here it describes "God's
purpose of grace" (p. 214).

Of this beautiful word Schrenk writes: *"Eudokia* is not a classical word. It is almost completely restricted to Jewish and Christian literature and occurs for the first time in the Greek Bible" (TDNT, 2:742). Concerning its use here he says: "The meaning of Phil. 2:13 is that the operation of God, which evokes the will and work of believers, takes place in the interests of the divine counsel, i.e., fulfils the ordination therein foreseen." The term expresses "His gracious resolution to save" (*ibid.,* pp. 746-47).

Arndt and Gingrich suggest the translation here: *"in his* (God's) *good will"* (p. 319). This stresses the fact that the divine sovereignty is on the side of man's best good. God's pleasure is man's well-being.

Murmuring (2:14)

The Greek word *gongysmos* sounds like the buzzing of bees. It is what is called an onomatopoetic term: the sound suggests the sense. Robertson comments: "It is the secret grumblings that buzz away till they are heard" (WP, 3:72). In the Septuagint it is used for the murmuring of the children of Israel in the wilderness. The phrase in this passage may be translated "without complaining" (NIV). We are to do our assigned work cheerfully, not grumblingly (cf. RSV—"without grumbling"). Whispering tongues sometimes sound like buzzing bees, about ready to sting!

Disputing (2:14)

This is the word *dialogismos,* from which we get *dialogue.* It means "a thought, reasoning, inward questioning" (A-S, p. 109). But it sometimes, as here, signifies "doubt, dispute, argument" (AG, p. 185). Whereas *gongysmos* occurs only 4 times in the NT (John 7:12; Acts 6:1;

Phil. 2:14; 1 Pet. 4:9), *dialogismos* is found 14 times. It is a favorite term in Luke's Gospel (6 times).

Lightfoot gives an interesting comparison of these two terms. He says: "As *gongysmos* is the moral, so *dialogismos* is the intellectual rebellion against God" (p. 117). The latter word may be rendered "arguing" (Phillips, NIV) or "wrangling" (NEB).

Blameless (2:15)

The adjective *amemptos* means "free from fault" (A-S, p. 24), or "deserving no censure" (Thayer, p. 31). It is found commonly in epitaphs on tombs of this period. Trench points out that the precise sense of the word is "unblamed" (p. 380).

Harmless (2:15)

This adjective, *akeraios,* means "unmixed, pure," and so "guileless, simple" (A-S, p. 17). It occurs only two other places in the NT (Matt. 10:16; Rom. 16:19). Trench says that the rendering "harmless" is based on a misunderstanding of the derivation of the word. The correct translation is "simple" or "sincere," the fundamental idea being that of "the absence of foreign admixture" (p. 206).

Concerning these adjectives in verse 15, Lightfoot writes: "Of the two words here used, the former *(amemptoi)* relates to the judgment of others, while the latter *(akeraioi)* describes the intrinsic character" (p. 117). In essential agreement is the observation of Ellicott. He says the desire for the Philippians was "that they might both outwardly evince *(amemptoi)* and be inwardly characterized by *(akeraioi)* rectitude and holiness, and so become examples to an evil world around them" (p. 66).

Faultless (2:15)

"Without rebuke" is one word in Greek, the adjective *amōmos*. In the Septuagint it is used for sacrificial animals, indicating "without blemish." That is the correct translation here (cf. RSV). The adjective is appropriately applied to Christ, who offered himself "without spot" to God (Heb. 9:14). As Christians we should seek to be both "unblamed" *(amemptos)* and "blameless" *(amōmos)*. Goodspeed translates the latter "faultless," NIV "without fault."

Crooked (2:15)

The Greek word is *skolios*. Literally it means "curved, bent, winding" (Luke 3:5), metaphorically "crooked, perverse, unjust" (A-S, p. 409)—Acts 2:40; Phil. 2:15; 1 Pet. 2:18—or "unscrupulous, dishonest" (AG, p. 763). It might be translated "warped" (Phillips, NEB).

Perverse (2:15)

This is the perfect passive participle of *diastrephō*, which means "distort, twist, pervert." So it signifies being in a perverted state—"perverse, corrupt, wicked" (Thayer, p. 142). Arndt and Gingrich say it means *"perverted* in the moral sense, depraved" (p. 188). Lightfoot renders it "distorted" (p. 117).

Nation or Generation? (2:15)

The Greek word is *genea*. It means "race, stock, family," but in the NT always "generation" (A-S, p. 89). That is the translation here in most modern versions. Arndt and Gingrich note that the term means "literally, those descended from a common ancestor," but "basically, the sum total of those born at the same time, expanded to include all those living at a given time, *generation, contemporaries"* (p. 153).

Jesus denounced His contemporaries as "a wicked and adulterous generation" (Matt. 16:4), as a "faithless and perverse generation" (Matt. 17:17). The passage in Philippians is an echo of this. And how sadly true are these words as applied to our generation!

Offered or Poured? (2:17)

The Greek word for "offered" is *spendomai,* which means *"I am poured out or offered as a libation* (in the shedding of my life-blood)" (A-S, p. 413). It occurs only here and in 2 Tim. 4:6—"For I am now ready to be offered" (cf. NEB—"As for me, already my life is being poured out on the altar"). Paul wrote to the Philippians during his first Roman imprisonment, knowing it might end soon in death. He wrote his second letter to Timothy shortly before his second Roman imprisonment terminated in his execution. In the latter instance he knew that martyrdom for the faith was almost inevitable.

The correct translation here is: "But even if I am being poured out like a drink offering on the sacrifice and service coming from your faith" (NIV). It has sometimes been objected that the drink offerings (libations) of the Jews were poured around the altar, not "upon" the sacrifice. But the same Greek preposition as here, *epi,* is used in Lev. 5:11 (LXX) for this. Lightfoot comments: "On the other hand, as St. Paul is writing to converted heathens, a reference to heathen sacrifice is more appropriate (comp. II Cor. ii. 14); while owing to the great prominence of the libation in heathen rites the metaphor would be more expressive" (p. 119).

Service or Offering? (2:17)

Instead of "service," Phillips, RSV, and NEB all have "offering." Is the change justified?

The Greek word is *leitourgia,* from which comes "liturgy." It occurs only six times in the NT. In Luke 1:23 it is used of Zechariah's priestly "ministration" in the Temple. In 2 Cor. 9:12, Paul employs it for the "service" which the Gentile Christians were rendering to their Jewish brethren in the form of a love offering. It is used similarly in Phil. 2:30. Finally, it occurs twice in Hebrews: for Christ's "ministry" (8:6), and for the "ministry" in the Tabernacle.

The word has a long history. In ancient Athens it was used for "the discharge of a public office at one's own expense" (A-S, p. 266). Then it came to be employed for referring to religious service, which is what it always means in the LXX and NT. Moulton and Milligan give instances in the papyri of the term as applied to the Egyptian priesthood (VGT, p. 373). It would appear that "service" is the best translation here.

Nevertheless it is closely related to "sacrifice" *(thusia).* Lightfoot points up the connection of the whole clause in these words: "The Philippians are the priests; their faith (or their good works springing from their faith) is the sacrifice: St. Paul's life-blood the accompanying libation" (p. 119).

Rejoicing Together (2:17-18)

It has been said that the Philippian letter might be summed up in four words: "I rejoice; rejoice ye!" That is based on the last part of verse 17 with verse 18. Paul says, "I am rejoicing *(chairō)* and rejoicing together *(synchairō)* with all of you. In the same way do you rejoice *(chairete)* and rejoice together *(synchairete)* with me."

Paul is especially fond of compounds with *syn* (cf. *synthetic*), which means "with" or "together." The average Greek lexicon has some half a dozen pages listing words in the NT that begin with *syn* as a prefix. A large part of these are found only in Paul's Epistles. He had a great appreciation of "togetherness" in the Christian life.

Comfort or Courage? (2:19)

The verb *eupsycheō* is translated "be of good comfort." RSV, NIV, and Phillips have "be cheered" (cf. NEB —"it will cheer me"). Abbott-Smith gives as its meaning "to be of good courage" (p. 191). Thayer has "to be of good courage, to be of a cheerful spirit" (p. 264); Arndt and Gingrich, "be glad, have courage" (p. 330). Since the verb comes from the adjective *eupsychos,* "courageous," it would seem that the best translation is: "so that I also may be encouraged when I learn of your condition" (NASB).

Likeminded (2:20)

Paul says of Timothy: "For I have no man likeminded." The adjective is *isopsychos,* from *isos,* "equal," and *psychē,* "soul," just as the word above was from *eu,* "good," and *psychē* (lit., "good-souled"). Both terms occur only here in the NT.

For the adjective, Thayer gives "equal in soul." Arndt and Gingrich suggest "of like soul or mind." NASB translates it "of kindred spirit."

Hope or Trust? (2:19, 24)

One would assume that "I trust" in verses 19 and 24 is the same in the Greek. But such is not the case. In verse

19 it is *elpizō,* "I hope," from the noun *elpis,* "hope." In verse 24 it is *pepoitha,* the perfect tense of *peithō,* "have confidence." So it would mean, "I have a settled confidence." Paul seemed to have a firm conviction that he was going to be released from prison. This is one reason why we date the Epistle to the Philippians near the close of his first Roman imprisonment (probably in A.D. 61).

Suppose or Think? (2:25)

The verb is *hēgeomai.* It means "think, consider, regard" (AG, p. 344). Phillips translates the phrase, "I have considered it desirable." RSV and NASB both use "thought." Weymouth has "I deem it important." Thayer says that *hēgeomai* denotes "a belief resting not on one's inner feeling or sentiment, but on the due consideration of external grounds, the weighing and comparing of facts . . . deliberate and careful judgment." So "thought" is better than "supposed."

Fellow Worker and Soldier (2:25)

As has been noted before, Paul is particularly fond of words beginning with *syn,* the Greek preposition which means "with" or "together with." Two of these occur here.

The first is *synergon,* translated "companion in labour." This is the only place (out of 13 times in NT) where it is rendered this way. Four times it is correctly translated "fellow-labourer." The literal meaning is "fellow worker" (RSV, NIV)—*ergon* means "work."

The other word, *systratiōtēs,* is accurately rendered "fellow soldier." To Paul the Christian life was both work and warfare. Fortunately there were a few faithful souls who were engaged in both with him.

Messenger (2:25)

Paul says that Epaphroditus was the "messenger" of the Philippians, conveying their love offering to him in prison, probably so that he could dwell "in his own hired house" (Acts 28:30)—"in his own rented apartment" (Phillips)—at Rome instead of in a miserable dungeon.

The word for "messenger" is *apostolos*. In 78 out of the 81 times this significant word occurs in the NT it is rendered "apostle." In only one other place (2 Cor. 8:23) is it translated "messenger." In John 13:16 it is rendered "he that is sent."

This noun comes from the verb *apostellō*, which means "send on an errand or mission." The Philippian church had sent Epaphroditus as its "apostle" to Paul, to minister to his needs.

Heavy or Distressed? (2:26)

Epaphroditus was longing for the Philippians and was "full of heaviness" because they had heard he was sick. The word is *adēmonōn*, the present participle of *adēmoneō*, "be troubled or distressed." In recent translations it is usually rendered "distressed" (Weymouth, RSV, NEB, NIV) or even "greatly distressed" (Goodspeed).

Sent or Send? (2:28)

"I sent" is in the aorist indicative *(epempsa)*, which normally signifies past time. But this is what is called the "epistolary aorist"—writing from the standpoint of the reader. When the Philippians received the letter, the messenger would have already been sent by Paul. But he had not yet gone when the apostle wrote this statement. So the correct translation is, "I am sending him"—that is, with this letter. Epaphroditus was now to be Paul's "apostle," carrying his letter to the Philippian church.

Carefully or Eagerly? (2:28)

Paul said that he was sending the bearer of the Epistle "the more carefully." This is all one word in the Greek, *spoudaioterōs*, the comparative degree of the adverb *spoudaiōs*. It comes from *spoudē*, which means "haste." So the adverb means *"with haste or zeal, i.e. earnestly, zealously, diligently . . . hastily, speedily"* (A-S, p. 415). Probably the best translation is "all the more eagerly" (NASB).

Receive or Welcome? (2:29)

Though many versions have "receive," the compound verb *prosdechomai* is perhaps better represented by "welcome" (Phillips, NEB, NIV). *Pros* means "to." So the idea is "welcome to oneself."

Reputation or Honor? (2:29)

"In reputation" is one word in Greek, *entimos*. It is from *timē* (tee-*may*), "honor," and so means "esteemed, highly honored." The best translation here is "hold men like him in high regard" (NASB), or simply "honor men like him" (NIV).

Grievous or Irksome? (3:1)

Paul says that to repeat what he has already written is not "grievous." The Greek word is *oknēros*. Its basic meaning is "shrinking, hesitating, timid." It is translated "slothful" in Matt. 25:26 and Rom. 12:11. Here it means "troublesome" or "irksome" (ASV, RSV).

Safe or Safeguard? (3:1)

"Safe" is the literal meaning of *asphales,* which inherently means "not in danger of being tripped up," and so "certain, secure, safe" (A-S, p. 66). The thought of the passage is better indicated, however, by rendering the phrase "your safety" (Charles B. Williams) or "a safeguard for you" (NEB, NASB, NIV).

Dog (3:2)

The Greek word is not *kynarion,* which means "little dog" or "pet dog" and might be rendered "doggie" (Matt. 15:26-27; Mark 7:27-28). Rather it is *kyon,* a term used for the scavenger dogs and which Phillips here translates "curs." This was the term of reproach and contempt which the Jews commonly used for the Gentiles. But Paul here turns the tables and applies it to the Judaizers themselves. They were the ones who were actually barking and biting.

Concision or Mutilation? (3:2)

The Greek word is *katatomē* (pronounced ka-ta-to-*may*). It is found only here in the NT. In the LXX the corresponding verb is used for mutilations of the body practiced in heathen religions but forbidden to the Israelites (Lev. 21:5). What Paul is saying here is that the Jews have lost the sacredness of circumcision as a sign of God's covenant with Abraham (Gen. 17:10). What they are actually doing is just mutilating the body, as the heathen did. So the apostle refers to them as "the mutilation faction" (Berk.), "those mutilators of the flesh" (NIV).

Circumcision (3:3)

The Greek word *peritomē* literally means "a cutting

around." That exactly represents the physical operation. The English word "circumcision" comes from the Latin and means the same thing. Paul is emphasizing here that the true circumcision is that of the heart, not the body.

Rejoice or Glory? (3:3)

It might be assumed that "rejoice" in verse 3 is the same as "rejoice" in verse 1. But such is not the case. In the first verse it is *chairō,* which most versions render as "rejoice." But here it is *kauchaomai,* which means "boast" or "glory." Most modern translations correctly render it "glory."

Trust or Confidence? (3:3-4)

The word "confidence" occurs in the last part of verse 3 and the first part of verse 4. In the latter part of verse 4, "hath whereof he might trust" is the same verb in the Greek as "have confidence" in the two previous cases. It would seem more consistent to translate it the same way, "have confidence," in all three places, as is done in the ASV (1901) and most translations since.

Stock or Nation? (3:5)

The Greek word is *genos.* Used rather widely in the NT, it is translated 10 different ways in the KJV.

It comes from the verb meaning "become," the root stem of which is *gen.* So it signifies "family . . . offspring . . . race, nation" (A-S, p. 91). Arndt and Gingrich give the following meanings: "1. *descendants* of a common ancestor . . . 2. *family relatives* . . . 3. *nation, people"* (p. 155). The best translation here is "people" (RSV, NIV) or "nation" (NASB).

Excellency or Surpassing Value? (3:8)

The Greek word is *hyperechon.* It is a participial form
of the verb *hyperechō,* which means "to rise above, over-
top," and so metaphorically "to be superior, excel, surpass." Here it means "the surpassing worth" (A-S, p. 458).
Arndt and Gingrich suggest "the surpassing greatness"
(p. 848). The best translation is probably "the surpassing
worth" (RSV) or "the surpassing value" (NASB).

Gnōsis (3:8)

This is the Greek word translated "knowledge." It literally means "a seeking to know, inquiry, investigation,"
but in the NT is used especially for "the knowledge of spiritual truth" (A-S, p. 94). Arndt and Gingrich would translate the phrase here "personal acquaintance with Christ
Jesus" (p. 163).

Since the Gnostics claimed a special, superior *gnōsis*
which others did not possess, it may well be that Paul is
here countering their ideas. He asserts that the supreme
gnōsis is "the knowledge of Christ Jesus."

Dung or Refuse? (3:8)

The Greek term is *skybala,* found only here in the NT.
Abbott-Smith gives its meaning as *"refuse,* especially
dung" (p. 410). Arndt and Gingrich give "refuse, rubbish,
leavings, dirt, dung" (p. 765). The choice seems to lie between "refuse" (ASV, RSV, Moffatt) and "rubbish"
(Goodspeed, NASB, NIV). "Garbage" (NEB) seems a little far out. Paul is using the strongest term he could get
hold of to show how little he valued everything else in
life in comparison with possessing Christ.

Attained or Obtained? (3:12)

The Greek word is *elabon,* the second aorist of *lambanō.* This verb occurs 263 times in the NT and is translated some 20 different ways in the KJV. Only here is it rendered "attain." In all but 24 instances it is translated either "receive" (133 times) or "take" (106 times).

By way of definition Abbott-Smith gives: "1. to take, lay hold of . . . 2. to receive" (p. 263). For this passage Thayer suggests "to get possession of, obtain, a thing" (p. 370). Arndt and Gingrich take a somewhat different slant: *"make one's own, apprehend* or *comprehend* mentally or spiritually (class.) of the mystical apprehension of Christ . . . *I have made (him) my own"* (p. 466). That is, Paul has not fully comprehended Christ.

It seems clear that "obtain" (RSV, NASB, NIV) is preferable to "attain." Weymouth has: "already gained this knowledge." Goodspeed reads: "Not that I have secured it yet." Phillips gives a good paraphrase: "I do not consider myself to have 'arrived' spiritually."

Perfect or Mature? (3:12)

The verb is *teleioō.* It comes from the adjective *teleios* (v. 15). This, in turn, is derived from the noun *telos,* "end." So the adjective means "having reached its end, mature, complete, perfect." For verse 15, Abbott-Smith gives "full-grown, mature." In this chapter Thayer thinks the verb means "to bring one's character to perfection" (p. 618).

Arndt and Gingrich think that *teleios* is used here as "a technical term of the mystery religions, which refers to one initiated into the mystic rites . . . the *initiate"* (p. 817), and that the verb carries the same connotation. Many scholars, however, object to this interpretation. It does not seem justifiable to make that connection.

With regard to the adjective, Lightfoot writes: "The *teleioi* are 'grown men' as opposed to children . . . They are therefore those who have passed out of the rudimentary discipline of ordinances (Gal. iv. 3, 4), who have put away childish things (I Cor. xiii. 10-12)" (p. 153).

On the basis of the same Greek root in verses 12 and 15 it would seem that KJV and NASB were more consistent in using "perfect" in both places. But since Paul denies perfection in verse 12 and seems to claim it in verse 15, it may well be that one is justified in using "perfect" in verse 12 and "mature" in verse 15 (RSV, NEB, NIV). A. T. Robertson comments on verse 15: "Here the term *teleioi* means relative perfection, not the absolute perfection so pointedly denied in verse 12" (WP, 4:455). The context suggests that in verse 12 Paul is denying resurrection perfection. We may say that in verse 15 he claims what John Wesley called Christian perfection.

Follow After or Press On? (3:12)

The verb is *diōkō*, translated "press" in verse 14. Properly it means "pursue." But here it is used with no object. So Abbott-Smith suggests: *"follow on, drive, or speed on"* (p. 119). Thayer gives for this passage: *"to press on:* figuratively, of one who in a race runs swiftly to reach the goal" (p. 153). Arndt and Gingrich have: "hasten, run, press on" (p. 200). It would seem that the best translation here is "press on" (RSV, NEB, NASB, NIV), which makes it consistent with the translation of the same verb in verse 14.

Apprehend or Lay Hold of? (3:12)

The word is *katalambanō*, a compound of the simple verb translated "attain" in this same verse. Thus there is a word play in Greek which does not come out in English.

The verb *katalambanō* means "to lay hold of, seize, appropriate" (A-S, p. 235). Of its use in this passage Thayer writes: "in a good sense, of Christ by his holy power and influence laying hold of the human mind and will, in order to prompt and govern it" (p. 332).

It would appear that the best translation is "lay hold of that for which also I was laid hold of by Christ Jesus" (NASB), or "take hold of that for which Christ Jesus took hold of me" (NIV).

Reaching Forth or Stretching Forward? (3:13)

The verb (only here in NT) is *epekteinō*. It is a double compound of *teinō*, "stretch" or "strain," with *ek*, "out" and *epi*, "upon." So it means "stretch forward." Here it is in the middle voice, and so means "stretching myself forward to." A. T. Robertson says that it is the "metaphor of a runner leaning forward as he runs" (WP, 4:455). Bengel comments: "The eye goes before (outstrips) and draws on the hand, the hand goes before (outstrips) and draws on the foot" (*Gnomon*, 4:147). The best translation is probably "stretching forward" (Weymouth, ASV).

Mark or Goal? (3:14)

Skopos means "*a mark* on which to fix the eye" (A-S, p. 410). It is found only here in the NT. Since the figure Paul is using is that of a runner in a race, the correct translation here is "goal," as in most modern versions.

Prize or Reward? (3:14)

The Greek word is *brabeion*. It comes from *brabeus*, "umpire," and so properly means a prize won in a race or in the games. Phillips translates it "reward." But the entire context favors "prize." Ignatius wrote in his letter to Polycarp (ii): "Be temperate as God's athlete. The prize is incorruption and eternal life."

Attained or Reached? (3:16)

The verb *phthanō* originally meant "come before." But in later Greek it simply meant "come" or "arrive." Weymouth gives an excellent translation of this verse: "But whatever be the point that we have already reached, let us persevere in the same course."

Followers Together (3:17)

This is one word in the Greek, *synmimētai,* found only here in the NT. The prefix *syn* is the preposition meaning "with" or "together with." The simple noun *mimētai,* meaning "imitators," occurs six times in the NT, always in Paul's Epistles. Apparently Paul made up the compound here, for it is not found elsewhere in Greek literature. It means "a fellow imitator" or "an imitator with others." Arndt and Gingrich give "fellow-imitator," but suggest for the whole phrase: *"join* (with the others) in following my example" (p. 786). That is, the readers were to join other Christians in following Paul's example in imitating Christ (cf. 1 Cor. 11:1). Lightfoot suggests for here: "Vie with each other in imitating me" or "one and all of you imitate me" (p. 154).

Mark or Observe? (3:17)

The verb is *skopeō.* It means "to look at, behold, watch, contemplate"; in the NT it is used only in the metaphorical sense, "to look to, consider" (A-S, p. 140). Arndt and Gingrich offer "notice" here. The TCNT has "fix your eyes on" (cf. *skopos* in v. 14). Weymouth says "carefully observe." Perhaps the simplest translation is "observe" (NASB) or "take note" (NIV).

Ensample or Pattern? (3:17)

The Greek word is *typos,* from which we get "type." Originally it meant "the *mark* of a blow" (John 20:25), and so "an *impression, impress,* the *stamp* made by a die; hence, a *figure, image"* (Acts 7:43); "form" (Rom. 6:17); "an example, pattern"; once, *"type"* (Rom. 5:14)—the meaning which has been taken over into English (A-S, p. 452).

Obviously, "ensample" is an obsolete form of "example." The choice here lies between "example" (RSV) and "pattern" (NASB, NIV).

Conversation or Citizenship? (3:20)

We have noted before that there are three Greek words which are translated "conversation" in the KJV, and not one of them signifies what we mean by conversation today. The one here is *politeuma* (only here in NT). It is derived from the verb *politeuō,* which occurs only in Phil. 1:27 (see notes there) and Acts 23:1.

It comes from *polis,* "city." Properly it means "an act of administration" or "a form of government" (A-S, p. 371). But in the NT it is equivalent to *politeia,* "a commonwealth" or "state." Moulton and Milligan say that most quotations from the papyri and inscriptions favor "community" or "commonwealth" (VGT, pp. 525-26).

Moffatt made a bold departure when he translated the opening part of this verse: "But we are a colony of heaven." This finds added appropriateness in the fact that Philippi, to which this letter was written, was a colony of

Rome. But Moulton and Milligan question whether this meaning is supported in Greek literature.

Goodspeed has: "But the commonwealth to which we belong is in heaven." Similarly, Arndt and Gingrich prefer: "Our commonwealth is in heaven" (so RSV). But it seems to us just as accurate and more meaningful to say: "Our citizenship is in heaven" (NASB, NIV)—cf. "We are citizens of heaven" (Phillips, NEB, Beck).

Change or Transform? (3:21)

The verb is *metaschēmatizō*. It is composed of *meta*, which has the idea of exchange or transfer, and *schēma*, which means "appearance" or "form." The compound means *"to change in fashion or appearance"* (A-S, p. 288). Thayer gives: "to change the figure of, to transform" (p. 406). It seems to us that the literal meaning of the Greek word is best represented in English by "transform" (NASB).

Vile or Lowly? (3:21)

In the KJV it is stated that Christ will change our "vile body." This is a completely unjustifiable translation. The *Oxford English Dictionary* (13 vols.) does not seem to give any example of exactly this usage.

The Greek has here simply "the body of our humiliation." The word *tapeinōsis* means "abasement, humiliation, low estate" (A-S, p. 440). This is the way it is used by Plato, Aristotle, and later writers. Arndt and Gingrich have: "humility, humble station, humiliation" (p. 812). Cremer gives the essential meaning as "humiliation" or "lowness" (p. 541).

It should be obvious that the correct translation is not "vile body" but "lowly body" (RSV). Phillips seems off-beat when he uses "wretched body." Far more accurate is "the body belonging to our humble state" (NEB). This gives exactly the sense of the Greek. Lightfoot says: "The English translation, 'our vile body,' seems to countenance the Stoic contempt of the body, of which there is no tinge in the original" (pp. 156-57). It is also contrary to the teaching of the NT.

Fashioned like or Conformed to? (3:21)

For the clause "that it may be fashioned like," the best Greek text has simply one word, the adjective *symmorphos* (only here and in Rom. 8:29). This is compounded of *syn*, "with," and *morphē*, "form." So the English equivalent is "conformed to." The first definition given by Arndt and Gingrich is: "having the same form" (p. 786).

The NEB has here: "give it a form like that of his own resplendent body." The best translation is: "will transform our lowly bodies so that they will be like his glorious body" (NIV).

Yokefellow (4:3)

The Greek word for "yokefellow" is *syzygos,* found only here in the NT. It is an adjective (used here as a substantive) meaning "yoked together." Concerning this word Thayer says:

> Used by Greek writers of those united by the bond of marriage, relationship, office, labor, study, business, or the like; hence, *a yokefellow, consort, comrade, colleague, partner.* Accordingly, in Phil. iv. 3 most interpreters hold that by the words *gnesie syzyge* Paul addresses some particular associate in labor for the gospel. But as the word is found in the midst of (three) proper names, other expositors more correctly take it as a proper name . . . and Paul, alluding (as in Philem.

11) to the meaning of the word as an appellative, speaks of him as "a genuine Synzygus", i.e., a colleague in fact as well as in name *(p. 594)*.

The fact that the Epistle is addressed "to all the saints . . . at Philippi" makes it impossible to identify this "loyal comrade" (NEB) unless it is taken as a proper name.

Fellow Labourers or Fellow Workers? (4:3)

This might seem like a distinction without a difference. But the objection we make to the former in the KJV is that it would naturally be thought of as parallel to "laboured with" in the first part of the verse. However, the Greek roots are entirely different. The verb "laboured with" is *synathleō*, found only here and in 1:27 (see notes there). Our word "athletics" comes from it. So it is properly translated "shared my struggles" (NEB).

"Fellow labourers" is one word in the Greek, *synergon*. It is compounded of *syn*, "with," and *ergon*, "work." The correct translation is "fellow workers."

Moderation or Gentleness? (4:5)

This word has perhaps been more variously translated in modern versions than any other term in the NT. It is difficult to settle on a "best" translation.

Actually it is an adjective, *epieikes*. In Homer it meant "seemly, suitable" and later "equitable, fair, mild, gentle" (Thayer, p. 238). Arndt and Gingrich give "yielding, gentle, kind," and for this passage "your forbearing spirit" (p. 292).

Lightfoot adopted "your forbearance" (cf. RSV). He says: "Thus we may paraphrase St. Paul's language here: 'To what purpose is this rivalry, this self-assertion? The end is nigh, when you will have to resign all. Bear with others now, that God may bear with you then'" (p. 160).

Preisker makes this helpful observation: "Because the *kyrios* (Lord) is at hand, and the final *doxa* (glory) promised to all Christians will soon be a manifest reality, they can be *epieikeis* towards all men in spite of every persecution" (TDNT, 2:590).

Trench gives careful attention to the meaning of the related noun, *epieikeia*. He says: "It expresses exactly that moderation which recognizes the impossibility cleaving to all formal law, of anticipating and providing for all cases that will emerge, and present themselves to it for decision; which, with this, recognizes the danger that ever waits upon the assertion of *legal* rights, lest they should be pushed into *moral* wrongs . . . which, therefore, urges not its own rights to the uttermost" (p. 154). That is, one should not insist on his lawful rights, contrary to the law of love.

On the difficulty of translation he makes this interesting comment:

> It is instructive to note how little of one mind our various Translators from Wiclif downward have been as to the words which should best reproduce *epieikeia* and *epieikes* for the English reader. The occasions on which *epieikeia* occur are two, or reckoning to *epieikes* as an equivalent substantive, are three (Acts xxiv. 4; II Cor. x. 1; Phil. iv. 5). It has been rendered in all these ways: "meekness," "courtesy," "clemency," "softness," "modesty," "gentleness," "patience," "patient mind," "moderation." *Epieikes,* not counting the one occasion already named, occurs four times (I Tim. iii. 3; Tit. iii. 2; Jam. iii. 17; I Pet. ii. 18), and appears in the several versions of our Hexapla as "temperate," "soft," "gentle," "modest," "patient," "mild," "courteous." "Gentle" and "gentleness," on the whole commend themselves as the best; but the fact remains . . . that we have no words in English which are full equiv-

alents of the Greek. The sense of equity and fairness which is in them so strong is more or less wanting in all which we offer in exchange *(pp. 156-57)*.

It would seem to us that "gentleness" (NIV) might be the best translation, though inadequate.

Careful or Anxious? (4:6)

The verb is *merimnaō*, which primarily means to "be anxious." It comes from *merizō*, "be drawn in different directions." So it suggests the idea of being distracted by many cares.

The KJV rendering is obviously incorrect. Paul is not forbidding us to be careful! He would doubtless agree with the ABC of safety: "Always Be Careful." What he is saying is "Do not be anxious about anything" (NIV). Phillips has caught the idea rightly in his rendering: "Don't worry over anything whatever." Carefulness is a Christian virtue. Worry, as John Wesley declared, is a sin.

Passes or Surpasses? (4:7)

The verb is *hyperechō*. It means "rise above, surpass, excell" (AG, p. 848). The correct translation here is "sur- passes" (NASB) or "transcends" (NIV).

Keep or Guard? (4:7)

The word is *phroureō*. It comes from *phrouros*, "a guard." So it means *"to guard, keep under guard, protect or keep* by guarding" (A-S, p. 474). Thayer gives as the literal meaning: "to guard, *protect by a military guard."* The English word "keep" may mean "hold on to" and so is not satisfactory.

The better translation here is "guard" (NASB, NIV).

Phillips expresses it well: "And the peace of God, which transcends human understanding, will keep constant guard over your hearts and minds as they rest in Christ Jesus."

Through or In? (4:7)

There seems to be no justification for the rendering "through Christ Jesus." The Greek says *en*, "in." Practically all modern translations give it correctly: "in Christ Jesus." What this means is well represented by Phillips, as quoted above. As long as our hearts and minds are resting in Christ, the peace of God stands guard over them.

Honest or Honorable? (4:8)

It is the adjective *semnos*, which means: "1. *reverend, august, venerable*, in classics of the gods and also of human beings. 2. *grave, serious;* of persons: I Tim. 3:8, 11; Tit. 2:2; of things: Phil. 4:8" (A-S, p. 404). For its use with things Arndt and Gingrich give: "honorable, worthy, venerable, holy" (p. 754).

Trench says of *semnos:* "It is used . . . constantly to qualify such things as pertain to, or otherwise stand in any very near relation with, the heavenly world" (p. 346). After noting that in Greek literature it is often associated with such adjectives as "holy," "great," "valuable," he observes: "From all this it is plain that there lies something of majestic and awe-inspiring in *semnos*" (p. 347). He speaks of "honest" as "an unsatisfactory rendering," and suggests "honorable" *(ibid.)*. This is the choice of most modern versions (ASV, RSV, NASB), though "noble" (NIV) is also good.

Lovely or Lovable? (4:8)

The adjective *prosphilēs* occurs only here in the NT. Arndt and Gingrich give its meaning as: "pleasing, agreeable, lovely, amiable" (p. 727). Vincent says it means "adapted to excite love, and to endear him who does such things" (3:459). While the favorite rendering is "lovely," several translators offer "lovable" (TCNT, Weymouth, NEB). It would be difficult to decide between the two.

Of Good Report or Gracious? (4:8)

The adjective (only here in NT) is *euphēmos*. It comes from *eu*, "well," and *phēmi*, "say." Abbott-Smith gives its meaning as: "primarily, *uttering words* or *sounds of good omen*, hence, 1. *avoiding ill-omened words, religiously silent.* 2. *fair-sounding, auspicious*" (p. 190). Thayer says that here it is used of "things spoken in a kingly spirit, with goodwill to others" (p. 263). Arndt and Gingrich say that in this passage it "can be interpreted in various ways: *auspicious, well-sounding, praiseworthy, attractive, appealing*" (p. 327).

H. A. A. Kennedy affirms that the exact meaning is "high-toned" (EGT, 3:468). Lightfoot says: "Not 'well-spoken of, well-reputed,' for the word seems never to have this passive meaning; but with its usual active sense, *'fair-speaking,'* and so 'winning, attractive'" (pp. 161-62). A good translation is "gracious" (NEB).

Virtue or Excellence? (4:8)

The Greek noun *aretē* occurs outside this passage only in the Epistles of Peter (1 Pet. 2:9; 2 Pet. 1:3, 5). Abbott-Smith gives its meaning as follows: "properly, whatever procures pre-eminent estimation for a person or thing, in

Homer any kind of conspicuous advantage. Later confined by philosophical writers to intrinsic eminence—*moral goodness, virtue*" (p. 58).

Thayer notes that it is "a word of very wide signification in Greek writers; *any excellence of a person* (in body or mind) or *of a thing, an eminent endowment, property, or quality*" (p. 73). Here he thinks it means "moral excellence."

Praise or Praiseworthy?

"Praise" is the literal meaning of the noun *epainos*. But "praiseworthy" (NIV) or "worthy of praise" (RSV, NASB) seems to be more appropriate in English.

Do or Practice? (4:9)

The verb is *prassō*. It sometimes is used as synonymous with *poieō*, "do." But here it would seem that the better translation is "practice" (NASB, NIV). The NEB gives an excellent paraphrase of this passage: "The lessons I taught you, the tradition I have passed on, all that you heard me say or saw me do, put into practice."

Flourish Again or Revive? (4:10)

The verb is *anathallō*, found only here in the NT. Since *ana* means "again," and *thallō* means "flourish," the KJV rendering is accurate. Intransitively the word means *"grow up again, bloom again"*; transitively it signifies *"cause to grow or bloom again"* (AG, p. 53). Arndt and Gingrich say that in this passage both meanings are possible: either "You have revived, as far as your care for me is concerned" or "You have revived your care for me" *(ibid.)*. The second one is more commonly adopted today.

Care or Concern? (4:10)

"Care" and "ye were . . . careful" are different forms of the same verb, *phroneō*. The first is the present infinitive, treated as a substantive. The second is the imperfect indicative, signifying continual concern for the apostle.

The verb *phroneō* means: "1. to have understanding . . . 2. to think, to be minded . . . 3. to have in mind, be mindful of, think of" (A-S, p. 474). It is obviously in the third sense that it is used here.

Weymouth gives an excellent translation of this passage: "But I rejoice in the Lord greatly that now at length you have revived your thoughtfulness for my welfare. Indeed you have always been thoughtful for me, although opportunity failed you." The idea is well expressed thus: "You have revived your concern for me; you were indeed concerned for me" (RSV; cf. NASB, NIV).

Content or Self-sufficient? (4:11)

The Greek word (only here in NT) is *autarkēs*. It is compounded of *autos*, "self," and *arkeō*, "suffice." Abbott-Smith says: "As in classics, in philosophical sense, *self-sufficient, independent*" (p. 69). Vincent writes: "A stoic word, expressing the favorite doctrine of the sect, that man should be sufficient to himself for all things; able by the power of his own will, to resist the shock of circumstance. Paul is *self-sufficient* through the power of the *new self*: not *he*, but *Christ* in him" (3:460-61).

Though most of the English versions have "content," the TCNT reads: "For, however I am placed, I, at least, have learnt to be independent of circumstances" (cf. NEB). Arndt and Gingrich say that here the word means "*content*, perhaps self-sufficient" (p. 122).

Instructed or Initiated? (4:12)

The verb is *mueō*. In classical Greek, as Abbott-Smith notes, its main meaning was "to initiate into the mysteries" (p. 297). Many of the modern versions have: "I have learned the secret," which is an excellent rendering. The TCNT translates this verse: "I know how to face humble circumstances, and I know how to face prosperity. Into every human experience I have been initiated—into plenty and hunger, into prosperity and want."

Communicate or Share? (4:14)

The verb is *synkoinōneō*. It means "to become a partaker together with others" or "to have fellowship with a thing" (Thayer, p. 593). The best translation here is "share."

Odor or Fragrance? (4:18)

"Odour of a sweet smell" is two words in Greek— *osmēn euōdias*. The first means "smell," the second "fragrance." So it is literally "a smell of fragrance"; that is, "a fragrant smell." Today the word "odor" is offensive. Perhaps the best translation here is simply "a fragrant offering" (RSV, NEB, NASB, NIV), or "the *sweet fragrance* of a sacrifice" (TCNT).

COLOSSIANS

Fellow Servant (1:7)

The Greek word is *syndoulos,* which literally means "fellow slave." Only in Colossians (1:7; 4:7) does Paul use this term. It is found five times in Matthew—four times in the parable of the unmerciful servant (18:28, 29, 31, 33), plus 28:49. Elsewhere in the NT it occurs only in Revelation, once of fellow saints (6:11) and twice of angels (19:10; 22:9). Paul had a strong sense of "togetherness" with his fellow laborers in the Kingdom.

Knowledge (1:9)

Paul desires that his readers might be filled with the "knowledge" of God's will. The Greek word is *epignōsis.*

The prefix *epi* perhaps intensifies the meaning of *gnōsis,* "knowledge." Should an attempt be made to bring out this distinction in English?

Paul uses *epignōsis* 15 out of the 20 times it is found in the NT. But he also uses *gnōsis* 23 out of its 29 occur-

rences. He has the cognate verb *epiginōskō* 12 out of its 42
appearances. He uses the simple verb *ginōskō* 48 times
(out of 223 in NT). So it can hardly be said, as sometimes
has been claimed, that Paul prefers the stronger terms and
so uses them as synonymous with the simple verb and
noun.

Arndt and Gingrich feel that in some cases (e.g., 1 Cor.
13:12) *epiginōskō* means "know completely," but that
most of the time it is simply equivalent to *ginōskō*. The
same would go for the nouns *epignōsis* and *gnōsis*.

Thayer puts the case more strongly. After noting that
"*epi* denotes mental direction towards, application to,
that which is known," he gives as the first definition for
epiginōskō: "to become thoroughly acquainted with, to
know thoroughly; to know accurately, know well" (p. 237).
For *epignōsis* he gives: "precise and correct knowledge."
Trench agrees with this when he writes: "Of *epignōsis,* as
compared with *gnōsis,* it will be sufficient to say that *epi*
must be regarded as intensive, giving to the compound
word a greater strength than the simple possessed" (p.
285). Likewise Cremer says that *epignōsis* signifies *"clear
and exact knowledge,* more intensive than *gnōsis,* because
it expresses a more thorough participation in the object
of knowledge on the part of the knowing subject" (p. 159).
Lightfoot concurs. Commenting on this passage, he writes:
"The compound *epignōsis* is an advance upon *gnōsis,*
denoting a larger and more thorough knowledge" (p. 138).

But J. Armitage Robinson takes exception to all this.
In his scholarly commentary on the Greek text of Ephesians he has a long additional note (seven pages) on the
meaning of *epignōsis.*

He first notes: "The word *epignōsis* is not found in
Greek writers before the time of Alexander the Great" (p.
248). The cognate verb does occur a few times in the classical writers. But after citing a number of passages from

the older writers, Robinson affirms: "There is no indication that *epiginōskein* conveys the idea of a fuller, more perfect, more advanced knowledge" (p. 249). He adds: "We find a large number of compounds in *epi*, in which the preposition does not in the least signify *addition*, but rather perhaps *direction*" *(ibid.)*. His conclusion is: "Thus *ginōskein* means 'to know' in the fullest sense that can be given to the word 'knowledge': *epiginōskein* directs attention to some particular point in regard to which 'knowledge' is affirmed. So that to perceive a particular thing, or to perceive who a particular person is, may fitly be expressed by *epiginōskein*" *(ibid.)*. The difference between the nouns may be stated thus: "*Gnōsis* is the wider word and expresses 'knowledge' in the fullest sense: *epignōsis* is knowledge directed towards a particular object, perceiving, discerning, recognizing: but it is not knowledge in the abstract: that is *gnōsis*" (p. 254).

The latest thorough study of *ginōskō* and its derivatives is by Bultmann. Speaking of early Christian usage, he says: "*Epiginōskein* is often used instead of *ginōskein* with no difference in meaning. . . . In fact the simple and compound forms are used interchangeably in the papyri, where *epiginōskein* really means 'to affirm' or 'to confirm.'" (TDNT, 1:703). He adds: "In the Septuagint the two terms are often used as equivalents," as well as in Philo. He cites several parallel passages in the Gospels where he finds no distinction in meaning between these words (p. 704). So it would seem that any supposed difference should not be overemphasized.

Made Us Meet or Qualified Us? (1:12)

The verb is *hikanoō*. It comes from the adjective *hikanos,* which means "sufficient, competent, fit." So it signifies "make sufficient, render fit" (A-S, p. 215), or "qualify" (AG, p. 375). Probably the best translation in this passage is: "who has qualified us" (RSV, NASB).

It should be noted, in passing, that the Bible Society Greek text has "you" instead of "us." The two oldest uncial manuscripts, Vaticanus and Sinaiticus, have "you." But the bulk of the early as well as late manuscripts have "us." Unfortunately, the still earlier papyri do not help us at this point, because of breaks in the fragile material. The NIV reads "who has qualified you."

Image (1:15)

The Greek word is *eikōn,* from which comes the English "icon." It means a "likeness"—not, however, an accidental similarity, but a derived likeness such as that of "the head on a coin or the parental likeness in a child" (A-S, p. 131). Thayer says the term is here applied to Christ "on account of his divine nature and absolute moral excellence" (p. 175).

In the Synoptic Gospels this word is used for the image of the emperor on a silver coin, the denarius (Matt. 22:20; Mark 12:16; Luke 20:24). Josephus uses it repeatedly in the same way. It thus signifies an exact representation. Philo employs this term to describe the Logos. Paul himself speaks of Christ as "the image of God" in an earlier Epistle (2 Cor. 4:4).

Lightfoot writes: "Beyond the very obvious notion of *likeness,* the word *eikōn* involves two other ideas: (1) *Representation . . . eikōn* implies an arche-type of which it is a copy. . . . (2) *Manifestation . . .* The Word, whether pre-incarnate or incarnate, is the revelation of the unseen Father" (p. 145). Ellicott comments: "Christian antiquity has ever regarded the expression 'image of God' as denoting the eternal Son's perfect equality with the Father in respect of His substance, nature, and eternity" (p. 134).

Eadie has a beautiful approach to the study of this passage. He writes: "The clause dazzles by its brightness, and awes by its mystery. . . . The invisible God—how dark and dreadful the impenetrable veil! Christ His image— how perfect in its resemblance, and overpowering in its brilliance! We must worship whilst we construe; and our exegesis must be penetrated by a profound devotion" (p. 43).

He further comments: "Visibility is implied in the very notion of an image. The spirit of the statement is, that our only vision or knowledge of the Father is in His Son" (p. 45). He goes on to say: "In His incarnate state He brought God so near to us as to place Him under the cognizance of our very senses—men saw, and heard, and handled him—a speaking, acting, weeping, and suffering God" (pp. 45-46). But he adds: "Still, too, at the right hand of the Majesty on high, is He the visible administrator and object of worship" (p. 46).

Kleinknecht writes part of the article on *eikōn* in Kittel's TDNT. He says: "Thus *eikōn* does not imply a weakening or a feeble copy of something. It implies the illumination of its inner core and essence" (2:389). Kittel himself says that in Col. 1:15 "all the emphasis is on the equality of the *eikōn* with the original" (2:395).

Phillips has a happy phrasing of this passage. He translates it: "Now Christ is the visible expression of the invisible God." Jesus himself said: "He that hath seen me hath seen the Father" (John 14:9). Paul is simply affirming the same truth about his Lord.

Every Creature or All Creation? (1:15)

The Greek word *ktisis* may be translated either "creature" or "creation." Unfortunately the Greek does not distinguish between "all" and "every." The same word is used for both. So there is an option between the two renderings given above. But there is a general agreement today that the better translation is "all creation" (NIV).

The Firstborn of Every Creature (1:15)

To say that Christ is "the firstborn of all creation" certainly poses a problem. Ever since the days of Arianism in the Early Church, those who deny the deity of Jesus have seized on this verse as proof that He was a created being—even though the first one created by God.

The Greek word for "firstborn" is *prōtotokos,* from *prōtos*, "first," and *tiktō*, "beget." Abbott-Smith thinks it was "originally perhaps a Messianic title" (p. 392). Lightfoot quotes a rabbinical interpretation and says: "Hence 'the firstborn' *ho prōtotokos* used absolutely, became a recognized title of Messiah" (p. 146). He states that the expression conveys two ideas: priority to all creation and sovereignty over all creation. He then adds: "In its Messianic reference this secondary idea of sovereignty predominated in the word *prōtotokos,* so that from this point of view *prōtotokos pasēs ktiseōs* would mean 'Sovereign Lord over all creation by virtue of primogeniture'" (p. 147). (Cf. "His is the primacy over all created things," NEB.)

Eadie holds that the genitive ("of all creation") "may be taken as that of reference. . . . The meaning therefore is, 'first-born in reference to the whole creation'" (p. 51).

The clauses immediately preceding and following this passage show clearly that it cannot be interpreted as meaning that Christ was a created being. For it is explicitly stated: "By him were all things created" (cf. John 1:3). The NIV has "over all creation."

Thrones (1:16)

Verse 16 enumerates four things that were created by

Christ (cf. a similar list in Eph. 1:21). To what do these refer? Lightfoot says: "Some commentators have referred the terms used here solely to earthly potentates and dignities. There can be little doubt however that their chief and primary reference is to the orders of the celestial hierarchy, as conceived by these Gnostic Judaiziers" (p. 152). He adds: "The names, too, more especially *thronoi*, are especially connected with the speculations of Jewish angelology" *(ibid.)*. But he thinks that earthly dignitaries may also be meant.

"Thrones" comes directly from the Greek *thronoi*. Lightfoot writes: "In all systems alike these 'thrones' belong to the highest grade of angelic beings, whose place is in the immediate presence of God" (p. 154). Paul is here declaring that Christ is supreme, far superior to all the celestial powers postulated in the Gnostic schools of thought.

Dominions (1:16)

The Greek word *kyriotēs* (from *kyrios*, "lord") means "power or position as lord" (Foerster, TDNT, 3:1096). Its literal meaning would be "lordships."

Consist or Hold Together? (1:17)

The last word is *synestēken*, from *synistēmi*. A better translation than "consist" is "cohere" or "hold together." Lightfoot says of Christ: "He is the principle of cohesion in the universe. He impresses upon creation that unity and solidarity which makes it a cosmos instead of a chaos" (p. 156).

Christ is not only Creator but Coherer. He upholds that which He brought into being (cf. Heb. 1:3).

Some years ago a noted scientist said: "If the creative

force residing in the universe should be withdrawn for a moment, the whole universe would collapse." This is what Jeans wrote about in *The Spiritual Nature of the Physical Universe*. The Bible tells us that this creative force is Christ.

Preeminence or First Place? (1:18)

The Greek verb is *prōteuō,* found only here in the NT. It comes from *prōtos,* "first," and so means "be first" or "have first place." The best translation of this clause is: "so that He Himself might come to have first place in everything" (NASB), or "might have the supremacy" (NIV).

Fulness (1:19)

A favorite term with the Gnostics was *plērōma.* In Colossians, Paul was concerned to oppose the incipient Gnosticism which was invading the churches of the Lycus valley. His answer to all the Gnostic heresies consisted essentially of one word: Christ. He alone was "fulness." Lightfoot comments that this was "a recognized technical term in theology, denoting the totality of the Divine powers and attributes" (p. 159).

Delling has an excellent statement on this. He writes: "The word *plērōma* emphasizes the fact that the divine fulness of love and power acts and rules in all its perfection through Christ" (TDNT, 6:303).

Dwell (1:19)

This is a strong term, *katoikeō.* It means "dwell permanently."

Reconcile (1:20-21)

The strong double compound *apokatallassō* occurs only here and in Eph. 2:16. It means "reconcile completely" (A-S, p. 51). Lightfoot comments: "The false teachers aimed at effecting a partial reconciliation between God and man through the interposition of angelic mediators. The Apostle speaks of an absolute and complete reconciliation of universal nature to God, effected through the mediation of the Incarnate Word" (p. 159). He adds: "Their mediators were ineffective, because they were neither human nor divine. The true mediator must be both human and divine" *(ibid.).* He must have the fullness of the divine nature, and at the same time be born as a man. Jesus Christ was the only One who ever fulfilled these conditions (1 Tim. 2:5).

Unreproveable (1:22)

The adjective *anegklētos* is found only in Paul's Epistles. It is composed of *alpha*-negative and the verb *egkaleō*, "call in" or "bring a charge against." So it literally means "not to be called to account" or "that cannot be called to account." The meaning is that before God no charge can be laid to our account. We are accepted before Him, because, and only because, we are in Christ.

Continue (1:23)

There is a condition attached to the above promise: "If ye continue in the faith." The word for "continue" is a compound, *epimenō*. The simple verb *menō* means "remain." So *epimenō* means "remain on" or "stay." Figuratively it has the sense of "persist" or "persevere."

Grounded or Established? (1:23)

The Greek has the perfect passive participle of *theme-lioō*, "lay the foundation of." Figuratively it means "firmly established" (NASB). That is perhaps the best translation. But the background sense should be kept in mind. It means to have one's foundations securely laid.

Settled or Steadfast? (1:23)

The adjective is *hedraios*. Elsewhere in the NT it occurs only in 1 Corinthians (7:37; 15:58), where it is translated "stedfast." It comes from *hedra*, "seat," and so literally means "sitting" or "seated." The best rendering is probably "steadfast."

Not Moved or Not Shifting? (1:23)

The verb is *metakineō* (only here in NT). It means to "remove" or "shift." Since it is a present participle, indicating continuous action, it should be rendered "not constantly shifting"—or, perhaps, "not being moved away."

Fill Up (1:24)

The word is a double compound *antanaplēroō* (only here in NT). It is composed of *anti*, "over against"; *ana*, "again"; and *plēroō*, "fill." So it means "I fill up in turn" (A-S, p. 40) or "I fill up on my part." Lightfoot suggests that the force of the *anti* here is to signify that "the supply comes *from an opposite corner* to the deficiency" (p. 165).

That Which Is Behind (1:24)

This is an awkward clause in English. The Greek has

simply *ta hysterēmata,* "the things lacking" or "that which is lacking." (A neuter plural in Greek may often be translated as a singular in English.)

But what does Paul mean by saying that he is completing what is lacking in the sufferings of Christ for the Church? Roman Catholics have used this passage as a basis for their doctrine of the merit of the saints, and so the system of indulgences.

As usual, Lightfoot gives a helpful explanation. He says that the sufferings of Christ may be considered from two different points of view. "From the former point of view the Passion of Christ was the one full perfect and sufficient sacrifice, oblation, and satisfaction for the sins of the whole world." But—"From the latter point of view it is a simple matter of fact that the afflictions of every saint and martyr do supplement the afflictions of Christ. The Church is built up by repeated acts of self-denial in successive individuals and successive generations." He adds: "But St. Paul would have been the last to say that they bear their part in the atoning sacrifice of Christ" (p. 166). In a very real sense it is still true today that only a suffering ministry can be a saving ministry. The preacher of the gospel must live redemptively if he is going to be used by his Master in redeeming men from sin.

Dispensation or Stewardship? (1:25)

Again we meet this word *oikonomia,* which clearly means "stewardship." The term "dispensation" has come so generally to be used in a prophetic sense for a period of history that it fails completely to convey the correct idea here. The Christian's task today, as was Paul's in the first century, is a stewardship from God.

Preach or Proclaim? (1:28)

The verb is *katangellō,* which occurs 17 times in the NT (6 in Paul, 11 in Acts). Ten of these times it is rendered "preach" in KJV. Thayer gives its meaning as: "to announce, declare, promulgate, make known; to proclaim publicly, publish" (p. 330). Schniewind says: "As with all the *angel*-verbs . . . it has the constant sense of 'proclaiming'" (TDNT, 1:70). The preferable translation is "proclaim" (RSV, NEB, NASB, NIV).

Warn or Admonish? (1:28)

The verb *noutheteō* is translated "warning" in most versions. But the only meanings that Abbott-Smith gives are: "to admonish, exhort" (p. 304). Thayer adds "warn" and Arndt and Gingrich "instruct." The verb is compounded of *nous,* "mind," and *tithēmi,* "put." So it literally means "put in mind." It would seem that "admonish" (ASV, NASB, NEB) is a little closer to the original. Actually KJV renders it "warn" four times and "admonish" four times.

Labour or Toil? (1:29)

The verb *kopiaō* occurs in Luke 5:5—"We have toiled all the night" (see also Matt. 6:28; Luke 12:27). In John 4:6 it is translated "being wearied." Elsewhere (19 times) it is rendered "labour" or "bestow labour." Thayer notes that in the contemporary writers Josephus and Plutarch the word means *"to grow weary, tired, exhausted,* (with toil or burdens of grief) . . . in biblical Greek alone, *to labor with wearisome effort, to toil"* (p. 355). Arndt and Gingrich say that the general idea is "work hard." For this passage they suggest: "This is what I am toiling for" (p. 444).

Hauck notes that the word means "to make great exertions" or "to wear oneself out" (TDNT, 3:828). It was used in burial inscriptions for severe, strenuous work. So it would seem that "I toil" (RSV) or "I am toiling" (C. B. Williams) expresses it well.

Striving or Struggling? (1:29)

Our word "agonize" comes directly from the Greek *agōnizō,* which is used here. Occurring only seven times in the NT, it is rendered "strive" three times (here; Luke 13:24; 1 Cor. 9:25), "fight" three times (John 18:36; 1 Tim. 6:12; 2 Tim. 4:7), and "labour fervently" once (Col. 4:12).

The root of this word is the noun *agōn.* Literally this means "a gathering." But since the main gatherings in the Graeco-Roman world were for athletic contests—as in America today—the word came to be applied to the contests themselves. Thus the verb meant "to contend for a prize" or "to compete in an athletic contest." The thought is conveyed correctly by Beck's rendering: "struggling like an athlete." Paul did not go at his work for the Lord in any halfhearted manner. He struggled as strenuously as any athlete would do to win. Weymouth words it beautifully: "To this end, like an eager wrestler, I exert all my strength in reliance upon the power of Him who is mightily at work within me."

Eadie translates the participle *agōnizomenos* "intensely struggling." He writes: "It was no light work, no pastime; it made a demand upon every faculty and every moment" (p. 104). He continues: "It would seem from the following verses, that it is to an agony of spiritual earnestness that the apostle refers—to that profound yearning which occasioned so many wrestlings in prayer, and drew from him so many tears" (pp. 104-5). Eadie concludes:

When we reflect upon the motive—the presentation of perfect men to God, and upon the instrument—the preaching of the cross, we cease to wonder at the apostle's zeal and toils. For there is no function so momentous—not that which studies the constitution of man, in order to ascertain his diseases and remove them; nor that which labours for social improvement, and the promotion of science and civilization; nor that which unfolds the resources of a nation, and secures it a free and patriotic government—far more important than all, is the function of the Christian ministry *(p. 105)*.

This is a truth which every minister of Christ needs to recall frequently to spur him on.

Working or Energy? (1:29)

The noun is *energeia*. Abbott-Smith says it signifies *"operative power* (as distinct from *dynamis, potential* power)" (p. 153).

It is a bit difficult to translate this verse satisfactorily. "Working" and "worketh" are cognate noun and verb in the Greek *(energeia, energeō)*. This connection is missed in RSV—"For this I toil, ...iving with all the energy which he mightily inspires within me." Probably the most literal translation is: "according to His energy which is being energized in me in powe " *(dynamis)*.

It is comforting to know that though we must strive earnestly, yet it is only God's power which enables us to do this successfully, and so we rely on that dynamic energy. Eadie expresses this thought beautifully. He says:

It was, indeed, no sluggish heart that beat in the apostle's bosom. His was no torpid temperament. There was such a keenness in all its emotions and anxieties, that its resolve and action were simultaneous movements. But though he laboured so industriously, and suffered so bravely in the aim of winning souls to

Christ and glory, still he owned that all was owing to
Divine power lodged within him—

> *The work to be perform'd is ours,*
> *The strength is all His own;*
> *'Tis He that works to will,*
> *'Tis He that works to do;*
> *His is the power by which we act,*
> *His be the glory too (p. 105).*

Conflict or Struggle? (2:1)

The Greek word for "conflict" is *agōna*, from the same
root as in *agōnizō* in the previous verse. We noted there
that the term is primarily an athletic one, referring to
engaging in an athletic contest. It would seem that this connection should somehow be brought out. With its "striving" (1:29) and "conflict" (2:1) KJV fails to do this. The
RSV does maintain the relationship by using "striving"
and "how greatly I strive for you." But in order to do this
it changes the noun here into a verb.

The NASB misses the connection by using "striving"
and "struggle." Beck has "struggling like an athlete" in
1:29 and "how much I'm struggling for you" in 2:1.

Comforted or Encouraged? (2:2)

The verb is *parakaleō;* literally, "call to one's side." In
usage it has three distinct connotations: (1) beseech, en-
treat; (2) admonish, exhort; (3) cheer, encourage, comfort
(A-S, p. 340). Thayer says that here it means "to encourage, strengthen" (p. 483). Arndt and Gingrich prefer "comforted" (p. 623). But the majority of recent translations
use "cheered" (Weymouth, Goodspeed, Berk.) or "encouraged" (TCNT, Moffatt, Phillips, RSV, NASB, NIV).
Lightfoot says it means "'comforted' in the older and

wider meaning of the word . . . but not with its modern and restricted sense" (pp. 172-73).

Knit or Bound? (2:2)

The verb is a compound, *symbibazō*. It means "to join together, put together." So the passive here signifies "united" or "knit together." Weymouth, followed by Berkeley, has "welded together."

A thoughtful reader might ask why Moffatt has: "May they learn the meaning of love!" It is because *symbibazō* in the Septuagint always has the sense of "instruct." So in this passage the Vulgate has *instructi*. This is the correct meaning in 1 Cor. 2:16 and Acts 19:33. But Lightfoot argues well that here it must be taken as "united" (NIV), the connotation it clearly has elsewhere in Colossians and Ephesians.

Full Assurance or Conviction? (2:2)

The Greek word is *plērophoria*, from *plērēs*, "full," and *phoreō*, "bear." So the literal meaning is "fullness"; or "abundance," which Thayer prefers here. Abbott-Smith and Arndt and Gingrich give "full assurance" as the first meaning. It may also denote "certainty" or "confidence." Moffatt uses "conviction" in this passage (cf. TCNT, Beck). Lightfoot feels that the word always means "full assurance" in the NT, though "fullness" might possibly fit most passages (p. 173). Arndt and Gingrich agree. Delling suggests "superabundance" (TDNT, 6:311).

Acknowledgment or Knowledge? (2:2)

The word *epignōsis* is translated "knowledge" in KJV in 16 out of its 20 occurrences in the NT. Three times it is

rendered "acknowledging" and only here "acknowledgement." Abbott-Smith gives only three meanings: "acquaintance, discernment, recognition"; Thayer, "precise
and correct knowledge." Since we have already discussed
this word at length in connection with its use in 1:9, we
shall simply note that here "knowledge" (RSV) or "true
knowledge" (NASB) is probably preferable to "acknowl-
edgment."

Hid or Hidden? (2:3)

The adjective *apocryphos* (only here; Mark 4:22; Luke
8:17) is the basis for the expression "apocryphal books."
This was used not only for the noncanonical (more accurately, deutero-canonical) books of the OT, but also for the
secret writings of the Gnostics. Against their claims to
esoteric knowledge, Paul asserts that all true knowledge is
hidden—"stored up, hidden from view" (Weymouth)—in
Christ.

Since *apocryphos* is an adjective, it would seem that
"hidden" (NASB, NIV) is more accurate than "hid"
(KJV, RSV).

Beguile or Deceive? (2:4)

The term *paralogizomai* occurs only here and in Jas.
1:22. It first meant "to miscalculate," and then "to reason
falsely" and so "mislead" (A-S, p. 341). Thayer gives: "to
deceive by false reasoning," and so, as here, "to deceive,
delude" (p. 484). For this passage Arndt and Gingrich
give "deceive, delude." It would seem that "delude" (RSV,
NASB) or "deceive" (NIV) is more exact than "beguile."

Enticing Words or Persuasive Argument? (2:4)

This is one word in Greek, the compound *pithano-*

logia (only here in NT). It comes from the adjective *pithanos,* "persuasive" or "plausible," and *logos,* "speech." So it means "persuasive speech." Arndt and Gingrich say that here it means *"plausible* (but false) arguments" (p. 663). Probably the best translation is "persuasive argument" (NASB) or "fine-sounding arguments" (NIV).

T. K. Abbott (ICC) makes the following observation on the two significant words of this verse: *"Pithanologia* expresses the subjective means of persuasion, the personal influence; *paralogizomai* the objective, the appearance of logic" (p. 242).

Steadfastness or Firmness? (2:5)

The Greek word *stereōma* (only here in NT) first meant "that which has been made firm," and finally "firmness, steadfastness" (Thayer, p. 587). The preference perhaps lies slightly with "firmness" (RSV, cf. NIV).

Lightfoot feels that both "order" *(taxis)* and "steadfastness" are military terms. He suggests for the former "orderly array" and for the latter "solid front" or "close phalanx" (p. 176). Apparently this is the basis for the popular translation "solid front" (TCNT, Weymouth, Moffatt). For the two terms NEB has: "your orderly array and the firm front."

Bertram translates here, "orderly and firm." He also calls attention to the fact that *taxis* is a military term and adds that *stereōma* "might also suggest a military metaphor in the sense of a castle or bulwark." He goes on to say that the righteous, as at Colosse, "are pressed by enemies, but they can stand fast in the stronghold of their faith and trust" (TDNT, 7:614).

To all of this Abbott takes exception. He writes: "But neither word has this military sense of itself, but from the context, and here the context suggests nothing of the kind." He concludes: "Here the idea of a well-ordered state lies much nearer than that of an army. The apostle rejoices in the orderly arrangement of the Colossian Church" (p. 243).

Meyer agrees with this. He says: "Hence, if we would avoid arbitrariness, we can only abide by the view that here *taxis* means the *orderly state of the Christian church,* which has hitherto not been disturbed by sectarian divisions or forsaken by the readers." He adds: "To this *outward* condition Paul then subjoins the *inner* one, by which the former is conditioned: *and the solid hold of your faith in Christ"* (p. 287).

It would be our feeling that the military metaphor might be used homiletically as an illustration of one kind of order and firmness. This could be done without insisting that this is the only, or even primary, application of the words.

Walk or Live? (2:6)

The verb is *peripateō,* which literally means "walk around." It may be translated "go about," as in Mark 12: 38. More often it has the general meaning "walk."

But in the NT it is frequently used in the figurative sense. This is especially true of Paul's Epistles, where it has this metaphorical meaning 32 times. The same usage is found in the three Johannine letters 10 times. It occurs 4 times in the Epistle to the Colossians. Used thus it means "to regulate one's life, to conduct one's self" (Thayer, p. 504).

The majority of recent translations prefer "live." While the NASB follows the ASV in retaining "walk," Goodspeed has: "So just as you once accepted the Christ, Jesus, as your Lord, you must live in vital union with him." Since *peripateō* is in the continuous present tense here, a better rendering is: "continue to live in him" (NIV).

Rooted and Built Up (2:7)

Paul here portrays the Christian as being rooted in Christ and built upon Christ as the Foundation. In Eph. 3:17 he speaks of being "rooted and grounded in love." These are the only two passages in the NT where the Greek verb for "root" occurs. (The noun is found 16 times.)

In this verse "rooted" is a perfect passive participle, whereas "built up" is a present passive participle. The NASB seeks to carry this distinction over into English by saying: "having been firmly rooted and now being built up in him." Charles B. Williams has: "with your roots deeply planted in Him, being continuously built up in Him."

Spoil or Capture? (2:8)

The verb is *sylagōgeō,* found only here in the NT. It comes from *sylē,* "booty," and *agō,* "carry." So it literally means "to carry off as spoil, lead captive." Arndt and Gingrich say that it is used "figuratively of carrying someone away from the truth into the slavery of error" (p. 784). So "capture" is the correct meaning here, and some form of this verb is found in most modern versions. In the KJV here the verb "spoil" is used in its earliest meaning, "to strip or despoil, or to strip (persons) of goods or possessions by violence or force; to plunder, rob, despoil" (OED, 10:650). The *Oxford English Dictionary* gives several examples of this usage at about 1611, when the KJV was translated. But this is not what the term connotes today.

Philosophy (2:8)

This comes directly from the Greek *philosophia* (only

here in NT). Literally it means "love of wisdom." Of its usage here, Thayer writes: "Once in the N.T. of the theology, or rather theosophy, of certain Jewish-Christian ascetics, which busied itself with refined and speculative inquiries into the nature and classes of angels, into the ritual of the Mosaic law and the regulations of Jewish tradition respecting practical life" (p. 655).

The term "philosophy," taken in itself, carries no bad connotation. It is said to have come as the result of the humility of Pythagoras, who called himself "a lover of (divine) wisdom." Lightfoot observes: "In such a sense the term would entirely accord with the spirit and teaching of St. Paul; for it bore testimony to the insufficiency of the human intellect and the need of a revelation. But in his age it had come to be associated generally with the idea of subtle dialectics and profitless speculation; while in this particular instance it was combined with a mystic cosmogony and angelology which contributed a fresh element of danger" (p. 179). Phillips translates the word here "intellectualism."

Vain or Empty? (2:8)

The literal meaning of *kenos* is "empty." That fits best here. Deceit is always an empty thing. Only what is true is solid. Goodness is positive; evil is negative.

Rudiments or Elements? (2:8)

The Greek word *stoicheia* occurs only seven times in the NT. Here and in verse 20 it is translated "rudiments." In Hebrews 5:12 it is "principles." But four times it is rendered "elements" (Gal. 4:3, 9; 2 Pet. 3:10, 12). Some recent versions (RSV, NEB) have "elemental spirits."

Probably a more acceptable translation would be "elementary principles" (NASB) or "basic principles" (NIV).

The primary meaning of *stoicheia* was "the letters of the alphabet." So it came to mean "rudimentary instruction." Many Early Church fathers interpreted this expression as referring to the heavenly bodies. But this seems a mistake. The application to "elemental spirits" also seems questionable.

Godhead or Deity? (2:9)

The Greek word is *theotēs* (only here in NT). It comes from *theos,* "God." The preferable translation is "deity" (RSV, NASB, NIV). That is a simpler and more commonly used term today than "Godhead." It means the essence of the divine nature.

Complete or Filled? (2:10)

The Greek form here is *peplērōmenoi.* Since it is based on the same root as *plērōma* ("fulness") in the previous verse, it would seem wise to show the connection. The RSV expresses it well: "You have come to fulness of life in him." The NIV reads: "You have this fullness in Christ."

Principality or Rule? (2:10)

The Greek word is *archē.* Most frequently in the NT it means "beginning." But in a number of passages in Paul's Epistles it has the sense of "dominion" or "rule." It always signifies "primacy," whether in time or in rank (TDNT, 1:479).

Power or Authority? (2:10)

The word is *exousia,* which properly means "author-

ity"—in distinction from *dynamis,* "power." The correct
combination here is "rule and authority" (RSV, NASB).

Of the Operation or In the Working? (2:12)

It is obvious that the expression "through the faith of
the operation of God" is meaningless. The word for "operation" is *energeia,* from *ergon,* "work." It means "working." A meaningful translation is: "through faith in the
working of God" (RSV, NASB).

Sins or Trespasses? (2:13)

The word is *paraptōma*—literally, "a falling beside."
The proper Greek word for "sin" is *hamartia.* The preferable translation here is "trespasses" (RSV).

Blotting Out or Canceled? (2:14)

The KJV gives the literal meaning. The verb *exalei-
phō* is used in the LXX in the sense of "to plaster, wash
over," and so came to mean "to wipe off, wipe out" (p.
159). This literal connotation is found in Rev. 7:17; 21:4.
It has the idea of "erase" in Rev. 3:5. But here it is used in
a metaphorical sense. Most of the recent versions follow
TCNT, Moffatt, and Goodspeed in translating it "can-
celed."

Handwriting or Bond? (2:14)

The Greek word is found only here in the NT. It is the
adjective *cheirographon;* literally, "handwritten." Here it
is used as a substantive, meaning "a handwriting." Thayer notes that it meant "specifically a note of hand, or
writing in which one acknowledges that money has either
been deposited with him or lent to him by another, to be

returned at an appointed time . . . metaphorically applied in Col. ii. 14 . . . to the Mosaic law, which shows men to be chargeable with offences for which they must pay the penalty" (p. 668).

Lohse says the word has the sense of "promissory note." He continues: "The reference is to God's pronouncement that the note which testifies against us is cancelled. The phrase is obviously based on a thought which is common to Judaism, namely that God keeps an account of man's debt . . . and that He imposes the penalty" (TDNT, 9:435). Lohse concludes: "God has forgiven sins. He has cancelled the note of indebtedness by taking it and fixing it to the cross of Christ" (p. 436).

Deissmann points out the fact that the idea of canceling a promissory note has been abundantly illustrated by the ancient Egyptian papyri discovered in modern times. He writes: "We have learnt from the new texts that it was generally customary to cancel a bond (or other document) by crossing it out with the Greek cross—letter Chi (X). In the splendid Florentine papyrus, of the year 85 A.D. . . . the governor of Egypt gives this order in the course of a trial:

'Let the handwriting be crossed out.' . . .
We have moreover recovered the originals of a number of 'crossed-out' I. O. U.'s" (LAE, pp. 333-34).

"Cancelled the bond" is the TCNT wording. This rendering has been followed by many versions (e.g., RSV, NEB). NASB reads: "having cancelled out the certificate of debt." The NIV has "the written code."

Ordinances or Decrees? (2:14)

The Greek word is *dogma,* which has been taken over into English. It meant a public decree. In the NT it is used for the decrees of Roman rulers (Luke 2:1; Acts 17:7), of the Jewish law (Eph. 2:15; Col. 2:14), and of the apostles (Acts 16:4).

Since Paul is here addressing the Gentiles as well as Jews, Lightfoot suggests: "The *dogmata* [plural] therefore, though referring primarily to the Mosaic ordinances, will include all forms of positive decrees in which moral or social principles are embodied or religious duties; and the 'bond' is the moral assent of the conscience, which (as it were) signs and seals the obligation" (p. 187). Josephus uses *dogma* for the Mosaic law.

In the KJV, "decrees" is used in the three passages written by Luke, but "ordinances" here and in the parallel passage in Eph. 2:15. Inconsistently the NASB has *"contained* in ordinances" in Eph. 2:15 but "consisting of decrees" here. Either term will fit in these two Pauline passages. (NIV has "regulations.")

Contrary to or Stood Against? (2:14)

The Greek word (only here and in Heb. 10:27) is *hypenantios,* an adjective which literally means "set over against, opposite" (A-S, p. 457), and so "opposed, contrary, hostile" (AG, p. 846). Lightfoot translates the clause: "which was directly opposed to us" (p. 188). Moulton and Milligan assert that this strong sense is illustrated by its use in a second-century papyrus from Oxyrhynchus (VGT, p. 651). Charles B. Williams gives a good brief rendering of this passage: "cancelled the note that stood against us, with its requirements." But the full force of the Greek is best brought out in TCNT: "the bond standing against us, which was in direct hostility to us."

Spoiled or Stripped? (2:15)

The strong double compound *apekduō* means *"to strip*

off clothes or arms" (A-S, p. 46). Here the form is the aorist middle participle, which literally would mean "having stripped off from himself." Lightfoot argues for that meaning here (cf. NEB). Others feel that the middle is used in this case for the active. This is perhaps the best conclusion, giving the translation "disarmed" (RSV, NIV, NASB) or "stripped" (C. B. Williams, Beck). This seems to fit in more naturally with the last two clauses of the verse.

Shew or Display? (2:15)

Deigmatizō is a "very rare verb" (VGT, p. 137). Thayer speaks of it as "a word unknown to Greek writers" (p. 126). But it has now been found in a Tebtunis papyrus from about 14 B.C. Lightfoot says that it means "'*displayed,*' as a victor displays his captives or trophies in a triumphal procession" (p. 191). He also asserts: "Nowhere does the word convey the idea of 'making an example' *(paradeigmatisai)* but signifies simply 'to display, publish, proclaim'" *(ibid.)*.

However, Arndt and Gingrich give as their definition "expose, make an example of" and suggest for this passage: "mock, expose" (p. 171). The last word is adopted by Phillips here, while the RSV has: "made a public example of them." A more neutral rendering, in line with Lightfoot's protest, would be "made a public display of them" (NASB).

In either case, the picture is made clear by the last clause of the verse. This is brought out in the paraphrase: "He made a public spectacle of them and led them as captives in his triumphal procession" (NEB). It was the familiar scene of a conqueror returning to Rome and leading the captured kings and warriors in chains in his triumphal procession. This is what Christ did on the Cross.

Meat or Food? (2:16)

Brōsis is found eleven times in the NT. In the KJV it is most frequently translated "meat." But the use of "meat" for "food" is now obsolete.

Literally the word meant "eating," and this is the sense in Matt. 6:19-20, where it is translated "rust." Lightfoot (p. 193) renders the double phrase here: "in eating and in drinking" (cf. TCNT, C. B. Williams). Arndt and Gingrich support this meaning here. Many translators prefer "by what you eat or drink" (NIV).

Holyday or Festival? (2:16)

The word *heortē* occurs 27 times in the NT and is translated "feast" in every place but here. The reference is to the annual "feasts" of the Jews, mentioned frequently in both Testaments.

But the term "feast" is not entirely satisfactory. It emphasizes the idea of eating. But one of the annual "feasts" was the Day of Atonement. On that day the people fasted, not feasted. So the word "festival," in the sense of a celebration, is better. This is what is used here by most modern translations.

Body or Substance? (2:17)

The word *sōma* literally means "body." It is used frequently in the NT for the physical body. Paul uses it many times for the Church as the body of Christ.

But here we have something different from either of these senses. The meaning is rather clearly that of "substance" in contrast to shadow. Most recent translations have "substance." The sacred rites of the Hebrew religion "have at most only a symbolical value" (Phillips). The "reality" (NIV) is found in Christ. This is the sense preferred here by Schweizer (TDNT, 7:1066).

Beguile or Disqualify? (2:18)

The expression "beguile you of your reward" does not adequately communicate to the modern reader the real meaning of *katabrabeuō* (only here in NT). This comes from *brabeus*, "an umpire." So it means *"to decide as an umpire against* one, *to declare* him *unworthy of the prize; to defraud of the prize of victory"* (Thayer, p. 330).

It is in the last sense that Lightfoot takes the word. He writes:

> The Christian's career is the contest of the stadium. . . . Christ is the umpire, the dispenser of the rewards (2 Tim. iv. 8); life eternal is the bay wreath, the victor's prize (*brabeion*, I Cor. ix. 24, Phil. iii. 14). The Colossians were in a fair way to win this prize; they had entered the lists duly; they were running bravely: but the false teachers, thrusting themselves in the way, attempted to trip them up or otherwise impede them in the race, and thus to rob them of their just reward *(p. 195).*

For this extremely rare word Arndt and Gingrich give these meanings: *"decide against* (as umpire), *rob of a prize, condemn"* (p. 410). It is certainly a much stronger term than "judge" in verse 16. Perhaps the best rendering is either "disqualify" (RSV, NIV) or "rob you of your prize" (ASV, Lightfoot).

Humility or Self-abasement? (2:18)

The word *tapeinophrosynē* carried a bad connotation in the pagan world. To heathen moralists humility was a vice. It was Christianity that made it a virtue. But Lightfoot well observes: "Humility, when it becomes self-conscious, ceases to have any value" (p. 196).

And that is the situation described here. "Voluntary" is in Greek the present participle *thelōn.* It means "taking delight in" or "devoting himself to." Goodspeed translates the phrase: "persisting in studied humility." Probably the best rendering is: "delighting in self-abasement" or "delights in false humility" (NIV). These false teachers made a religion out of asceticism.

Intruding into or Taking His Stand? (2:18)

The verb *embateuō* (only here in NT) seems to be related to *embainō,* and so to mean "enter." But just what it means here has been much debated.

It ought first to be noted that the object following this verb—"those things which he hath not seen"—should be "those things which he has seen." There is no negative in the best Greek text.

Arndt and Gingrich call attention to two possible meanings of *embateuō.* The first is: *"enter into* a subject, to investigate it closely, *go into detail* . . . hence in Col. 2:18 perhaps *entering at length upon the tale of what he has seen* in a vision" (p. 253). With regard to the second they write: "Three inscriptions of Asia Minor (second century A.D.) . . . show that *embateuō* was a technical term of the mystery religions. Then perhaps . . . *taking his stand on what he had seen* in the mysteries" *(ibid.).* This last idea is developed at length by Moulton and Milligan (VGT, p. 206).

The passage is admittedly difficult. About the best that can be done is: "goes into great detail about what he has seen" (NIV).

Will Worship or Self-made Religion? (2:23)

The compound *ethelothrēskia* is found only here in the

NT. It means *"voluntary, arbitrary worship . . .* i.e. worship which one devises and prescribes for himself, contrary to the contents and nature of the faith which ought to be directed to Christ; said of the misdirected zeal and practices of ascetics: Col. ii. 23" (Thayer, p. 168). Abbott-Smith gives "self-imposed worship" (cf. NEB). Arndt and Gingrich have "self-made religion." Probably as good a translation as any of this verse is: "Such regulations indeed have an appearance of wisdom, with their self-imposed worship, their false humility and their harsh treatment of the body, but they lack any value in restraining sensual indulgence" (NIV).

Affection or Mind? (3:2)

"Set your affection" is one word in Greek, the verb *phroneite*. It comes from the noun for "mind" *(phrēn)*. Homer and other early writers used it in the sense of "have understanding." Then it meant "to think." Here it means: "to have in mind, be mindful of, think of" (A-S, p. 474). For this passage Arndt and Gingrich suggest "set one's mind on, be intent on" (p. 874). Thayer has: "to direct one's mind to a thing" (p. 658). The best translation is probably, "Set your mind on things above" (NIV).

Mortify or Put to Death? (3:5)

Nekrōsate is from *nekros,* "dead." So it literally means "put to death." Thayer suggests that here it means "to deprive of power, destroy the strength of" (p. 424). But why dilute the full force of the verb? Arndt and Gingrich translate the clause: "Put to death what is earthly in you" (p. 537). "Mortify" is hardly an adequate rendering because it is used too loosely today.

Inordinate Affection or Passion? (3:5)

The KJV has a long translation for a short word—
pathos. This comes from the second aorist stem *(path)* of
paschō, "suffer." Basically it means "that which befalls
one, that which one suffers," and so "a passion, passionate desire" (A-S, pp. 332-33). It occurs only here, in Rom.
1:26, and in 1 Thess. 4:5. Thayer notes that, while it was
"used by the Greeks in either a good or a bad sense," yet
"in the N. T. (only) in a bad sense, *depraved passion*"
(p. 472). Doubtless "passion" is a more meaningful rendering today, and so it is found in most modern translations.

Concupiscence or Desire? (3:5)

The former (KJV) is also an antiquated expression,
unused today. The Greek *epithymia* means "desire." It is
used in the NT for the natural desire of hunger (Luke 15:
16; 16:21). But in Paul's Epistles it usually has a bad connotation. Buechsel writes: "The essential point in *epithymia* is that it is desire as impulse, as a motion of the
will. . . . *Epithymia* is anxious self-seeking" (TDNT,
3:171). Since the adjective "evil" is affixed to the term
here, clearly the best translation is "desire."

Blasphemy or Slander? (3:8)

The Greek word is *blasphēmia*. But originally this did
not have the modern connotation of blasphemy. It meant
"slander, detraction, speech injurious to another's good
name," and only later "impious and reproachful speech
injurious to the divine majesty" (Thayer, p. 102). So the
correct translation here, as in numerous other places in the
NT, is "slander."

Filthy Communication or Foul Talk? (3:8)

This is one word in the Greek; *aischrologia* (only here
in NT). It means "abusive language" (A-S, p. 14). Thayer
says: "Foul speaking . . . low and obscene speech" (p. 17).
Arndt and Gingrich have: *"Evil speech* in the sense of
obscene speech . . . or *abusive speech"* (p. 24).

Lightfoot combines both these ideas in his translation,
"foul-mouthed abuse." After noting that the word is
defined by Clement of Alexandria as "filthy-talking" and
used by Polybius in the sense of "abusive language," he
continues: "If the two senses of the word had been quite
distinct, we might have some difficulty in choosing between them here. . . . But the second sense is derived
from the first. The word can only mean 'abuse' when the
abuse is 'foul-mouthed.' And thus we may suppose that
both ideas, 'filthiness' and 'evil-speaking,' are included
here" (p. 214).

Trench insists that the meaning of the word should
not be confined to obscene discourse, as the Greek Fathers
usually took it, but should also include *"every* license of
the ungoverned tongue employing itself in the abuse of
others" (p. 121). T. K. Abbott feels that "the connexion
here shows that it means 'abusive' rather than 'filthy' language," and adds that "the sins of uncleanness have been
dealt with in ver. 5, and the other substantives here regard
want of charity" (p. 283).

In the light of all this discussion it would seem that
"foul talk" (RSV), "abusive speech" (NASB), and "filthy
language" (NIV) are all correct.

Barbarian (3:11)

The Greek word is the adjective *barbaros*. It is probably an onomatopoetic word; that is, its sound suggests its

sense. Thayer gives this ample definition: "1. properly, *one whose speech is rude, rough, harsh,* as if repeating the syllables *barbar* . . . hence 2. *one who speaks a foreign* or *strange language which is not understood by another.* . . . 3. The Greeks used *barbaros of any foreigner ignorant of the Greek language and the Greek culture* . . . with the added notion, after the Persian war, of rudeness and brutality" (p. 95).

Scythian (3:11)

This word refers to "an inhabitant of Scythia, i.e., Russia and Siberia, a synonym with the Greeks for the wildest of barbarians" (A-S, p. 410). Lightfoot comments: "The savageness of the Scythians was proverbial" (p. 218). But in Christ there are no distinctions of race or color, of culture or education.

Windisch points out that each of the other three pairs in this verse is in the form of an antithesis; so presumably this one (Barbarian/Scythian) is also. He suggests that Paul "contrasted the barbarians generally with a particularly notorious barbarian people" (TDNT, 1:553).

Bowels or Heart? (3:12)

Again we meet this word *splanchna,* which literally means "bowels," but is used metaphorically for the seat of the affections. Instead of "bowels of mercies" we should read "a heart of compassion" (NASB).

Forbearing or Bearing with? (3:13)

In the active the verb *anechō* means "hold up." But in the NT it is always in the middle and means "bear with." Though most versions retain "forbearing," it would seem that "bearing with" (NASB) is slightly more meaningful (cf. "bear with," NIV).

Forgiving or Freely Forgiving? (3:13)

The verb is *charizomai*. It comes from *charis*, which means "grace." So it means "forgive graciously." The more common word for "forgive" in the NT is *aphiēmi*, which literally means "leave off." But the word here carries a deeper sense of wholehearted forgiveness. It should be translated "freely forgiving" (C. B. Williams). Weymouth has "readily forgiving." That is the right idea. Our forgiveness of others must be given, not grudgingly, but gladly.

Quarrel or Complaint? (3:13)

The Greek word *momphē* occurs only here in the NT. It literally means "blame" or "complaint." The correct translation here is "complaint" or "grievances" (NIV). Even if we have a just cause for complaint against someone, we should "forgive as freely as the Lord has forgiven you" (Phillips). We want God's forgiveness of us to be immediate, gracious, and complete. That is the kind of forgiveness we must extend to others.

Charity or Love? (3:14)

This is one of the most unfortunate renderings found in the King James Version. The Greek word is *agapē*, which means the highest kind of unselfish, holy love. Yet 27 times the KJV renders it "charity," which today suggests handouts and cast-off clothes. The word should always be translated "love."

Bond of Perfectness (3:14)

The Greek phrase is a bit difficult to translate into English. This is shown by the fact that one can hardly find two versions that agree exactly.

"Bond" is *syndesmos*. It comes from the verb *syndeō,* which means "bind together." So it signifies "that which binds together."

"Perfectness" is *teleiotētos* (only here and in Heb. 6: 1), which means "completeness." It comes from *telos,* "end."

What this passage states is that love is "the power, which unites and holds together all those graces and virtues, which together make up perfection" (Lightfoot, p. 222). Since the figure that Paul uses here is that of putting on clothing (v. 12), it would seem that love may be thought of here as the belt which holds all the rest in place. This is to be put on "above all these things," to tie them together. Phillips perhaps suggests this when he says that "love is the golden chain of all the virtues." Lightfoot thinks of love rather as the outer garment, to be worn over all the rest. He paraphrases this passage: "And over all these robe yourselves in love; for this is the garment which binds together all the graces of perfection" (p. 220).

Rule or Arbitrate? (3:15)

The Greek word for "rule" is *brabeuō* (only here in NT). It comes from *brabeus,* which means "an umpire." So it properly means "act as an umpire," and thus "arbitrate, decide" (A-S, p. 85). Lightfoot paraphrases this clause: "And let the one supreme umpire in your hearts, the one referee amidst all your difficulties, be the peace of Christ" (p. 220). He comments on this passage: "Wherever there is a conflict of motives or impulses or reasons, the

peace of Christ must step in and decide which is to pre-
vail" (p. 223).

It is true that some commentators object to adopting
the literal meaning of *brabeuō* here. For instance, Meyer
writes:

> It means primarily: *to arrange and conduct the
> contest* . . . then *to confer the prize of victory,* to be
> *brabeus, i.e.* umpire; finally: *to govern* generally. Con-
> sidering its very frequent occurrence in the latter sense,
> and its appropriateness in that sense to (in your
> hearts), and seeing that any reference to the Messianic
> *brabeion* (comp. ii. 18) is foreign to the context, the
> majority of modern expositors have rightly interpreted
> it: the peace of Christ must *rule, govern* in your hearts
> *(p. 362).*

Moulton and Milligan cite several examples of this
more general meaning in papyri of the second century
B.C. But they find also definite reference to the athletic
games in other cases. They conclude: "We may endorse
accordingly . . . Lightfoot's insistence on the element of
award or *decision* in a conflict between two impulses, in
the remarkable phrase of Col. 3:15: whether the figure of
the games is present we need not argue" (VGT, p. 116).
In connection with this passage Stauffer says: "Paul uses
the verb of the peace which settles all strife and preserves
the unity of the Christian community" (TDNT, 1:638).
So it seems to us that the idea of "arbitrate" fits well here.
C. B. Williams has: "Let the peace that Christ can give
keep on acting as umpire in your hearts." He also brings
out the force of the (continuous) present imperative in the
last clause of this verse by rendering it: "And practice
being thankful."

Submit or Be Subject? (3:18)

The verb is *hypotassō*. It was first used as a military

term, with the sense "place under" or "arrange under."
In the middle, as here, it means "subject oneself, obey"
(A-S, p. 463). Perhaps the better rendering here is "be
subject to" (RSV, NEB, NASB).

Fit or Duty? (3:18)

Paul says that the subordination of the wife to the
husband is "fit" in the Lord. The Greek word is the verb
anēkō. Thayer gives this definition: "In Greek writers *to
have come up to, arrived at, to reach to, pertain to* . . .
hence in later writers . . . *something appertains to one, is
due to him* . . . and then ethically *what is due, duty* . . .
impersonal *hōs anēke, as was fitting* . . . Col. III. 18" (p.
45). Charles B. Williams brings out this idea of obligation
when he translates this clause: "For this is your Christian
duty."

Bitter or Harsh? (3:19)

The verb is *pikrainō*. It comes from *pikros*, which is
found only in Jas. 3:11, 14. This adjective is defined by
Abbott-Smith as follows: "1. *sharp, pointed.* 2. *sharp* to
the senses; of taste, *bitter* . . . metaphorically, *harsh*, bitter" (p. 360). So the verb in the passive, as here, means
"to be embittered, irritated" (Thayer, p. 509). But many
of the translations use "harsh" (RSV, NEB, NIV), and this
seems to fit well. T. K. Abbott writes: "The word would
seem, then, to correspond more nearly with the colloquial
'cross' than with 'bitter'" (p. 293). As usual, Phillips gives
a free but meaningful paraphrase: "Husbands, be sure you
give your wives much love and sympathy; don't let bitter-
ness or resentment spoil your marriage."

Provoke or Exasperate? (3:21)

The problem here is partly as to which Greek word is original. The Textus Receptus, on which the KJV is based, has *parorgizete* (only here and in Rom. 10:19). This means "provoke to anger." But the reading found in the very earliest manuscripts (Papyrus 46, Vaticanus) is *erethizete*. In the only other place in the NT where it occurs it has a good sense—"stir up, stimulate." But here it has the bad sense—"stir up, provoke" (A-S, p. 179). Arndt and Gingrich say that it means: *"Arouse, provoke* mostly in a bad sense, *irriate, embitter"* (p. 308). It would seem that the best translation here is "irritate" (TCNT, Moffatt, Goodspeed, Beck) or "exasperate" (NEB, NASB). Weymouth gives a rather full paraphrase: "Fathers, do not fret and harass your children, or you may make them sullen and morose." In line with this, Lightfoot comments: "'Irritation' is the first consequence of being too exacting with children, and irritation leads to moroseness" (p. 227).

Discouraged or Disheartened? (3:21)

The verb *athymeō* (only here in NT) is compounded of *a*-negative and *thymos*. The latter comes from *thyō*, which means "rush along" (cf. thymus gland). The idea of *athymeō* is "to be disheartened, dispirited, broken in spirit" (Thayer, p. 14). This is a tragic thing to have happen to children. Lightfoot suggests that the idea here is that irritated children will "go about their task in a listless, moody, sullen frame of mind" (p. 227). Probably the best translation is "disheartened" (TCNT, NEB) or "lose heart" (Goodspeed, NASB), though "discouraged" is also accurate and meaningful.

Do or Work? (3:23)

The KJV reads: "Whatsoever ye do, do it heartily."
But this ignores the fact that whereas the first *do* is the
common verb of that meaning, *poieō*, the second *do* is
ergazō, which means "work." The correct translation is:
"Whatever you do, work at it with all your heart" (NIV).

Heartily or From the Heart? (3:23)

The latter is a little nearer the Greek, which has *ek
psychēs*—literally, "out of the soul." Like the English
word "soul," the Greek *psychē* has many meanings. The
one that fits here is apparently "heart." This admonition
means: "Let your hearts be in your work" (Weymouth).
Phillips' paraphrase is excellent: "Put your whole heart
and soul into it."

Reward or Recompense? (3:24)

The Greek word *antapodosis* is found only here in the
NT. It is a double compound, composed of *didōmi*, "give";
apo, "from"; and *anti*, "in exchange for." It comes from
the verb *antapodidōmi*, which Abbott-Smith defines as:
"To give back as an equivalent, recompense, requital (the
anti expressing the idea of full, complete return)" (p. 40).
For the noun he gives "recompense." The point is that we
shall receive our heavenly inheritance as a full reward or
recompense for all that we have relinquished down here.
We shall be paid in full.

Receive or Paid Back? (3:25)

The verb is not the same as the one translated "receive" in verse 24. There it was the more general word

apolambanō, which has the idea mainly of receiving from another. Here it is *komizō*, which Abbott-Smith defines as: "1. *to take care of.* 2. *to carry off safe.* 3. *to bear or carry:* Lk. 7:37. Middle, *to bear for oneself,* hence *(a) to receive . . . (b) to receive back, recover . . .* metaphorically, of requital . . . Col. 3:25" (p. 253).

Thayer writes: "Since in the rewards and punishments of deeds, the deeds themselves are as it were requited and so given back to their authors, the meaning is obvious when one is said *komizesthai* (to be requited) *that which he has done,* i.e. either the reward or punishment of the deed" (p. 354).

Perhaps the best translation is "be paid back" (Goodspeed, RSV). Moffatt puts it exactly: "The wrongdoer will be paid back for his wrongdoing."

Give or Grant? (4:1)

The verb translated "give" is not the common *didōmi* or one of its compounds. It is *parechō*. Lightfoot renders it "exhibit on your part" and comments: "The middle *parechesthai,* 'to afford from oneself,' will take different shades of meaning according to the context. . . . Here the idea is 'reciprocation,' the master's duty as corresponding to the slave's" (p. 230).

Possibly "grant" is a little more nearly exact than "give." All versions, however, present the meaning well.

Equal or Fair? (4:1)

The Greek word is *isotēs,* which literally signifies "equality." But in this passage it probably means "equity" or "fairness." Lightfoot writes: "It seems a mistake to suppose that *isotēs* here has anything to do with the treatment of slaves as *equals* (comp. Philem. 16). When connected with *to dikaion* ("that which is just"), the word naturally suggests an even-handed, impartial treatment, and is equivalent to the Latin *aequitas.* . . . Thus in Aristotle . . . *to dikaion* and *to ison* are regarded as synonymns, and in Plutarch . . . the relation of *isotēs* to *dikaiotēs* is discussed" (p. 230).

T. K. Abbott is in essential agreement. He says: *"Isotēs* differs from *to dikaion* nearly as our 'fair' from 'just,' denoting what cannot be brought under positive rules, but is in accordance with the judgment of a fair mind" (p. 296). So it would seem that the best translation here is: "Masters, provide your slaves with what is right and fair" (NIV).

Continue or Continue Steadfastly? (4:2)

The Greek has a strong compound, *proskartereō.* It is composed of *pros,* "to," and *karteros,* "strong, steadfast." So it means: "to occupy oneself diligently with something," "to pay persistent attention to," or "to hold fast to something" (TDNT, 3:618). This word is used in connection with praying in Acts 1:14; 2:42; 6:4; and Rom. 12:12.

It is obvious that "continue" is an inadequate rendering. The compound verb demands "continue steadfastly" (RSV) or "persevere" (NEB).

Watch (4:2)

The verb is *grēgoreō,* which means "to be awake" or "to keep awake." Arndt and Gingrich would translate it here: "be wide awake about it" (p. 166). Since the form here is a present participle, a better rendering than "watch" is "being watchful" (NIV).

Lightfoot makes a helpful comment. He observes: "Long continuance in prayer is apt to produce listlessness.

Hence the additional charge that the heart must be *awake*, if the prayer is to have any value." He adds that "thanksgiving" is "the crown of all prayer" (p. 231).

Of Utterance or For the Word? (4:3)

Paul solicits the prayers of the Colossian Christians that God might open for him (apparently at Rome) "a door of utterance." In the Greek the last term is *logos*, which means "word." So the better translation is "a door for the word" (RSV, NASB). What is meant is well expressed thus: "that God may open a door for our message" (NIV). That he received this open door is indicated by Acts 28:31.

Walk or Conduct? (4:5)

The Greek word *peripateō* properly means "walk." It is used in this literal sense countless times in the Gospels and Acts. But Paul employs it over 30 times in a figurative sense. With him it means "live" or "conduct oneself." In this passage a better translation is, "Conduct yourselves" (RSV, NASB). Weymouth catches the thought of this clause well in his paraphrase: "Behave wisely in relation to the outside world."

Redeeming or Making the Most of? (4:5)

The verb *exagorazō* literally means to buy something "out of" *(ex)* the marketplace *(agora)*. But it came to be used technically in the sense of "ransom" or "redeem" slaves. That is the basis of its metaphorical use in Gal. 3:13; 4:5. But here and in Eph. 5:16 (the only other places it occurs in NT) it is found in the present middle participle. Used this way it means "buying up for oneself." Thayer says that in these two passages "the meaning seems to be *to make a wise and sacred use of every opportunity for doing good,* so that zeal and well-doing are as it were the purchase-money by which we make the time our own" (p. 220).

A meaningful translation is: "making the most of the time" (RSV; cf. NASB). Since the word for "time" is *kairos,* which means "opportune time," a good rendering is: "make the most of every opportunity" (NIV). Lightfoot gives this full paraphrase: "Walk wisely and discreetly in all your dealings with unbelievers; allow no opportunity to slip through your hands, but buy up every passing moment" (p. 230).

Salt and Grace (4:6)

Paul writes: "Let your speech be alway with grace, seasoned with salt." It would seem that *salt* is closely related to *grace.* Weymouth brings it out this way: "Let your language be always seasoned with the salt of grace."

In the Greek comic writers the verb *artyō,* "season," referred to the seasoning with the salt of wit. But too often this degenerated into off-color jokes. Paul says that the Christian's speech should be "with grace," or "gracious."

Salt gives both flavor and preservation, making food tasty and wholesome. A very helpful translation of this verse is: "Let your conversation be always gracious, and never insipid; study how best to talk with each person you meet" (NEB).

Your Estate or Our Circumstances? (4:8)

The KJV says that Paul was sending Tychicus to the Colossian church "that he might know your estate." Why do the NASB and NIV have "that you may know about our circumstances"?

The answer is that the latter translation represents what scholars believe to be the best Greek text, though admittedly the manuscript evidence in this case is rather evenly balanced. But the reading adopted by most modern translators is parallel to that in Eph. 6:22, where Paul is apparently saying the same thing.

In any case, "estate" is an archaic rendering here. Today "estate" means property belonging to someone. Here the Greek literally says: "the things concerning us *(or you)."* The correct idea is: "that you may know how we are" (RSV).

Comfort or Encourage? (4:8)

The verb *parakaleō* literally means "call alongside (to help)." It is variously translated as "beseech," "exhort," "comfort," or "encourage." Only the context can decide the choice. It would seem that "encourage" fits best here, as most translators have agreed. The correct thought is expressed by such a rendering as "put fresh heart into you" (NEB). Lightfoot feels that in this passage, as in Eph. 6:22 and 2 Thess. 2:17, the real meaning is "encourage you to persevere" (p. 235).

Sister's Son or Cousin? (4:10)

The KJV presents Mark as the nephew of Barnabas. But the Greek word *anepsios* (only here in NT) really meant "cousin" at the time. Lightfoot writes: "The term *anepsioi* is applied to cousins german, the children whether of two brothers or of two sisters or of a brother and sister, as it is carefully defined in Pollux iii. 28" (p. 236). (Pollux wrote his famous Greek dictionary, entitled *Onomasticon,* in the second century after Christ.) Abbott says of *anepsios:* "The use of it for 'nephew' is very late" (p. 300).

Receive or Welcome? (4:10)

Paul says that he had already given instructions that if Mark should come, the Colossians were to "receive" him. The verb is *dechomai* (not the same word as "received" earlier in the verse). It means "accept" or "welcome." Most of the recent translations have adopted "welcome" or "make him welcome." The importance of this idea is underlined by T. K. Abbott. After calling attention to the correct term above, "cousin," he says: "The relationship explains why Barnabas was more ready than Paul to condone Mark's defection, Acts xv. 37-39. At the same time the passage throws light in turn on the rather remarkable form of commendation here, 'if he comes unto you, receive him.' The Pauline Churches, which were aware of the estrangement, might not be very ready to give a very hearty welcome to Mark" (p. 300). So Paul is urging: "Give him a hearty welcome" (Phillips).

Comfort or Encouragement? (4:11)

The Greek noun here is not from the same root as the verb for "comfort" in verse 8. There it was *parakaleō*. Here it is *parēgoria* (only here in NT). Lightfoot notes that the latter has an even wider range of meaning than the former. He writes: "The verb *parēgorein* denotes either (1) 'to exhort, encourage' . . . (2) 'to dissuade' . . . (3) 'to appease,' 'quiet' . . . or (4) 'to console, comfort.' The word, however, and its derivatives . . . were used especially as medical terms, in the sense of 'assuaging,' 'alleviating' . . . and perhaps owing to this usage, the idea of consolation, comfort, is on the whole predominant in the word" (p. 239). The English word *paregoric* comes from this Greek term. The NASB has "encouragement," but almost all recent translations have adopted "comfort" (so NIV).

Labouring Fervently or Wrestling? (4:12)

The verb *agōnizō* has given us our English word "agonize." As we have noted in previous studies, this was primarily an athletic term. Properly it meant "to contend for a prize" (A-S, p. 8), or "engage in a contest" (AG, p. 15). Here the thought is that of "wrestling in prayer." It would seem that "wrestling" is the best translation here (so Weymouth, NIV).

Complete or Fully Assured? (4:12)

This is again a matter of variant readings. "Complete" is based on *peplēromenoi,* the perfect passive participle of *plēroō,* which means to fill, complete, or fulfill. "Fully assured" (RSV, NASB, NIV) is the rendering preferred by Lightfoot, Abbott, and the other best commentators. It is based on *peplērophoremenoi,* the perfect passive participle of *plērophoreō.* This verb means: "1. to bring in full measure . . . fulfill, accomplish . . . 2. to persuade, assure or satisfy fully" (A-S, p. 365). Though Delling prefers the former sense (TDNT, 6·310), the latter is its meaning in the papyri, as Deissmann has demonstrated.

Great Zeal or Deep Concern? (4:13)

The word "zeal" is the translation of *zēlon.* But the oldest Greek manuscripts have *ponon.* The original meaning of this word was "labor" or "toil." Then it came to mean "great trouble, intense desire" (Thayer, p. 531). Aside from this passage the word *ponos* occurs only in Revelation (16:10-11; 21:4), where it means "pain" or "distress." Most recent translations have "is working hard" (NIV) or something similar. But there is much to be said for "deep concern" (NASB; cf. Weymouth).

FIRST THESSALONIANS

Without Ceasing (1:3)

This is an adverb in the Greek, *adialeiptōs*. It comes from *a* (negative) and the verb *dialeipō*, "leave off (for a time)." So it means "not leaving off." Paul prayed for his converts "constantly" (RSV, NASB) or "continually" (NEB, NIV). His unremitting prayer life is a challenge to all of us in our day when busy activity too often takes the place of prayer.

It is interesting to note that this word occurs three times in this Epistle (1:3; 2:13; 5:17), and elsewhere in the NT only in Rom. 1:9. It underscores the faithful, unselfish character of the great apostle.

Patience or Steadfastness? (1:3)

The Greek word *hypomonē* is translated "patience" (KJV) in 29 out of its 32 occurrences in the NT. In the other three places it is more correctly rendered "enduring" (2 Cor. 1:6), "patient continuance" (Rom. 2:7), and "patient waiting" (2 Thess. 3:5). The word "patience" is too passive a term to represent the Greek original. *Hypomonē* means "endurance" or "patient endurance." It is more adequately translated "steadfastness" (RSV, NASB). Phillips brings out the full force of it in his paraphrase: "The hope that you have in our Lord Jesus Christ means sheer dogged endurance."

Lohmeyer puts it well: "*hypomonē* is an endurance which is grounded in waiting, a waiting which expresses itself in endurance" (TDNT, 4:588).

Election or Choice? (1:4)

The word "election" is a powerful and polemical term in theological circles. Those who have heard it used frequently and expounded at great length may be surprised to learn that it occurs only six times in the entire Bible (Rom. 9:11; 11:5, 7, 28; 1 Thess. 1:4; 2 Pet. 1:10). The Greek word is found also in Acts 9:15, where it is translated "chosen."

The term is *eklogē*. It signifies a "choice" or "selection" and is used this way in the papyri of the period. Because of the sometimes unfortunate theological overtones of "election," it is better to translate *eklogē* as "choice" (NASB).

Followers or Imitators? (1:6)

The Greek word *mimētai* is found seven times in the NT and always translated "followers" (KJV). It comes from *mimos,* "a mimic" or "an actor." Both the verb *mimeomai* and the noun *mimētēs* are used always in the NT in a good sense. "Followers" is not an adequate translation. The word *mimētai* should be rendered "imitators" (RSV, NASB, NIV).

Ensample or Example? (1:7)

The Greek word is *typos,* from which comes "type." It is used in this sense in Rom. 5:14. But in a majority of instances in the NT it carries the connotation of "example" (so most translations here) or "pattern" (Weymouth). "Ensamples" is obviously an archaic form. Goppelt says that here it means "a model for others" (TDNT, 8:249).

Sounded Out (1:8)

The word *echeō* is found only here in the NT. It comes from *ex,* "out," and *echos* (Eng. "echo"), "noise" or "sound." Abbott-Smith says the verb means "*to sound forth* (as a trumpet, or thunder)" (p. 160). Milligan thinks of it here as "pointing to the clear, ringing nature of the report as of a trumpet" (p. 12). (Cf. "rang out," NEB, NIV.)

Spread Abroad (1:8)

The form here is *exelēlythen,* the perfect tense of *exerchomai,* which means "go out." So rather than "is spread abroad," the correct translation is: "has gone forth" (RSV, NASB).

Shew or Report? (1:9)

The word *apangellō* is used "of a messenger, speaker, or writer, *to report, announce, declare*" (A-S, p. 14). It is obvious that "shew" is hardly an exact rendering. More accurate is "report" (RSV, NASB, NIV).

Entering In or Welcome? (1:9)

The Greek word *eisodos* literally means "a way into."

Here it signifies the act of entering. Probably the idea of the passage is well conveyed by "welcome" (RSV) or "reception" (NASB, NIV). However the same word is rendered "visit" (RSV, NIV) and "coming" (NASB) in 2:1.

Wait or Await? (1:10)

The term *anamenō* is found only here in the NT. It is a compound of *menō*, "remain," and *ana*, "up." Milligan comments: "The leading thought here seems to be to wait for one whose coming is expected . . . perhaps with the added idea of patience and confidence" (p. 14). Probably "await" (Weymouth) best conveys the meaning (so Abbott-Smith).

Suffered Before (2:2)

This is one word in Greek, *propathontes,* found only here in the NT. It is the second aorist participle of the verb *propaschō,* which literally means "suffer before." But "already suffered" (RSV, NASB) is smoother English. The fact that Paul had suffered at Philippi just before coming to Thessalonica (Acts 17) is brought out well by "just suffered" (C. B. Williams).

Shamefully Entreated (2:2)

This is a single term in Greek, the verb *hybrizō.* It is a strong word found five times in the NT (cf. Matt. 22:6; Luke 11:45; 18:32; Acts 14:5). It comes from *hybris,* the basic meaning of which was "insolence" or "insult." Thayer adds: "In Greek usage the mental injury and the wantonness of its infliction being prominent" (p. 633).

So the verb means: "treat in an arrogant or spiteful manner, mistreat, scoff at, insult" (AG, p. 839). Milligan comments: "More than the bodily suffering it was the personal indignity that had been offered to him as a Roman citizen . . . that had awakened a sense of *contumely* (humiliation) in St. Paul's mind" (p. 16). It may be that "insulted" (NIV) is the best rendering here.

With Much Contention (2:2)

The KJV gives an entirely wrong connotation. It suggests that Paul preached with a very contentious spirit. But the correct thought is "in spite of strong opposition" (NIV) or "amid much opposition" (NASB).

Literally the text says "in much conflict" *(en pollō agōni)*. The Greek word *agōn* (cf. "agony") was originally an athletic term, referring to the "contest" or "struggle" of the Olympic Games. The Christian life is compared to an athletic competition in which the participants strive to win. Christians need this same spirit if they are to be winners in the game of life.

Exhortation or Appeal? (2:3)

The word *paraklēsis* is difficult to translate into English. Occurring 29 times in the NT, it is rendered "consolation" (14 times), "exhortation" (8), "comfort" (6), and "intreaty" (1). It comes from the verb *parakaleō,* which literally means "call alongside (to help)." In the NT the verb carries three main connotations: beseech, comfort, exhort.

For this passage Thayer suggests that the meaning of the noun is: "persuasive discourse, stirring address—instructive, admonitory, consolatory; powerful hortatory discourse" (p. 483). Milligan says that *paraklēsis* "implies something more in the nature of an appeal . . . having for its object the direct benefit of those addressed, and which may be either hortatory or consolatory according to circumstances" (p. 17). It is interesting to note that the general word "appeal," suggested by Milligan, has been adopted for many translations (e.g., TCNT, Weymouth, Moffatt, Goodspeed, RSV, NEB, NIV).

Deceit or Error? (2:3)

The Greek word *planē* means: *"a wandering, a straying about,* whereby one, led astray from the right way, roams hither and thither. . . . In the N.T. metaphorically mental straying, i.e. *error, wrong opinion* relative to morals or religion" (Thayer, p. 514).

Milligan says that *planē* is used "apparently always in the N.T. in the passive sense of 'error' rather than in the active sense of 'deceit'" (pp. 17-18). The word "deceit" is a proper rendering of *dolos* ("guile") at the end of the verse (cf. NASB).

Allow or Approve? (2:4)

The KJV "allowed of God" is taken from Tyndale (1525), which surprisingly was followed by the Geneva Version (1560). More accurate was the first English Bible, that of Wyclif (1382), which had "preued" (proved). The Catholic Rheims Version (1609) was still better. It had "approved."

The Greek word is *dokimazō* in the perfect passive indicative. Thayer defines the verb as follows: "1. *to test, examine, prove, scrutinize* (to see whether a thing be genuine or not), as metals. . . . 2. *to recognize as genuine* after examination, *to approve, deem worthy.*" For this passage he suggests: "We have been approved by God to be intrusted with the business of pointing out to men the way of salvation" (p. 154). Arndt and Gingrich have: "We have been found worthy" (p. 201).

Milligan translates the clause: "But according as we have been approved by God," and comments: *"Dokimazō* means originally 'put to the test' . . . but in the N.T. generally conveys the added thought that the test has been successfully surmounted, in accordance with the technical use of the word to describe the passing as fit for election to a public office" (p. 18). Most recent translations correctly have "approved by God" in this passage.

It is the same verb, *dokimazō*, which is translated "trieth" at the end of this verse. A better rendering is "tests" (NIV). Because it is the present participle which is used here, a more adequate translation is: "who is continually testing our hearts" (NEB). Charles B. Williams brings out the double meaning of the verb in his rendering: "who proves and finds approved our hearts."

Flattery (2:5)

Lightfoot says of the Greek term here: "*Kolakeia,* a word which occurs here only in the New Testament, is defined both by Theophrastus . . . and Aristotle . . . to involve the idea of selfish motives. It is flattery not merely for the sake of giving pleasure to others but for the sake of self-interest" (p. 23).

In the same vein Milligan writes that *kolakeia* "carries with it the idea of tortuous methods by which one man seeks to gain influence over another, generally for selfish ends." He adds: "How easily such a charge might be brought against the Apostles is evident from what we know of the conduct of the heathen rhetoricians of the day" (p. 19).

Cloak or Pretext? (2:5)

Thayer defines the Greek word here, *prophasis,* as follows: "A pretext (alleged reason, pretended cause) . . . such as covetousness is wont to use, I Th. ii. 5 (. . . the meaning being, that he had never misused his apostolic office in order to disguise or hide avaricious designs)" (p. 552). Arndt and Gingrich note that originally the word *prophasis* meant "actual motive or reason, valid excuse," but that it soon came to mean "falsely alleged motive, pretext, ostensible reason, excuse"—and so here "pretext" (pp. 729-30). This is probably the best rendering.

Burdensome or Authority? (2:6)

The Greek literally says "to be in a burden" *(baros).* Milligan gives a clear explanation of this word. He writes: "*Baros* is here understood (1) in its simple meaning of 'weight,' 'burden' . . . with reference to the Apostle's right of maintenance . . . or (2) in its derived sense of 'authority,' 'dignity' . . . pointing to the honour they might have expected to receive at the Thessalonians' hands" (p. 20). He goes on to say: "The two meanings are however compatible, and it is probable that St. Paul plays here on the double sense of the phrase" (pp. 20-21). Lightfoot agrees (p. 24).

The standard lexicons favor the second meaning here. For instance, Arndt and Gingrich have for this passage: "Wield authority, insist on one's importance" (p. 133). So also do most of the modern translations. Weymouth, for example, has: "We might have stood on our dignity" (cf. NASB—"We might have asserted our authority").

Schrenck says that "the reference can hardly be to financial cost . . . it is rather to conscious self-assertion. Though the apostle maintains his apostolic authority, he does not think it necessary to support it by a particularly imposing appearance" (TDNT, 1:556).

Gentle or Children? (2:7)

The difference is only one letter in the Greek. "Gentle" is *ēpioi;* "children" (C. B. Williams, Beck) is *nēpioi.* Undeniably the latter has the stronger support of the earliest manuscripts. But the former seems to fit better in the context. Milligan writes: "The reading here is doubtful. If *nēpioi* . . . be adopted, the whole clause is the avowal on the writers' part of their becoming as children to children, speaking . . . baby-language to those who were still babes in the faith. . . . On the other hand, if the well-attested *ēpioi* . . . be preferred, the Apostolic 'gentleness' is placed in striking contrast with the slanders that had been insinuated against them. . . . This agreement with the context leads most modern editors and commentators to favour *ēpioi*" (p. 21). However, Lightfoot seems to defend *nēpioi* (p. 24).

The extreme difficulty of deciding between these two readings is shown by the fact that of two equally good scholars, Moffatt has, "We behaved gently when we were among you," while Goodspeed has, "We were children when we were with you." Probably we shall prefer to go along with the majority of recent versions (e.g., RSV, NEB, NASB, NIV) in reading "gentle" here. This fits perfectly with the next clause, "even as a nurse cherisheth her children."

Nurse or Nursing Mother? (2:7)

The Greek word is *trophos* (only here in NT). It comes from the verb *trephō,* which means to give food to, and is used of a mother nursing a baby at her breast (Luke 23:29). So some (e.g., Weymouth, Moffatt, Goodspeed, C. B. Williams, NASB) prefer "nursing mother" here. But "nurse" is still widely used (e.g., RSV, Phillips, NEB). NIV has simply "mother."

Cherisheth (2:7)

Of the verb *thalpō* Thayer says: "1. properly *to warm, keep warm* . . . 2. . . . *to cherish* with tender love, *to foster* with tender care" (p. 282). The word is found only here and in Eph. 5:29. Probably the best translation for our day is "tenderly cares for" (NASB).

Affectionately Desirous (2:8)

The verb is *homeiromai*. It means "to desire earnestly, yearn after" (A-S, p. 316). Charles B. Williams gives the sense well: "We were yearning for you so tenderly."

Labour and Travail (2:9)

The first noun is *kopos*, the second *mochthos*. Lightfoot points out very well the distinction between the two when he writes: "*Kopos* (from *koptō*) is properly a 'blow' or 'bruise,' and hence signifies 'wear and tear,' the fatigue arising from continued labour, and hence the labour which brings on lassitude. In *mochthos* on the other hand the leading notion is that of struggling to overcome difficulties" (*Notes,* p. 26). Perhaps the best translation is "labor and hardship" (NASB) or "toil and hardship" (NIV).

Chargeable or A Burden? (2:9)

The Greek has the infinitive of the verb *epibareō*. This is from *baros,* the noun which occurs in verse 6 above. So it literally means "be a burden upon" *(epi)*. Paul had labored and toiled night and day, so that he might not be a financial burden upon his first converts at Thessalonica. This shows the unselfish love and consecrated devotion of this man of God.

Forbidding or Hindering? (2:16)

The verb *kolyō* is translated "forbid" 17 times in the NT (KJV) and "hinder" only twice. Once (Rom. 1:13) it is rendered "let," which in modern language is just the opposite of what the Greek word means. It occurs also in Acts 11:17 ("withstand"), Acts 27:43 ("keep from"), and Heb. 7:23 ("not suffer").

The word comes from *kolos*, which means "lopped" or "clipped." So it literally means to "cut off" or "cut short," and so "to hinder, prevent, forbid" (Thayer, p. 367). It would seem that "hindering" is slightly more exact than "forbidding." In view of the fact that it is the present participle here, the most accurate translation may be: "trying to keep us from speaking" (C. B. Williams).

Taken from (2:17)

The word (only here in NT) is *aporphanizō*. It is compounded of *apo*, "away from," and the adjective *"orphanos,"* meaning "orphan" or "fatherless." This adjective is used literally in Mark 12:40 and Jas. 1:27, and metaphorically in John 14:18 ("comfortless")—the only places in the NT where it occurs. So the verb means "to bereave of a parent" (Thayer, p. 67). Arndt and Gingrich say that the passive form here is used "figuratively, of the apostle separated from his church . . . *made orphans by separation from you*" (p. 97). Lightfoot seeks to bring out the full force by a double rendering: "bereft of and separated from" (*Notes*, p. 36).

Presence or Person? (2:17)

"In presence" is *prosōpō,* the dative of *prosōpon,* "face." Arndt and Gingrich translate the phrase here: *"orphaned by separation from you in person, not in heart or outwardly, not inwardly"* (p. 728). It would seem that "person" (NIV) is somewhat clearer than "presence."

Endeavored or Were Eager? (2:17)

The verb *spoudazō* occurs 11 times in the NT and is translated 7 different ways in the KJV: "be forward" (Gal. 2:10); "endeavor" (Eph. 4:3; 1 Thess. 2:17; 2 Pet. 1:15); "study" (2 Tim. 2:15); "do diligence" (2 Tim. 4:9, 21); "be diligent" (Titus 3:12; 2 Pet. 3:14); "labour" (Heb. 4:11); "give diligence" (2 Pet. 1:10).

The literal meaning of *spoudazō* is "hasten" or "hurry," and so "be zealous or eager, take pains, make every effort" (AG, p. 771). Milligan comments on this passage: "a sense of *eagerness* being present in *espoudasamen,* which we do not usually associate with our English 'endeavored' (A.V., R.V.)" (p. 33). A good translation here is: "were all the more eager with great desire to see your face" (NASB).

Would Have or Wanted to? (2:18)

The Greek literally says, "We wished *(ēthelēsamen)* to come to you." So the better rendering is "wanted to come" (Weymouth and most recent translations).

Once and Again (2:18)

The Greek is literally "once and twice" *(hapax kai dis)*. It means "repeatedly." The best English rendering is "more than once" (TCNT, Moffatt, NEB, NASB) or "again and again" (Weymouth, Goodspeed, RSV, NIV).

Hindered or Thwarted? (2:18)

This is not the same Greek word which we translated "hindering" in verse 16. Here it is *enkoptō*. Thayer gives this definition: *"to cut into, to impede one's course by cutting off his way;* hence universally to *hinder"* (p. 166). Arndt and Gingrich give: "hinder, thwart" (p. 215).

Stahlin notes that this word "took on its main sense of 'obstacle' . . . from the military practice of making slits in the street to hold up a pursuing enemy. Hence the basic meaning is 'to block the way'" (TDNT, 3:855). He also says that "the term is used in the metaphor of running on the racetrack" (p. 856). So it would seem that the best translation is "thwarted" (NEB, NASB).

Crown (2:19)

The word is *stephanos,* already noted in Phil. 4:1. Abbott-Smith gives this full definition: "1. *that which surrounds* or *encompasses* (as a wall, a crowd: Homer, others). 2. *a crown,* i.e. the wreath, garland or chaplet given as a prize for victory, as a festal ornament, or as a public honour for distinguished service or personal worth (so to sovereigns, especially on the occasion of a *parousia*)" (p. 417).

Rejoicing or Exultation? (2:19)

The Greek word *kauchēsis* occurs 12 times in the NT.

In the KJV it is translated "boasting" 6 times and "rejoicing" 4 times. Thayer defines the term as "the act of glorying" and thinks the meaning of the two Greek words here is "crown of which we can boast" (p. 342). Arndt and Gingrich say: *"crown of pride,* i.e. to be proud of" (p. 427). (Cf. NEB.) Some versions prefer "boasting" (e.g., RSV). But it seems to us that "exultation" (NASB) expresses better the point of view of the apostle (cf. NIV).

Forbear or Bear? (3:1, 5)

The verb *stegō* comes from the noun *stegē,* which means "roof." So it signifies: "1. *to protect* or *keep by covering, to preserve . . .* 2. *to cover over with silence: to keep secret; to hide, conceal . . .* 3. *by covering to keep off* something which threatens, *to bear up against, hold out against,* and *so to endure, bear, forbear"* (Thayer, p. 586). This is an excellent example of the way words change their meanings in the course of time.

This verb is found elsewhere in the NT only in 1 Cor. 9:12; 13:7. There, as here, it seems to carry the third sense given above. For the fifth verse of this chapter Arndt and Gingrich have: "since I could not bear it any longer" (p. 773). Kasch writes: "Paul, impelled by his missionary task, can no longer bear not to have an influence on the development of the young church in Thessalonica" (TDNT, 7:586).

Leave or Leave Behind? (3:1)

One of the weaknesses of the KJV is its failure, in many cases, to distinguish between simple verbs and their compounds. *Leipō* means "leave." But the verb here is *kataleipō,* which means "leave behind." What it implies in this passage is expressed well by Moffatt: "Paul shrank from loneliness, especially where there was little or no Christian fellowship; but he would not gratify himself at the expense of the Thessalonians. Their need of Timothy must take precedence of his" (EGT, 4:31). So he sent Timothy to them, and stayed behind in Athens alone, with only Silas as a companion. Calvin comments: "It is . . . a sign of unusual affection and anxious desire that he is willing to deprive himself of all consolation for the purpose of succouring the Thessalonians" (p. 352).

Establish or Strengthen? (3:2)

The verb *stērizō* is thus defined by Thayer: "a. *to make stable, place firmly, set fast, fix* . . . b. *to strengthen, make firm;* tropically [figuratively] (not so in profane authors) *to render constant, confirm, one's mind*" (p. 588). Most recent translations have "strengthen."

Comfort or Encourage? (3:2)

This is again the verb *parakaleō*. While it may be rendered "exhort" (RSV), most translators prefer "encourage." That seems to fit best here. It combines the ideas of "comfort" and "exhort."

Moved or Deceived? (3:3)

This might seem like a simple verb, but its meaning is a bit complicated. *Sainō* originally was used, as in Homer and in Aesop's fables, for a dog wagging its tail. Thus it came to mean "fawn," as a dog does when it wags its tail and meekly lowers its head. The term was then employed in a metaphorical sense for persons who "fawn upon, flatter, beguile" (A-S, p. 400). And so Milligan comments: "What the Apostles evidently dreaded regarding the Thessalonians was that they would allow themselves to be 'drawn aside,' 'allured' from the right path in the midst of *(en)* the afflictions . . . which were then . . . falling upon them" (p. 38).

Lightfoot follows the same trail. He says that *sainō* signifies "fondle, caress, flatter, coax, wheedle, allure, fascinate, deceive," and adds: "This seems to be the meaning here; 'that no one, in the midst of these troubles, desert the rough path of the truth, drawn aside and allured by the enticing prospect of an easier life" (*Notes,* p. 42). Frame (ICC) agrees with this (p. 128).

Arndt and Gingrich come to a different conclusion. After noting that many prefer "so that no one might be deceived," they say: "However, a more suitable meaning is the one preferred without exception by the ancient versions and the Greek interpreters [Church Fathers]: *move, disturb, agitate . . . so that no one might be shaken or disturbed"* (p. 747). On the other hand, Lightfoot asserts that no passages in Greek literature can be cited which bear this meaning.

This difference of opinion is reflected in modern translations. One finds "shaken" (TCNT, NEB), "disturbed" (Moffatt, NASB), and "moved" (RSV) on the one hand, and "led astray" (Goodspeed) or "deceived" (C. B. Williams) on the other. It is very difficult to decide the matter. But in view of the total scholarship represented on the translation committees of the RSV and the NEB, it would seem the part of wisdom to settle in favor of "moved" or "shaken." It should be noted that "beguiled away" is given as an alternative in the margin of NEB. The NIV has "unsettled."

Brought Us Good Tidings (3:6)

This is the verb *euangelizō.* Its most common rendering in the NT (KJV) is "preach" (23 times), or "preach the gospel" (22 times). But here and in Luke 1:19 it is used in the literal sense of "bring good tidings" (or "good news"). Of course, that is what the preaching of the gospel is— good news for the needy sinner.

Perfect or Complete? (3:10)

The verb is *katartizō*. Thayer notes that it means "properly to *render artios* i.e. *fit, sound, complete* . . . hence a. *to mend* (what has been broken or rent), *to repair* . . . to *complete*" (p. 336)—as in this passage. Arndt and Gingrich also give "complete" for this place (p. 418). Milligan notes that the verb "is used in the N.T. especially by St. Paul and in the Epistle to the Hebrews in the general sense of 'prepare' or 'perfect' anything for its full destination or use" (p. 42). Lightfoot comments: "This sense of completion is borne out by the not uncommon application of *katartizein* to military and naval preparation, e.g. in Polybius, where it is used of manning a fleet . . . of supplying an army with provisions" (*Notes,* p. 47). So the NIV has "supply."

Commandments or Instructions? (4:2)

Thayer says that *parangelia* properly means "announcement, a proclaiming or giving a message to," and so "a charge, command" (p. 479). It was used by Xenophon for a military order and by Aristotle for instruction. Arndt and Gingrich think that here is meant "instructions" (p. 618).

Milligan comments: *"Parangelia* . . . is found elsewhere in the Pauline Epistles only in I Tim. i. 5, 18, where it refers to the whole practical teaching of Christianity. Here the plural points rather to special precepts

. . . or rules of living, which the writers had laid down when in Thessalonica, and which they had referred to the Lord Jesus . . . as the medium through whom alone they could be carried into effect" (p. 47).

Body or Wife? (4:4)

Paul wants every one of his readers to "know how to possess his vessel in sanctification and honour." But what does "vessel" mean? The most natural answer would seem to be that it refers to the physical body. This is the interpretation of several recent translations—"learn to control his body" (Phillips); "learn to gain mastery over his body" (NEB, cf. NIV).

On the other hand, a large number of modern versions have "take a wife," or its equivalent. This is the rendering of Weymouth, Moffatt, Goodspeed, C. B. Williams, RSV, Beck. Why?

The answer lies partly in the true meaning of "possess." The Greek verb is *ktaomai*. It means "to procure for oneself, get, gain, acquire" (A-S, p. 259). One does not acquire a body, but he does acquire a wife.

The word *skeuos* (vessel) has a variety of uses—for containers, household utensils, etc. But it is clearly used for one's wife in 1 Pet. 3:7. On the other hand, it is rather obviously used for the human body in 2 Cor. 4:7. Which does it mean here?

Frame translates the passage: "That each of you get in marriage his own wife" (p. 150). He calls attention, as do others, to the fact that the verb *ktasthai* is used in both classical Greek and the Septuagint for getting a wife.

Milligan writes of this interpretation:

> The latter view, advocated by Theodore of Mopsuestia . . . and St. Augustine . . . has been adopted by the great majority of modern commentators, principal-

ly it would appear on account of the objections that can
be urged against the former. But though supported by
certain Rabbinic parallels . . . it is not, it will be admitted, at first sight the natural view, and is suggestive
of a lower view of the marriage-state than one would
expect in a passage specially directed to enforcing its
sanctity. . . . On the whole therefore it seems better to
revert to the meaning 'his own body' which was fa-
voured by the Greek commentators generally" (pp.
48-49).

The matter must be left open.

Maurer comments: "The most probable interpreta-
tion of 1 Th. 4:3f. is as follows: '. . . that every one of you
know how to hold his own vessel in sanctification and honour (i.e., live with his wife in sanctification and honour).'
. . . Material as well as linguistic considerations favour
'wife' rather than 'body' in interpretation of 1 Th. 4:4"
(TDNT, 7:366-67).

Lust or Passion? (4:5)

The Greek word is *pathos,* found elsewhere in the NT
only in Rom. 1:26 and Col. 3:5. In both of those it is rendered "affection." But the best translation is "passion."

Concupiscence or Lust? (4:5)

The word *epithymia* is generally translated "lust" in
the KJV. While "desire" is preferable in some instances,
"lust" seems to fit best here. So the phrase would mean
"passion of lust" (RSV). Arndt and Gingrich suggest "lust-
ful passion" (cf. Weymouth, NASB), but the NIV has
"passionate lust."

Any Matter or This Matter? (4:6)

The Greek has simply *en tō pragmati,* "in the matter"

(cf. NASB). There is no support for "any matter" (KJV). The context clearly suggests that the meaning is "this matter"; that is, the matter of fornication or adultery. Frame, quoting Lillie, would broaden it to be "a euphemistic generalization for all sorts of uncleanness" (p. 152).

Holiness or Sanctification? (4:7)

The word *hagiasmos* occurs 10 times in the NT and is translated "holiness" five times and "sanctification" five times. It has already occurred twice in this chapter (vv. 3, 4) where it is rendered "sanctification." But here it is "holiness." Which is preferable?

The word comes from the verb *hagiazō*, which means "sanctify." So it properly means "sanctification." There are other words *(hagiotēs, hagiosynē)* which signify the resultant state of holiness. Even though *hagiasmos* sometimes is used for the latter, it would seem better to translate it "sanctification." Here it is literally "in sanctification."

Despiseth or Rejects? (4:8)

The verg is *atheteō.* Out of the 16 times it occurs in the NT it is translated "despise" 8 times and "reject" 4 times. But the latter is more accurate. Thayer gives for this passage: "to reject, refuse, slight" (p. 14). It literally means "declare invalid, nullify, set aside," and so "reject, not recognize" (AG, p. 20). Abbott-Smith gives for this passage "reject" (p. 11). The reference is to those who deliberately reject God's prescribed way of holy living.

Brotherly Love (4:9)

The Greek word *philadelphia* is found six times in the

NT (Rom. 12:10; 1 Thess. 4:9; Heb. 13:1; 1 Pet. 1:22; 2 Pet. 1:7, twice). It was adopted by William Penn and his Quaker associates as the name for the new city which they founded as a haven of rest for persecuted people of Europe. Incidentally, Philadelphia was the first capital of the United States (1781-1800). In the NT the word refers to the love of Christian brethren for each other.

Of or By? (4:9)

The most overworked term in the KJV is the little word "of." It is used repeatedly in places where modern English usage would employ other prepositions.

"Taught of God" is one word in Greek—*theodidaktos,* from *theos,* "God," and *didaskō,* "teach." It is found only here in the NT. The correct translation is "taught by God."

Study or Be Ambitious? (4:11)

The word "study" occurs only here and in 2 Tim. 2:15, where it is a translation of *spoudazō,* "hasten, be eager." Here the Greek word is *philotimeomai.* It is compounded of *philos,* "love," and *timē,* "honor." So it literally means "to love or seek after honour," and hence "to be ambitious" (A-S, p. 471). Lightfoot suggests: "to make the pursuit of a thing one's earnest endeavour" (p. 61).

We would take issue with Phillips' rendering: "Make it your ambition to have no ambition!" This would be all right if revised to read: "no self-ambition." A preacher with no ambition to be and do something for God's cause does not belong in the pulpit or pastorate.

The verb here occurs elsewhere in the NT in Rom. 15:20 ("strived") and 2 Cor. 5:9 ("labour"). This is another example of how frequently the KJV translates the same

Greek word differently in various locations. This shows the inadequacy of using an English concordance to trace words through the NT. For the one who knows Greek, the *Englishman's Greek Concordance* is an invaluable tool. For those who do not use Greek, the same task can be accomplished, with somewhat more labor, by using Strong's *Exhaustive Concordance* or Young's *Analytical Concordance*. The latter is a bit easier to use.

Honestly or Becomingly? (4:12)

The adverb *euschemonōs* occurs elsewhere in the NT only in Rom. 13:13 ("honestly") and 1 Cor. 14:40 ("decently"). It comes from the adjective *euschemon,* which means: "of elegant figure, shapely, graceful, comely, bearing one's self becomingly in speech or behavior" (Thayer, p. 263). Arndt and Gingrich think that "walk honestly" is best translated "behave decently" (p. 327). The KJV "honestly" comes from the Latin Vulgate *honeste.* The etymology of the Greek term would suggest that the best translation here is "becomingly" (Weymouth). Greeven says that it "denotes the external aspect of the Christian life" (TDNT, 2:771).

Nothing or Nobody? (4:12)

The former is found in KJV, the latter in RSV. Which is correct?

The answer is that both are equally accurate translations. The Greek form *mēdenos* may be either masculine or neuter. Frame properly observes: "Nor does it matter logically, for in either case the reference is to dependence upon the brotherhood for support. . . . Contextually, the masculine is probable" (p. 163). What Paul is saying is that Christians should attend to their own business, earn

their own living, and not be dependent on others for
support.

Asleep (4:13, 14, 15)

The verb *koimaomai* occurs 18 times in the NT. In
four instances (Matt. 28:13; Luke 22:45; John 11:12; Acts
12:16) it is used in the literal sense of "be asleep." But in
all the other cases it is used metaphorically and euphemis-
tically for being dead. (In 1 Cor. 7:39 it is translated "be
dead.") This use of sleep for death goes as far back as
Homer's *Iliad.* But there is one marked difference here:
the Christians "sleep in Jesus." In the resurrection they
will awaken to live forever with Him.

Remain (4:15, 17)

Half a dozen different Greek words are translated
"remain" in the KJV. The one found here, and only here
in the NT, is *perileipō.* It comes from *peri,* "around," and
leipō, "leave." So it means "left around" or "left behind"
(C. B. Williams).

Prevent or Precede? (4:15)

The word is *phthanō.* In classical Greek it meant "to
come before, precede." Thayer interprets this passage as
meaning: "We shall not get the start of those who have
fallen asleep, i.e., we shall not attain to the fellowship of
Christ sooner than the dead, nor have precedence in
blessedness" (p. 652).

Because there is a double negative in the Greek preceding the verb, Arndt and Gingrich have: "We will by no
means precede those who have fallen asleep" (p. 864).
The Jews held the view that a special blessedness attached

to those who were alive at the setting up of the Messianic kingdom. A similar belief was found in the Early Church (e.g., Clementine, *Recognitions*). Paul is here emphatically refuting any such idea.

The word "prevent" comes from the Latin *prevenio,* which means "go before." But today "prevent" means "hinder" or "stop," which is not at all the idea here. It is interesting to note that Lightfoot still used "prevent" as the proper translation in his day (he died in 1889). But the ASV (1901) correctly gave "precede."

Shout or Cry of Command? (4:16)

The Greek word (only here in NT) is *keleusma.* It comes from *keleuō,* which means "command (mostly of one in authority)." So the noun signifies: "a call, sumons, shout of command" (A-S, p. 244). It is used in Herodotus for the word of command in battle. So it appears that the best translation here is "with a cry of command" (RSV, Arndt and Gingrich).

Times and Seasons (5:1)

The first noun is *chronos,* from which comes "chronology." It means: *"Time,* mostly in the sense *a period of time"* (AG, p. 896). The term occurs 53 times in the NT. It is rendered "time" 33 of these, and "season" four.

The second noun is *kairos.* It is found 86 times and is translated "time" in 63 of these and "season" in 13.

The same combination of words is found in Acts 1:7, where Jesus said to His disciples: "It is not for you to know the times or the seasons, which the Father hath put in his own power." Yet in a general way, Paul declares, Christians are aware of the times and seasons.

Kairos is a more distinctive term than *chronos,* as

shown by its rendering in these two passages. Trench points out the difference as follows: *"Chronos* is time, contemplated simply as such; the succession of moments. . . . *Kairos* . . . is time as it brings forth its several births" (p. 210). Commenting on Acts 1:7, he writes: " 'The times' *(chronoi)* are, in Augustine's words 'ipsa spatia temporum,' and these contemplated merely under the aspect of their duration, over which the Church's history should extend: but 'the seasons' *(kairoi)* are the joints or articulations in these times, the critical epoch-making periods foreordained of God" (p. 311).

Abbott-Smith summarizes well the early history of *kairos:* "1. *due measure, fitness, proportion* (Euripides, Xenophon, others). 2. Of Time (classical also) in the sense of a fixed and definite period, *time, season"* (p. 226). Arndt and Gingrich say that *kairos* means *"point of time* as well as period of time" (p. 395). They define it as "the right, proper, favorable time"—and so it may be translated "opportunity" in some passages in the NT—and so as "definite, fixed time can also refer to the last things, hence *kairos* becomes . . . one of the chief eschatological terms, *ho kairos, the time of crisis, the last times"* (pp. 395-96). On Acts 1:7 and this passage they say: *"Times and seasons,* which must be completed before the final consummation" (p. 396).

Delling notes that the sense of the "decisive moment" is found in Greek philosophers from the time of Sophocles. The Pythagoreans placed especially strong emphasis on *kairos.* In the Septuagint the term is used for the "decisive point of time," though not as markedly as in later Christian writings. In the NT it means: "The 'fateful and decisive point,' with strong, though not always explicit, emphasis (except at Acts 24:25) on the fact that it is ordained by God" (TDNT, 3:459).

Lightfoot sums up well the difference between these

two terms. He writes: "Here *chronoi* denotes the period which must elapse before and in the consummation of this great event, in other words it points to the date: while *kairoi* refers to the occurrences which will mark the occasion, the signs by which its approach will be ushered in" (p. 71).

It is interesting to note that in modern Greek *chronos* means "year," that is, a measurement of time, whereas *kairos* means "weather." This follows out of the idea of "season."

Safety or Security? (5:3)

The Greek word is *asphaleia*. It first meant "firmness," then "certainty" (Luke 1:4), and finally "security" (Acts 5:23; 1 Thess. 5:3; not elsewhere in NT). In the papyri it is used as a law term, in the sense of "proof, security" (A-S, p. 66). Moulton and Milligan say: "The noun occurs innumerable times in the commercial sense, 'a security'" (VGT, p. 88).

Many recent translations use "security" here instead of "safety." In this day of constant emphasis on "social security" and "national security" it would seem that this rendering is more meaningful. No vaunted "security" can guarantee against sudden disaster.

Sudden (5:3)

The adjective *aiphnidios* means "unexpected, sudden, unforeseen" (Thayer, p. 18). It is difficult to bring this out in a simple English translation. The word occurs elsewhere in the NT only in Luke 21:34, where it is rendered "unawares." Here it probably means that the destruction will come both suddenly and unexpectedly.

Children or Sons? (5:5)

The Greek word is *huioi,* which means "sons," not *techna,* which is the proper word for "children." "Sons of light" (so most recent translations) is a Hebrew idiom, meaning people who have the character of light. This feature occurs many times in the NT. We read of "sons of the kingdom" (Matt. 8:12), "son of Gehenna" (Matt. 21:5), a "son of peace" (Luke 10:6), "sons of this age" (Luke 16: 8), "sons of truth" (Eph. 2:2). The very expression here, "sons of light," is found in Luke 16:8. They are contrasted with the "sons of this age." As sons of God we are sons of light, for "God is light" (1 John 1:5).

Watch or Keep Awake? (5:6)

The verb *grēgoreō* means "to be awake," as well as "watch." In view of the previous part of the verse— "Therefore let us not sleep, as do others"—it seems evident that the best translation here is "keep awake" (RSV). The same verb is translated "wake" in verse 10, where it means "alive," not sleeping in death.

Be Sober (5:6)

The verb *nephō* was originally used in a literal sense of abstaining from drinking wine. But in the NT it is employed only in the figurative sense, "Be free from every form of mental and spiritual 'drunkenness,' from excess, passion, rashness, confusion, etc., *be well-balanced, self-controlled*" (AG, p. 540).

Edify or Build Up? (5:11)

The verb is *oikodomeō.* It comes from *oikos,* "house,"

and *demo*, "build." So at first it means "build a house." Then it came to be used in the general sense of "build." Probably "build each other up" (NIV) is more meaningful today than "edify one another."

Know or Respect? (5:12)

Here we have the infinitive of *oida*, which ordinarily means "know." But Thayer says that in this passage it is used Hebraistically in the sense of "to have regard for one, cherish, pay attention to" (p. 174). Abbott-Smith also notes that it is found here "in unique sense of *respect, appreciate*" (p. 311). For this verse Arndt and Gingrich give "respect."

Lightfoot holds that the word here means "'to know,'" with a pregnant meaning, i.e. 'to see in their true character, to recognize the worth of, to appreciate, to value'" (p. 79). Milligan agrees that this is "evidently" the sense here, though he declares that it is "a usage of the word for which no adequate parallel has yet been produced from classical or Biblical Greek" (p. 71).

Apparently the best translation is "respect" (Weymouth, Moffatt, Goodspeed, RSV, NIV) or "appreciate" (NASB, Beck).

Warn or Admonish? (5:14)

It is the same verb here that is translated "admonish" in verse 12. Why not here also?

Noutheteō is compounded of *nous*, "mind," and *tithēmi*, "place" or "put." So it literally means "put in mind." Abbott-Smith gives: "To admonish, exhort" (p. 305). Arndt and Gingrich have: "admonish, warn, instruct" (p. 546).

Unruly or Disorderly? (5:14)

The adjective is *ataktos,* found only here in the NT. It is derived from *a*-negative, and the verb *tassō,* "draw up in order" or "arrange." So it means "disorderly, out of the ranks" (Thayer, p. 83).

From the adjective *ataktos* comes the adverb *ataktōs* (long *o*), found in 2 Thess. 3:6, 11, and the verb *atakteō,* which occurs only in 2 Thess. 3:7. It is a striking fact that all three of these cognate terms are found only in the Thessalonian letters, the main emphasis of which is on preparation for the Second Coming. So the words must be interpreted in that light.

These three cognate terms are treated at considerable length in an additional note by Milligan. He starts with the adjective, "which means primarily 'out of order,' 'out of place,' and hence . . . is readily employed as a military term to denote a soldier who does not keep the ranks, or an army advancing in disarray." He goes on to say: "From this the transition is easy to disorderly or irregular living of any kind as in Plato's reference to *ataktoi hēdonai . . .* or in Plutarch's rebuke to those who, neglecting a 'sane and well-ordered life' . . . hurl themselves headlong into 'disorderly and brutal pleasures'" (p. 152).

Of the verb Milligan writes: "Like its adjective, it is frequently applied to soldiers marching out of order, or quitting the ranks, and hence is extended to every one who does not perform his proper duty" (p. 153).

Especially interesting and illuminating are two examples of the use of *atakteō* in the papyri. The first is in an Oxyrhynchus papyrus of A.D. 66, about 15 years after Paul wrote to the Thessalonians. It is a contract of apprenticeship. The boy's father agrees not to take away his son during the period specified. There is also the further stipulation that if there are any days on which the boy "plays the truant" *(ataktese),* the father is to return him for an equivalent number of days after the regular period has ended (p. 153).

The second Oxyrhynchus papyrus is dated about 120 years later. In it there is the specification that a weaver's apprentice is permitted to have 20 holidays in the year, "but if he exceeds this number of days from idleness *(ataktese)* or ill-health or any other reason," he must make up his absences without added pay (p. 154).

Milligan concludes: "If then these instances can be taken as typical of the ordinary colloquial sense of the verb, we can understand how readily St. Paul would employ it to describe those members of the Thessalonian Church who, without any intention of actual wrong-doing, were neglecting their daily duties, and falling into idle and careless habits, because of their expectation of the immediate Parousia of the Lord" *(ibid.).*

It is doubtless in the light of this papyrus usage that Arndt and Gingrich, after noting that *ataktos* means "disorderly, subordinate," conclude: "The sense *idle, lazy* is to be preferred here" (p. 119). It is also in line with this that Moffatt translates the clause, "keep a check on loafers"; and Goodspeed, "warn the idlers" (cf. RSV, NIV).

Feebleminded or Fainthearted? (5:14)

The word is *oligopsychos* (only here in NT). It is composed of *oligos,* "little," and *psychē,* "soul." So it might literally be rendered "little-souled." But all authorities agree that the correct meaning is "fainthearted." The rendering most widely used today is: "Encourage the fainthearted."

Wholly or Entirely? (5:23)

Sometimes we are asked: "Where do you get the expression, 'entire sanctification'? I don't find it in the New Testament."

The answer is 1 Thess. 5:23—"The very God of peace sanctify [aorist tense] you wholly." The last word is *holoteleis* (only here in NT).

It is compounded of *holos*—"whole, entire, complete" —and *telos*, "end." So it would require some such hyphenated expression as "wholly-completely" or "completely-entirely" to bring out the full force of this compound adjective. Martin Luther translated it *durch und durch*, "through and through" (cf. NIV).

Whole or Complete? (5:23)

The word is *holoklēros*. This is a compound of *holos* and *klēros*, "lot." Thayer defines it as "complete in all its parts, in no part wanting or unsound, complete, entire, whole," and says that in this passage it should be taken ethically as meaning "free from sin, faultless" (p. 443). Arndt and Gingrich translate it: "May your spirit be preserved complete or sound" (p. 567).

SECOND THESSALONIANS

❦

The Duty of Thanksgiving (1:3)

The first part reads literally: "We are obligated to give thanks to God always for you, brothers, even as it is fitting." The thought of this passage is expressed strikingly in the liturgy of the Church of England: "It is very meet, right, and our bounden duty that we should at all times and in all places give thanks."

The verb "be obligated" is *opheilō*, which originally meant to owe someone a financial debt. It is translated "owe" in Rom. 13:8. So here it carries a strong sense of obligation. Thayer says that when it is followed by an infinitive (as here) it means "to be under obligation, bound by duty or necessity, to do something" (p. 469).

Meet or Fitting? (1:3)

The word is *axios*. It is translated "worthy" (KJV) in 35 out of 41 of its occurrences in the NT. But when used impersonally, as here, it means "fitting" or "proper."

Superabundance (1:3)

Paul uses two strong verbs. He says that the faith of the Thessalonian believers grows abundantly and their love superabounds.

The first word, *hyperauxanō,* is found only here in the NT. The simple verb *auxanō* occurs 22 times. Twelve of these times it is rendered "grow," and seven times "increase." The compound here means "to increase beyond measure" (A-S), or "grow wonderfully, increase abundantly" (AG). The Greek *hyper* is equivalent to the Latin *super.*

The second term, *pleonazō,* is found nine times. It may be translated either "abound" or "superabound." Of these two verbs Lightfoot writes: "The words *hyperauxanei* and *pleonaxei* are carefully chosen; the former implying an internal, organic growth as of a tree; the other a diffusive, or expansive character, as of a flood irrigating the land" (p. 98).

Manifest Token or Proof? (1:5)

The word *endeigma* (only here in NT) comes from *endeiknymi* (11 times), which means "to mark, point out" and in the middle "to show forth, prove" (A-S). The patient endurance and faith of the Thessalonian Christians was a clear evidence of God's righteous judgment which would be poured out on their persecutors. The best translation here is "evidence" or "proof."

Tribulation . . . Trouble (1:6)

This combination fails to bring out the connection in the Greek. The noun is *thlipsis,* the verb *thlibō* (same in v. 7). The literal meaning of the verb is *"to press* (as grapes), *press hard upon*" (Thayer). Metaphorically it means "to trouble, afflict, distress" *(ibid.)*. The best way to indicate that the noun and the verb have the same root is to translate the phrase: "Repay with affliction those who afflict you" (RSV, NASB).

Rest or Relief? (1:7)

A superficial reading of KJV might suggest that "rest" is a verb. But it is the noun *anesis*. Literally it means "a loosening, relaxation," but here "relief" from afflictions (A-S). Arndt and Gingrich translate the whole expression: "Grant, in turn, rest to those who are oppressed." Either "rest" or "relief" (NIV) fits well. But the contrast with "afflictions" somewhat favors the latter (cf. NASB).

Pay the Penalty (1:9)

"Be punished" is in the Greek a combination of verb and noun. The verb *tinō* (only here in NT) means "pay."

Dikē has an interesting history, as given by Thayer. First it meant "custom" or "usage," then "right" or "justice." Then it came to have the technical meaning of "a suit at law." The next step was "a judicial hearing, judicial decision," especially "a sentence of condemnation." The final step was "execution of the sentence, punishment" (p. 151).

So the noun and verb together mean "pay the penalty" or "suffer punishment." The judicial sentence is "everlasting destruction from the presence [literally, 'face'] of the Lord."

Admired or Marveled at? (1:10)

The verb is *thaumazō*. Occurring 46 times in the NT,

it is translated (KJV) "marvel" 30 times and "wonder" 14 times. Only here is it rendered "admire," and once "have in admiration" (Jude 16). It is obvious that this is not its usual meaning.

The word is found most frequently in the Gospels (33 times), where it expresses the wonder and amazement caused by Jesus' miracles. It seems clear that the idea of wonder or astonishment is inherent in the term. The best translation here is "marveled at" (ASV, RSV, NASB, NIV).

Beseech or Request? (2:1)

The original meaning of *erōtaō* was "ask" in the sense of "ask a question." This is found not only in Homer but also in the papyri and nearly always in the Septuagint. It carries the same connotation regularly in the Gospels. But in the rest of the NT, except for Acts 1:6, its predominant meaning is "to request." Thus it becomes almost equivalent to *aiteō.* Greeven points out the slight difference thus: "In distinction from *aiteō,* which often suggests a claim or passion, *erōtaō* denotes a genuine request which is humble or courteous" (TDNT, 2:686).

Troubled or Alarmed? (2:2)

The verb *throeō* comes from a noun meaning "tumult." In classical Greek it was used in the active with the sense of "cry aloud, make an outcry." In the NT it is always passive and means *"to be troubled,* as by an alarm" (A-S). Thayer suggests: "to be troubled in mind, to be frightened, alarmed" (p. 292). For this passage Arndt and Gingrich give, *"be disturbed* or frightened" (p. 364).

Attention should be called to the fact that this verb is in the present, whereas the previous one (shaken) is in the aorist tense. Milligan observes: "The present tense should be noted as pointing to a continued state of agitation following upon a shock received" (p. 96).

Is at Hand or Has Come? (2:2)

The Greek has *enestēken*. This verb literally means "to place in." For this passage Thayer suggests "to be upon, impend, threaten." Abbott-Smith prefers "to be present." Arndt and Gingrich render the expression here: "The day of the Lord has come." Milligan agrees: "as if the day of the Lord is now present" (p. 97). He comments: "The verb is very common in the papyri and inscriptions with reference to the *current* year." Perhaps the best translation is "has already come" (NIV).

The Apostasy (2:3)

The KJV says "a falling away." But the Greek has *hē apostasia*, "The Apostasy." The noun occurs only here and in Acts 21:21. In the latter passage it is translated "to forsake." Abbott-Smith defines the term as follows: "defection, apostasy, revolt." Lightfoot writes: "The word implies that the opposition contemplated by St. Paul springs up from within rather than from without. In other words, it must arise either from the Jews or from apostate Christians, either of whom might be said to fall away from God" (p. 111).

This emphasis on an apostasy from within takes on added significance in the light of recent developments in the church world. There was a day when the Bob Ingersolls railed and ranted against Christianity. Now this opposition comes from within the church. When teachers of theology in leading theological seminaries in America tell their ministerial students that God is dead, and when a prominent denominational leader declares that it is a sin to believe in individual salvation, it would seem that "The Apostasy" has come.

Sin or Lawlessness? (2:3)

Instead of "man of sin" the two oldest Greek manuscripts have "man of lawlessness"—*anomias* rather than *hamartias*. It is the same word *(anomias)* which is translated "iniquity" in verse 7—"mystery of iniquity." Furthermore "that Wicked" in verse 8 is in the Greek "the Lawless One"—*ho anomos*. This striking connection in these three verses is entirely lost to the readers of the KJV. Those who are dependent on the KJV are deprived all too often of both the accuracy and the richness of a correct translation of the best Greek text.

Again we should note the application to the present day. Never before has there been such a spirit of lawlessness in the United States as we are witnessing now. It stalks our streets and ravages our university campuses. Apostasy in the church and lawlessness in the land—these are two dominant features of American life today.

Perdition or Perishing? (2:3)

The Greek word is *apōleias*. It comes from the verb *apollumi*, which means "perish." Frame (p. 254) notes that the phrase *ho huios tēs apōleias* ("the son of perdition") equals *ho apollumenos* (literally, "the perishing one"). The latter expression is found in the plural in verse 10—*tois apollumenois* ("in them that perish"; literally, "in those who are perishing"). So it would seem that the best translation here is "the son of perishing" or "the son of destruction."

What does this mean? Frame says the phrase is "a

Hebraism indicating the one who belongs to the class destined to destruction, as opposed to the class destined to salvation" *(ibid.).*

Thayer gives the passive meaning of *apōleia* as "a perishing, ruin, destruction" (p. 70). Arndt and Gingrich note that in the New Testament the term is used "especially of eternal destruction as punishment for the wicked" (p. 103). Oepke writes: "What is meant here is not a simple extinction of existence, but an everlasting state of torment and death" (TDNT, 1:397). It should be noted that exactly the same phrase is used for Judas Iscariot in John 17:12.

Let or Restrain? (2:6-7)

A typical vagary of translation in the KJV is found in verses 6 and 7. Exactly the same verb is translated "withholdeth" in verse 6 and "letteth" in verse 7. Neither rendering is correct today, though "withholdeth" comes closer.

The word is *katechō.* It means "to hold back, detain, restrain" (A-S, p. 241). Here it indicates "to restrain, hinder" (Thayer, p. 339).

The present participle (continuous action) is used in both verses. But in verse 6 the form is neuter, while in verse 7 it is masculine. Arndt and Gingrich correctly give the meaning as "that which restrains" and "he who restrains"; that is, "what prevents the adversary of God from coming out in open opposition to him, for the time being" (p. 423). They note that both the ancient church fathers and present-day interpreters take verse 6 as referring to the Roman Empire and verse 7 to the emperor. This would be the first application. Theodore of Mopsuestia referred verse 6 to the preaching of Christian missionaries and verse 7 to the Apostle Paul. Chrysostom mentions the Holy Spirit as the One who restrains. Does the passage mean that the Holy Spirit in the Church is restraining lawlessness in this age and that when He leaves this world in the rapture of the saints the man of lawlessness (the Antichrist) will be revealed? One cannot be dogmatic in insisting that only one possible interpretation is correct. But this is at least a live option.

Spirit or Breath? (2:8)

It is stated that the Lord will consume the lawless one with the "spirit" of His mouth. It is true that *pneuma* is almost always translated "ghost" or "spirit" in the NT. However, in John 3:8 it is rendered "wind"—"The wind blows where it wishes." The word *pneuma* comes from the verb *pneō* ("bloweth" in John 3:8). So the earliest meaning was "wind," then "breath." Then it came to signify "the spirit, i.e. the vital principle by which the body is animated" (Thayer, p. 520). When one breathes his last breath, the spirit leaves the body.

But the meaning which seems to fit best here, as Arndt and Gingrich note, is "the breathing out of air, blowing, breath" (p. 680). Christ, as it were, will blow His consuming breath upon the Antichrist, destroying him.

Incidentally "destroy" here is *katargeō*, which is translated the same way in Rom. 6:6. Some have argued for a weaker rendering there. But probably no one would deny that "destroy" is correct here, and the context of Rom. 6:6 demands it there.

Brightness or Appearance? (2:8)

Here we find two of the three words used in the NT for Christ's second coming. The most common term for this is *parousia,* translated "coming." The other is *epiphaneia,* rendered "brightness." (The third is *apocalypsis,* "revelation," taken over into English as *apocalypse.*)

In the NT, *epiphaneia* is found elsewhere only in the three Pastoral Epistles, where it is always translated (five times) "appearing." It comes from the verb *epiphainō,* which means "appear, become visible." In the transitive it can be rendered "manifest." So "manifestation" is sometimes used to translate the noun here. But Thayer gives "an appearing, appearance," and adds: "Often used by the Greeks of a glorious manifestation of the gods, and especially of their advent to help; in 2 Maccabees of signal deeds and events betokening the presence and power of God as helper" (p. 245). In a similar vein Arndt and Gingrich write: "As a religious technical term it means a visible manifestation of a hidden divinity, either in the form of a personal appearance, or by some deed of power by which its present is made known" (p. 304). For this passage they prefer "appearance." That seems to be the most accurate rendering. In his *The Letters of Paul: An Expanded Paraphrase* (Eerdmans, 1965), F. F. Bruce has "the bright shining of His advent."

A Working of Wandering (2:11)

That is the literal Greek of "strong delusion." The first noun, *energeia* (cf. energy), is translated "working" in verse 9. It means *"operative power* (as distinct from *dynamis, potential power*), working" (A-S). In the NT it is used only of superhuman power (God, Satan, demons).

The second noun is *planē* (*pla*-nay). It literally means "a wandering, a straying about" (Thayer). In the NT it is used of mental straying, and so means "error." Hence we find "a working of error" (ASV). Thayer thinks the phrase means "the power which error works." Arndt and Gingrich take the second noun as a descriptive genitive and translate the whole expression "a deluding influence" (cf. NASB).

J. Armitage Robinson writes: "In all the passages where it occurs in the New Testament *planē* will bear the passive meaning, 'error,' though the active meaning, 'deceit,' would sometimes be equally appropriate. There is no reason therefore for departing from the first meaning of the word, 'wandering from the way'; and so, metaphorically, 'error,' as opposed to truth" (p. 185).

Moulton and Milligan (VGT, p. 516) note that the word sometimes means "deceit" in the papyri, but add: "In the NT *planē* is generally, if not always, used in the passive sense of error" (VGT, p. 516). However, Ellicott renders the phrase: "an (effective) working of delusion" (p. 118).

A Lie or The Lie? (2:11)

The Greek says the latter. It is not that they should believe "a lie," but "the lie"—"this (great) Lie" (Milligan). The expression is in contrast to "the truth" in verse 12. The truth is the gospel of Jesus Christ, that one must accept Christ as his Saviour and live a holy life if he is to be saved. "The lie" is the teaching of the man of lawlessness (v. 3) that one can live in unrighteousness (vv. 10, 12) as long as he submits to the rule of the Antichrist (or to the dominion of Satan).

Damned or Judged? (2:12)

The verb *krinō* occurs no less than 114 times in the NT. In 88 of these instances it is correctly translated "judge." Only in this passage is it rendered by the strong Puritan term "damn." The compound *katakrinō* is twice translated "damned" (Mark 16:16; Rom. 14:23). It should not be necessary to try to convince any thoughtful person today that the use of "damned" three times in our common English Bible is unfortunate, to say the least. It certainly creates problems with our children that could easily be avoided by a correct translation.

But what does the verb *krinō* mean? In classical Greek it first meant "to separate, put asunder, to pick out, select, choose" (Thayer). Later it conveyed the sense: "to determine, resolve, decree," and then "to pronounce an opinion concerning right and wrong." In the passive (as here) it meant "to be judged," that is, "summoned to trial that one's case may be examined and judgment passed upon it." Thayer continues: "Where the context requires, used of condemnatory judgment, i.q. *to condemn*" (p. 361). Abbott-Smith notes that sometimes in the NT it is used as the equivalent of *katakrinō,* which properly means "condemn." In fact, the simple verb *krinō* is translated "condemn" five times in the KJV.

Arndt and Gingrich note that *krinō* came to be used as a legal technical term meaning "judge, decide, hale before a court, condemn . . . hand over for judicial punishment" (p. 452). They write: "Often the emphasis is unmistakably laid upon that which follows the Divine Judge's verdict, upon the condemnation or punishment." And so the verb comes to mean "condemn, punish" (p. 453).

The doctrine of divine judgment is not a minor emphasis in the NT. In the article on *krinō* in TDNT, Buechsel says of the preaching of Jesus in the Synoptic Gospels: "Here the thought of judgment is central. Jesus' call to repentance is urgent because God's judgment hangs over every man" (3:936). He repudiates the modern "rationalistic criticism" which rejects the NT concept of judgment as mythical and unethical. Buechsel declares: "In face of this we must stress the fact that in the NT judgment is not capricious or emotional. . . . It is an inwardly necessary consequence of the sin of man" (3:940). He concludes: "The concept of judgment cannot be taken out of the NT Gospel. It cannot even be removed from the centre to the periphery. Proclamation of the love of God always presupposes that all men are moving towards God's judgment and are hopelessly exposed to it" (3:941).

Altogether there are a dozen words which are translated "judge" or "judgment" in the KJV NT. This opens up a whole field of study in preparation for preaching on the Judgment—a topic which is surely relevant today.

Have Free Course or Run? (3:1)

It is one word in Greek, *trechō,* which simply means "run." It is used of those who run in a race. So it has here the metaphorical idea of swiftness—"proceed quickly and without hindrance." So say Arndt and Gingrich, who suggest for this passage: "that the word of the Lord might spread rapidly" (p. 833). This has been adopted by NASB and is probably a more adequate translation than the literal rendering "run" (ASV).

Unreasonable or Perverse? (3:2)

The Greek word *atopos* is composed of *a*-negative and *topos,* "place." So literally it means "out of place." It came to have the sense of "strange, paradoxical" (LSJ) or "unusual, surprising" (AG). In later Greek it took on the ethical connotation, "improper, wicked." That is its meaning here.

In his excellent commentary on the Greek text of the Thessalonian letters (reprinted by Eerdmans, 1952),

George Milligan cites an interesting use of *atopos* in a papyrus document of around A.D. 100. The parents of a prodigal son posted a public notice that they would no longer be responsible for his debts or for *atopon ti praxe*—whatever he did "out of the way." Milligan adds: "It is in this sense accordingly implying something morally amiss, that, with the exception of Ac. xxviii. 6, the word is found in the LXX and the N.T. . . . and in the passage before us it is best given some such rendering as 'perverse' or 'fro-ward' rather than the 'unreasonable' of A.V., R.V." (p. 110).

Concerning the second adjective ("wicked," KJV) he observes: "Similarly *ponēros* . . . is used not so much of passive badness as of active harmfulness, while the pre-fixed article shows that the writers have here certain defi-nite persons in view, doubtless the fanatical Jews who at the time were opposing their preaching in Corinth (Ac. xviii. 12ff.), as they had already done in Thessalonica and Beroea (Ac. xvii. 5, 13)" *(ibid.)*.

Keep or Protect? (3:3)

The verb *phylassō* comes from the noun *phylax*, "guard" or "sentinel." So it means "guard, protect" (AG). Thayer puts it this way: *"To guard* a person (or thing) *that he may remain safe,* i.e. lest he suffer violence, be despoiled, etc., i.q. *to protect."* It is obvious that "pro-tect" (NASB, NIV) is a more adequate translation than "keep" (KJV).

Lightfoot paraphrases the second part of the verse as follows: "He will not only place you in a firm position, but also maintain you there against assaults from without" (p. 125).

Evil or The Evil One? (3:3)

Ellicott holds to the rendering "from the Evil One." He writes: "Here as elsewhere in the N.T., it is extremely doubtful whether *tou ponērou* refers to evil in the abstract . . . or to the Evil One. . . . The context alone must decide; and this in the present case . . . seems rather in favour of the masculine,—(1) in consequence of the seeming reference to the Lord's prayer, where the Greek commentators (whose opinion in such points deserves full consideration) adopt the masculine,—and (2) from the tacit personal antithesis suggested by the preceding *Kyrios* [Lord]" (p. 125).

Milligan agrees with this. He comments:

> The precise sense to be attached to these words is best determined by the meaning assigned them in the petition of the Lord's Prayer (Mt. vi. 13), of which we have apparently a reminiscence here. . . . As the general consensus of modern scholarship is to understand *ponērou* there as masculine rather than as neuter in accordance with the predominant usage of the N.T. . . . and the unanimous opinion of the Greek commentators, we follow the same rendering here, and translate "from the evil one": a rendering, it may be noted further, which forms a fitting antithesis to *ho kyrios* of the preceding clause, and is moreover in thorough harmony with the prominence assigned shortly before to the persons of Satan and his representatives (ii. 1-12), and more especially to the *evil men (ponērōn anthrōpōn)* of the preceding clause (p. 111).

Patient Waiting or Steadfastness? (3:5)

The word *hypomonē* means "a remaining behind . . . patient enduring, endurance" (A-S). Arndt and Gingrich define it as follows: "Patience, endurance, fortitude, steadfastness, perseverance"; and add: "especially as they are shown in the enduring of toil and suffering." For this passage they give: *"a Christ-like fortitude,* i.e. a fortitude that comes from communion with Christ" (p. 854). But they also allow the meaning "(patient) expectation," which they think is clearly correct in Rev. 1:9 and perhaps here and in Rev. 3:10. Thayer prefers "a patient, steadfast waiting for" in all three of these passages. Abbott-Smith does not even cite this meaning.

Ellicott is rather adamant at this point. He says: "Analogy with what precedes would suggest (a) a genitive *objecti,* 'waiting for Christ' . . . but would introduce a meaning of *hypomonē* that is apparently not lexically defensible, and certainly is contrary to the usage of the N.T." (p. 127).

Again Milligan agrees. He declares that "the subjective interpretation of the second clause is rendered almost necessary by the regular meaning of *hypomonēn* in the N.T., 'constancy,' 'endurance' . . . not 'patient waiting'" (p. 112).

But Hauck takes exception to this. While agreeing that the verb *hypomenō* in the NT is "used comparatively rarely for 'to wait,' 'to wait for,' 'to expect,'" he yet goes on to say: "There is an example of the Godward use, corresponding to that of the LXX, in 2 Th. 3:5. The *hypomonē tou Christou* is here expectation of the Christ who will come again in glory. . . . Similarly in Rev. 1:9 the *hypomonē Jesou* is to be construed as expectation of Jesus, since the saying of the exalted Christ in 3:10 . . . is plainly intended to praise the loyal preservation of faith in the *parousia* in the community." Then he adds this beautiful comment: "Pious waiting for Jesus is the heart-beat of the faith of the NT community" (TDNT, 4:586).

It is obvious that both "patient waiting for Christ" (KJV) and "steadfastness of Christ" (RSV, NASB) are live options.

Ancient Hippies (3:6)

Today the hippies constitute one of the saddest seg-
ments of American society. These "flower children" who
talk volubly about love can also foment riots and break out
in violent demonstrations.

This is not a twentieth-century phenomenon alone.
There were plenty of these people in the Graeco-Roman
society of the first century, as writers of that day testify.
There were even some in the Church. Paul had to warn
the brethren at Thessalonica to disassociate themselves
from "every brother that walketh disorderly."

The last word is the adverb *ataktōs,* found only here
and in verse 11. The cognate adjective occurs only in 1
Thess. 5:14, where KJV renders it "unruly"; that is, not
living according to the rules. The verb *atakteō,* derived
from this, is also a *hapax legomenon,* being found only in
2 Thess. 3:7 (the next verse here). There it is translated
"behave disorderly." It will be seen, then, that these three
cognate terms do not occur in the NT outside the Thessalonian letters. It looks as though there was a hippie community at Thessalonica!

This suspicion is given further support when we look
at the contemporary usage of these terms. Moulton and
Milligan note that the verb *atakteō* has the "original connotation of riot or rebellion." One is reminded of the riots
and disorderly demonstrations precipitated by hippies on
our university campuses. But the authors go on to say:
"Like its parent adjective *ataktos,* and the adverb, this
verb is found in the NT only in the Thessalonian Epistles,
where their context clearly demands that the words should
be understood metaphorically. Some doubt, however, has
existed as to whether they are to be taken as referring to
actual moral wrong-doing, or to a certain remissness in
daily work and conduct. . . . The latter view is now sup-

ported by almost contemporary evidence from the *Koine*"
(VGT, p. 89).

This evidence is found in a papyrus contract of apprenticeship (A.D. 66). The father agrees that if there
should be any days when his son (the apprentice) "plays
truant" or "fails to attend," he must later make up for
them. Also in a papyrus of A.D. 183 a weaver's apprentice
is bound to appear for an equivalent number of days in
case he exceeds, from idleness or ill health, the 20 days'
vacation he is allowed during the year. These illustrations
show that the verb *atakteō* was used in that day for being
idle or failing to discharge one's responsibilities. For this
passage (2 Thess. 3:6) Arndt and Gingrich suggest the
rendering "live in idleness."

Follow or Imitate? (3:7)

The verb *mimeomai* occurs (in NT) only four times:
here; verse 9; Heb. 13:7; and 3 John 11. In the KJV it is
always translated "follow." Likewise the noun *mimētēs* (7
times in NT) is always "follower." But "follow" is *akoloutheō*. The correct meaning of *mimeomai* is "imitate."
Perhaps the best rendering here is "follow our example"
(NASB, NIV).

For Nought or Gratis? (3:8)

The Greek word *dōrean* comes from the verb *didōmi*,
"give." So it means "as a gift, without payment, gratis"
(AG). TCNT and NIV translate it "without paying for it."
That is still the best rendering. It is favored by Arndt and
Gingrich.

Chargeable or A Burden? (3:8)

The verb *epibareō* literally means "to put a burden

on, be burdensome" (A-S). In 1 Thess. 2:9 it is translated
as here, "be chargeable." The only other place where it
occurs in the NT is 2 Cor. 2:5, where it is rendered "over-
charge." Again TCNT gives the correct meaning: "so as
not to be a burden upon any of you" (cf. NIV).

Power or Right? (3:9)

The basic meaning of *exousia* was liberty of action or
freedom of choice. Paul is saying that he was free to accept
financial support. Later the word came to signify "right"
or "authority." The correct meaning here is "not because
we had not a right to receive support" (TCNT; cf. NASB,
NIV).

Not Busy but Busybodies (3:11)

There is a play on words in the Greek: "not at all
ergazomenous but *periergazomenous*." This is brought out
in the heading above about as nearly as can be done in
English. Literally the Greek means "not at all working,
but working around."

The second verb, *periergazomai,* is found only here in
the NT. It means "to bustle about uselessly, to busy one's
self about trifling, needless, useless matters." Thayer goes
on to say that the verb is "used apparently of a person
officiously inquisitive about others' affairs" (p. 502).
Demosthenes employs it in that sense. This seems also to
be the meaning in a papyrus letter written in A.D. 41 by the
Emperor Claudius to the Alexandrians. In it he says:
"And, on the other side, I bid the Jews not to busy themselves about anything beyond what they have held hitherto" (VGT, p. 505).

Have Company or Mix? (3:14)

The verb is a strong compound, *synanamignymi*. Literally it means "to mix up together," and so "to associate with" (A-S). Perhaps the best translation is: "Do not associate with him" (NASB, NIV). In the NT it is used only here and in 1 Cor. 5:9. The idea that Christians, and especially pastors, should be "good mixers" is not exactly scriptural.

Token or Mark? (3:17)

The Greek word *sēmeion* means *"the sign* or *distinguishing mark* by which something is known." Arndt and Gingrich translate the passage: "This is the mark of genuineness in every letter." The verse may be translated: "I, Paul, add this farewell in my own handwriting. Every letter of mine is signed in this way. This is the way in which I write" (TCNT; cf. NIV).

FIRST TIMOTHY

❧◉◍◉❧

God Our Saviour (1:1)

This unique phrase is used by Paul only in the Pastoral Epistles (1 Tim. 1:1; 2:3; 4:10; Titus 1:3; 2:10; 3:4). Elsewhere in the NT it occurs just twice and then in liturgical passages (Luke 1:47; Jude 25). It is also found in the Septuagint version of Deut. 32:15. It fits in perfectly with Old Testament theology, as well as that of Paul. There is no reasonable justification for using it as an argument against the Pauline authorship of the Pastoral Epistles. God is our Savior just as truly as Jesus Christ is our Savior.

My Own or True? (1:2)

The word *gnēsios* properly means "lawfully begotten, born in wedlock" (A-S), and so "true" or "genuine." The KJV "my own" suggests this, but is perhaps not strong enough. Strangely, NEB has "his true-born son" (cf. Moffatt, "his lawful son"). Probably the best translation is "my true son" (NIV).

A New Word (1:3)

Paul, unlike John, was particularly fond of compound words. Some of them he evidently coined himself. An example is found at the end of verse 3. "That they teach . . . other doctrine" is all one word in Greek—*heterodidaskalein.* It is composed of *heteros,* "different," and *didaskaleō,* "teach." The term (only here and 6:3 in NT) is used by Ignatius in his letter to Polycarp (ca. A.D. 115). Eusebius, in his *Ecclesiastical History* (A.D. 326) employs the cognate noun *heterodidaskaloi* to designate heretical teachers. In verse 7, Paul has *nomodidaskaloi,* "lawteachers." So the "different" teaching here in verse 3 was evidently that of Judaizers, who asserted that Gentile Christians had to keep the Jewish law (cf. Acts 15).

Fables or Myths? (1:4)

The Greek word is *mythos,* from which we get "myth." In the NT it is found four times in the Pastoral Epistles (1 Tim. 1:4; 4:7; 2 Tim. 4:4; Titus 1:14) and in 2 Pet. 1:16. In all five places it is rendered "fables" in KJV.

The term first meant "a speech, word, saying," then "a narrative, story"—whether true or fictitious—and finally "an invention, falsehood" (Thayer). It is thus distinguished from *logos,* "a historical tale" (Vincent, 4:203).

Kittel's TDNT devotes no less than 34 pages to this word alone. Because of the vague and varied ways in which the term is used today by biblical scholars, it might be well to give it some attention.

The article in TDNT is written by Staehlin. He notes that some use "myth" for that which is unhistorical and yet has religious value. Then he asserts: "But if the concept of myth is brought into antithesis to both historical reality and to truth as such, and if reality and truth are thought to be essential to genuine revelation and the only possible basis of faith, myth can have no religious value" (4:765). Two results follow. Either the NT stories are "dismissed as myths, as errors and deceptions," or a sharp line is drawn between Gospel and myth. He notes that the latter is "the judgment of the NT itself" which contrasts myth with history (2 Pet. 1:16) and with truth (2 Tim. 4:4; Titus 1:14). His conclusion is incisive: "The Christian Church, insofar as it is true to itself, accepts this judgment that myth is untrue and consequently of no religious value" *(ibid.)*. This is a welcome antidote to Bultmann!

Plato made much use of myth, but Aristotle argued that *logos* alone has educational value; myth merely pleases (4:775). For the Stoics myth was valid as a symbol (4:777). Staehlin concludes his study of myth in the Greek world by saying: "There is, however, no fundamental repudiation on religious grounds until we come to the NT and the Christian writers of the first centuries" (4:779).

In the Septuagint the word *mythos* is found only in the apocryphal books (twice). Later rabbis made use of Greek myths as parables (4:781).

Coming to "Mythoi in the NT," Staehlin reiterates his earlier statements. He says: "The position of the NT regarding what it calls *mythos* is quite unequivocal. . . . There is obviously a complete repudiation of *mythos*. It is the means and mark of an alien proclamation, especially of the error combatted in the Pastorals" *(ibid.)*.

What is the nature of these myths which Paul warns against? Staehlin says, "It is highly probable that the Pastorals are concerned with the early form of a Gnosticism which flourished on the soil of Hellenistic Jewish Christianity" (4:783).

Staehlin concludes that "myth as such has no place on biblical soil" (4:793). Against those who defend it as a form of religious communication he asserts: "In the Bible, however, we have from first to last the account and narration of facts. This may undergo certain changes in form and consciousness from the childlikeness of many of the ancient stories to the maturity of the Johannine view of Christ. But the essential theme is the same throughout, namely, what God says and what God does" (4:793-94).

Pagan myths were sometimes used as parables. But Staehlin insists that "the NT uses genuine parable rather than myths" (4:794). Myths were finally thought of as symbols. Staehlin's answer to this argument is clear and direct. He says: "The central symbol of the Gospel, however, is the cross, and this embodies a hard and unromantic historical reality. No myth can be integrated into or imposed upon this symbol in any form" *(ibid.)*. In a footnote he adds: "Hence the use of expressions like the Christ myth, which is common in form criticism, is to be strictly avoided."

This German writer maintains his position without equivocation. He raises the question as to whether there is some other way to make myth at home in the biblical world. He answers: "But no matter how the term is understood, and no matter how it is extended, as e.g., by Bultmann, there is within it an inherent antithesis to truth and reality which is quite intolerable on NT soil" *(ibid.)*.

We have quoted at unusual length from this article because it touches on a very relevant problem in current NT studies. It is the most scholarly, constructive treatment we have seen to date.

Minister or Cause? (1:4)

The word is *parechō,* which literally means "hold beside." As used here it signifies "cause, bring about" (AG). Vincent suggests "afford, furnish, give occasion for" (4:204).

Questions or Questionings? (1:4)

The Greek term *ekzētēsis* occurs only here in the NT
and is not found in the Septuagint or classical Greek. It
carries the idea of "seekings *out*" *(ek)*. For these two words
together in this verse Arndt and Gingrich suggest the
rendering, "give rise to speculations" (cf. RSV). Perhaps
the best translation is "cause questionings." N. J. D.
White defines the second term as: "*Questionings* to which
no answer can be given, which are not worth answering"
(EGT, 4:93). Lock suggests "out-of-the-way researches"
(p. 9).

Edifying or Stewardship? (1:4)

The best Greek text does not have *oikodomēn*, "edify-
ing," but *oikonomia*. The latter word primarily means
"stewardship" (cf. Luke 16:2-4). In later writers it came to
have the more general sense of "administration" or "dispensation" (A-S). Aside from the above passage in Luke,
the word occurs in the NT only in Paul's Epistles (1 Cor.
9:17; Eph. 1:10; 3:2; Col. 1:25), where it is always translated "dispensation" in KJV. Here Arndt and Gingrich
(p. 562) think the meaning is: "They promote useless
speculations rather than divine training that is in faith"
(cf. RSV). Michel, in TDNT (5:153), agrees. He writes: "In
1 Tim. 1:4 it is said of the false teachers that they proclaim
fables in which there is more questioning than godly instruction in faith." Lock (p. 9) gives what seems to us an
especially good interpretation: "'God's stewardship,' *i.e.*
they do not help them to carry out the stewardship entrusted to them by God."

End or Aim? (1:5)

The simple meaning of the word *telos* is "end." But it

also has in this passage the specialized sense, "the end to which all things relate, the aim, purpose" (Thayer, p. 620; cf. A-S, p. 443). Arndt and Gingrich give here: "The preaching has love as its aim" (p. 819).

Commandment or Charge? (1:5)

The noun here has the same stem as the verb "charge" in verse 3. The connection is retained by translating it similarly. The goal of Timothy's charge to the Ephesian Christians was "love out of a pure heart." And that is the ultimate aim of all true Christian preaching.

Unfeigned or Sincere? (1:5)

The adjective *anypocritos* is from *a*-negative and *hypocrites,* "hypocrite." So it literally means "unhypo-critical." Perhaps the best modern equivalent is "sincere" (NIV).

Swerved or Straying? (1:6)

The verb *astocheō* (only in the Pastorals) literally means "miss the mark." Arndt and Gingrich say that here it signifies "deviate, depart." Lock (p. 10) thinks the idea is "taking no pains to aim at the right path." A possible translation is "straying" (NASB) or "wandered" (NIV).

Vain Jangling or Empty Talk? (1:6)

This is one word in the Greek, *mataiologia* (only here in NT). Literally it means "vain talking, empty talk" (Thayer). It could be translated "empty prattle" (TDNT, 4:524) or "meaningless talk" (NIV). Arndt and Gingrich give the sense here as "fruitless discussion" (cf. NASB).

"law" or "Law"? (1:7)

"Teachers of the law" is all one word in the Greek, *nomodidaskaloi*—literally, "law-teachers." Since it is obviously the Mosaic law which is meant here, it is best to capitalize "Law" (cf. NASB).

Affirm or Confidently Affirm? (1:7)

The term is a strong compound, *diabebaiountai* (only here and Titus 3:8). It means "affirm strongly, assert confidently" (Thayer). The NIV renders it well: "They so confidently affirm."

Disobedient or Unruly? (1:9)

The adjective is a double compound, *anypotaktos*. It is formed from *a*-negative, *hypo* ("under"), and *tassō*. The last is a verb with primarily the military connotation of "draw up in order." So the compound means "that cannot be subjected to control . . . unruly" (Thayer). It may well be translated "disorderly" or "insubordinate." The first two adjectives here signify "the general refusal to obey all law" (Lock, p. 12). The next two, "ungodly and sinners," refer to "the general refusal to obey the law of God"; and the next two, "unholy and profane," to "the more detailed opposition to the law of God" *(ibid.)*. The verse finishes with the mention of patricides, matricides, and homicides. It is obvious that in this list of sinners (vv. 9-10) there is indicated a progression in sin.

Whoremongers or Adulterers? (1:10)

The latter term is preferable today for *pornois*, though "immoral persons" (RSV) may be better. "For them that defile themselves with mankind" is all one word in Greek, *arsenokoitais.* It is correctly translated "sodomites" (RSV), though the usual term used today for this is "homosexuals" (NASB). "Menstealers" (*andrapodistais,* only here in NT) refers to slave traders or "kidnapers." "Perjured persons" (*epiorkois,* only here in NT) is better translated "perjurers" (NIV).

Sound or Healthful? (1:10)

The term is *hygianousei,* from the verb *hygiainō* (cf. "hygiene"). This verb is found three times in the Gospel of Luke (5:31; 7:10; 15:10); eight times in the Pastoral Epistles, and once in 3 John (v. 2, "be in health"). It means "to be sound, to be well, to be in good health" (Thayer, p. 634). With regard to its use in the Pastorals, Arndt and Gingrich write: "Thus in accord with prevailing usage, Christian teaching is designated as the *correct* doctrine, since it is reasonable and appeals to sound intelligence" (p. 840). Some scholars prefer "healthful" or "wholesome." Lock specifically rejects the latter, choosing "sound" (p. 12). Vincent (4:209) supports both "sound" and "healthful." While the basic idea of the Greek verb may suggest "healthy" rather than "healthful," we know that teaching, like food, is either conducive to moral and spiritual health or a hindrance to it. For that reason, "healthful" seems to be a justifiable translation.

This list of common sins at Ephesus in the first century, for which there is abundant documentation from secular sources, is a shocking one. But every item mentioned here can be duplicated from contemporary society in America and Europe. Some of these sins are perhaps more prevalent now than at any time since Roman days.

Injurious or Insolent? (1:13)

The word *hybristēs* is found (in NT) only here and in Rom. 1:30, where it is translated "despiteful" (KJV). It is a noun meaning "a violent, insolent man" (A-S). It suggests "one who, uplifted with pride, either heaps insulting language upon others or does them some shameful act of wrong" (Fritzsche, quoted by Thayer). The great humility of Paul is seen in his describing his pre-Christian life in this way. Vincent writes: "*Hybristēs* is one whose insolence and contempt of others break forth in wanton and outrageous acts. Paul was *hybristēs* when he persecuted the church" (4:211).

First or Chief? (1:15-16)

The superlative degree form *prōtos* is defined thus by Abbott-Smith: "*first*, 1. of Time or Place. . . . 2. Of Rank or Dignity, *chief, principal.* . . . 3. Neuter, *proton*, as adverb, *first, at the first*" (pp. 389-90).

Prōtos is translated "chief" in verse 15 (second meaning above) and "first" in verse 16 (first meaning). Vincent defends this. He says of *prōtos* in verse 16: "Not the chief sinner, but the representative instance of God's long-suffering applied to a high-handed transgressor" (4:212). Arndt and Gingrich agree. They translate the phrase in verse 16: "in me as the first" (p. 733). A. T. Robertson interprets it this way: "Probably starts with the same sense of *prōtos* as in verse 15 (rank), but turns to order (first in line). Paul becomes the 'specimen' sinner as an encouragement to all who come after him" (WP, 4:564). Alford follows much the same line. He writes on verse 16: "It can hardly be denied that in *prōtō* here the senses of '*chief*' and '*first*' are combined. . . . Though he was not in time 'the first of sinners,' yet he was the first as well as the most notable example of such marked long-suffering, held up for the encouragement of the church" (3:309). Lock agrees with these interpretations (starting with "chief," but also implying "first") (p. 16).

In spite of this array of scholarly opinion we prefer to go along with J. H. Bernard in the *Cambridge Greek Testament*. He says that the Revised rendering "in me as chief," "certainly brings out the connection with . . . the preceding verse better than A.V. 'first'" (p. 33). The NASB preserves this connection by using "foremost" (v. 15) and "in me as foremost" (v. 16).

All His Long-suffering (1:16)

The KJV has simply: "that in me first Jesus Christ might shew forth all longsuffering." This could be interpreted as meaning Paul's patience with others. But the Greek has the definite article, with the possessive force. So the correct meaning is "all his longsuffering" (ASV); that is, the long-suffering of Christ toward Paul. The NASB has: "might demonstrate His perfect patience" (cf. NIV: "might display his unlimited patience").

Pattern or Example? (1:16)

Paul normally uses the simple word *typon* (9 times), from which comes "type." But here and in 2 Tim. 1:13 we find the compound *hypotypōsis*. Originally it meant an outline or sketch. Then it came to be used in the metaphorical sense of an example—"to show by the example of my conversion that the same grace which I had obtained would not be wanting also to those who should hereafter believe" (Thayer, p. 645). Arndt and Gingrich feel that here it suggests "prototype," whereas in 2 Tim. 1:13 it means "standard." The majority of recent translations have wisely adopted "example."

Only Wise God or Only God? (1:17)

The best Greek text does not have the adjective "wise." The Eternal King is not just the "only wise God" but the "only God"—period! There is no other real God of any kind, wise or unwise.

Went Before or Led the Way? (1:18)

The verb *proagō* was used transitively in the sense of "lead on, lead forth," and intransitively as "lead the way" or "go before." The English Revised Version (NT, 1881) followed the KJV in reading, "which went before on thee." But it also placed in the margin an alternative rendering, "led the way to thee." This marginal reading was adopted in the American Standard Edition of the Revised Version (ASV), put out in 1901. It is preferred by Abbott-Smith in his *Lexicon* and by Bernard (CGT).

But Thayer thinks the participle in this passage means "preceding i.e. prior in point of time, previous." Similarly Arndt and Gingrich suggest here: "in accordance with the prophecies that were made long ago" (p. 709).

Lock (p. 18) allows both of these meanings: "*Either* according to the previous . . . prophecies about thee . . . *or* according to the prophecies leading me towards you." But in his paraphrase he adopts the latter: "recalling to mind the words of the Christian prophets which led me to choose you to help me in my work" (p. 17). The reference seems to be to Timothy's ordination (4:14), although the quotation just given would relate it to Acts 16:3. At one time or the other—perhaps both—there were inspired utterances about Timothy's future.

Warfare or Fight? (1:18)

The KJV has "war a good warfare." Because there is a definite article in the Greek, the ASV has more accurately, "war the good warfare."

The NASB adopts the rendering given in Arndt and Gingrich: "fight the good fight." Perhaps this is too narrow. Of the noun Vincent says: "Not *fight (machēn)*, but covering all the particulars of a soldier's service" (4:215).

The verb is *strateuō*, which means "to serve as a soldier" (A-S); "do military service, serve in the army" (AG). The noun *strateia* was used for "an expedition, a campaign, warfare" (A-S). The point to emphasize, of course, is that the Christian's fight with evil is not a single battle; it lasts until death. It has been truly said: "There is no discharge in this war." Possibly "war the good warfare" is best, or "wage the good warfare" (RSV). On the other hand, "fight the good fight" (Weymouth, Moffatt, Goodspeed, NIV) may be a better contemporary translation.

Put Away or Thrust from Them? (1:19)

The KJV translation is not strong enough. The verb *apōtheō* means "to thrust away" and in the middle (always in NT) it signifies "to thrust away from oneself, refuse, reject" (A-S). Bernard says: "The verb is expressive of a wilful and violent act" (p. 35). Schmidt observes that it is "used in Greek poetry and prose from the time of Homer to the papyri with both the literal and figurative meaning of 'to repel' or 'reject'" (TDNT, 1:448).

Faith or Their Faith? (1:19)

The noun has the definite article in the Greek: "concerning the faith." A. T. Robertson writes: "Rather, 'con-

cerning their faith' (the article here used as a possessive
pronoun, a common Greek idiom)" (4:566). Lock agrees
with this. He feels that the context and the stress on faith
throughout the chapter "make the subjective meaning
more probable" (p. 19).

Variety in Praying (2:1)

In this verse we find four words for prayer: "supplica-
tions, prayers, intercessions, and giving of thanks"—the
only place in the NT where they all occur together. There
are some points of distinction between them.

The first term is *deēsis* (de-*ay*-sis), the second *proseuchē* (pro-seu-*chay*). *Deēsis* simply means "petition,"
whether made to God or man. But *proseuchē* is used only
for prayer to God.

The third noun is *enteuxis,* which occurs only here and
in 1 Tim. 4:5. In his classic work, *Synonyms of the New
Testament,* R. C. Trench notes that *enteuxis* "does not
necessarily mean what intercession at present commonly
does mean—namely, prayer in relation to others. . . .
[Rather] it is free, familiar prayer, such as boldly draws
near to God" (pp. 189-90).

Concerning these three words Thayer comments:
"*Deēsis* gives prominence to the expression of personal
need, *proseuchē* to the element of devotion, *enteuxis* to
that of childlike confidence, by representing prayer as the
heart's converse with God" (p. 126).

The fourth expression, "giving of thanks," is one word
in the Greek—*eucharistia.* Of this Trench writes: "Regarded as one manner of prayer, it expresses that which
ought never to be absent from any of our devotions (Phil.
iv. 6; Eph. v. 20; I Thess. v. 18; I Tim. ii. 1); namely, the
grateful acknowledgement of past mercies, as distinguished from the earnest seeking of future" (p. 191).

Now to look at each of these terms more closely. *Deēsis,* from the verb *deomai,* first meant "a wanting, need" and then "an asking, entreaty, supplication" (A-S, p. 99). Arndt and Gingrich note that it is used "with *proseuchē,* the more general term, to denote a more specific supplication" (p. 171). In the NT it is employed only for prayer to God. The word is "frequently used for intercession" (TDNT, 2:41). Occurring 19 times in the NT, *deēsis* is 12 times translated "prayer," 6 times "supplication," and once "request."

In contrast, *proseuchē* is found 37 times in the NT and is regularly translated "prayer" ("pray earnestly" in Jas. 5:17). It is the most general word for prayer in the NT.

The noun *enteuxis* comes from the verb *entynchanō,* which signifies "to fall in with a person; to draw near so as to converse familiarly." Vincent continues: "Hence, *enteuxis* is not properly *intercession* in the accepted sense of that term, but rather approach to God in free and familiar prayer" (4:216). Ellicott says that *enteuxis* refers to "prayer in its most individual and urgent form . . . prayer in which God is, as it were, sought in audience . . . and personally drawn nigh ᴜᴏ ' (p. 42).

The term *eucharistia* suggests another important aspect of prayer. It occurs 15 times in the NT and is variously rendered "thanksgiving," "giving of thanks," "thankfulness," and simply "thanks."

N. J. D. White thinks that Paul did not have in mind strong distinctions between the first three terms: "His object in the enumeration is simply to cover every possible variety of public prayer" (EGT, 4:102). In line with this J. H. Bernard, in his volume on "The Pastoral Epistles" in the *Cambridge Greek Testament,* writes: "The four words are not to be too sharply distinguished, inasmuch as they point to different moods of the suppliant rather than to the different forms into which public prayer may be cast" (p. 38). But he later goes on to say: "To sum up, then, we may (1) with Origen, regard the four words as arranged in an ascending scale: the needy suppliant *(deēsis)* as he goes on is led to ask for larger blessings *(proseuchē)*, and then becoming bold he presents his *enteuxis,* which being granted, his devotion issues in thanksgiving. Or (2) we may more simply take the words in two contrasted pairs, *deēsis* being related to *proseuchē* as the particular to the general, and *enteuxis* to *eucharistia* as petition to thanksgiving" (pp. 38-39).

Authority or High Office? (2:2)

The Greek word is *hyperochē.* It is found only here and in 1 Cor. 2:1, where it is translated "excellency." It was first used for an eminence, such as a mountain peak, and then metaphorically in the sense of "preeminence." The Greek phrase here occurs in an inscription of the second century B.C. at Pergamum. Deissmann (BS, p. 255) renders it "persons of consequence." Perhaps the best translation is "high office" (NEB).

Quiet and Peaceable (2:2)

The two Greek words, *ēremos* and *hēsychion,* are defined exactly the same way in Abbott-Smith's *Lexicon:* "quiet, tranquil." The former is found only here in the NT; the latter occurs also in 1 Pet. 3:4. Vincent points out the distinction between the two. *"Ēremos* denotes quiet arising from the absence of outward disturbance: *hēsychios* tranquillity arising from within" (4:217). We are to pray for our rulers, that we may enjoy the former. Meanwhile, God's grace can give us the latter.

Honesty or Dignity? (2:2)

The Greek word is *semnotēs*. Thayer gives this definition: "That characteristic of a person or a thing which entitles to reverence or respect, *dignity, gravity, majesty, sanctity*" (p. 573). The last two ideas apply especially to God, the other two to man. Abbott-Smith gives only "gravity." But this term is not commonly used today. Arndt and Gingrich say that when used of men *semnotēs* means: "Reverence, dignity, seriousness, respectfulness, holiness, probity."

Vincent opts for "gravity." He comments: *"Honesty, according to the modern acceptation, is an unfortunate rendering"* (4:217). In place of "godliness and honesty," if one likes alliteration he can use "godliness and gravity" (ASV) or "piety and probity" (Goodspeed). Perhaps the best translation for the second word is "dignity" (NASB) or "holiness" (NIV).

Will Have or Desires? (2:4)

The KJV rendering might be taken as indicating simple futurity. But the Greek word is *thelō*, which signifies "wish" or "will," in the sense of desire or purpose (cf. NIV: "wants"). Both ideas apply here.

Mediator (2:5)

Besides this passage, *mesitēs* occurs twice in Galatians (3:19-20) and three times in Hebrews (8:6; 9:15; 12:24). It is regularly translated "mediator" in most versions.

Thayer explains the term as meaning "one who intervenes between two, either in order to make or restore peace and friendship, or to form a compact, or for ratifying a covenant." Of this passage he writes: "Christ is called

mesitēs theou kai anthrōpōn, since he interposed by his
death and restored the harmony between God and man
which human sin had broken" (p. 401). Arndt and Gingrich refer to it as "this many-sided technical term of Hellenistic legal language" (pp. 507-8). It is used many times
in the papyri for an arbitrator in connection with both
legal and business transactions.

The word comes from *mesos,* "middle," and so means
a middleman; that is, "a man who stands in the middle
and who brings two parties together." The Greek term
occurs only once in the Septuagint, when Job complains:
"Neither is there any daysman betwixt us, that might lay
his hand upon us both" (Job 9:33). As indicated in the
Oxford English Dictionary, "daysman" is an archaic term
for "an umpire or arbitrator; a mediator" (3:53).

In his meaty little volume *A New Testament Word-
book,* William Barclay has an excellent discussion of
mesitēs. He says that it had two main meanings in classical Greek. The first was "arbiter." Both Greek and Roman
law gave considerable attention to arbitration. Barclay
writes: "An arbiter, a mediator, a *mesitēs,* is therefore
fundamentally a person whose duty it is to bring together
two people who are estranged and to wipe out the differences between them" (p. 86). He adds that this is what
Jesus did between us and God.

The second meaning is "a sponsor, guarantor, or
surety." Barclay says: "A man who went bail for another's
appearance in court was so called. But the words are especially used of guaranteeing or standing surety for a debt"
(ibid.). So Jesus stands surety for our debt to God. This
usage is found several times in the papyri of the second
and third centuries (VGT, p. 399).

In TDNT Oepke devotes to *mesitēs* 27 pages, much of
it in fine print. His thorough survey of the history of this
term and its theological significance ends with a twofold

observation. After noting the almost complete absence of *mesitēs* in early Christian writings, he says: "In Roman Catholicism the Church and its agent largely took over the mediatorial function. In contrast, Reformation theology looked to the one Mediator, Christ." And then he adds this striking statement: "It is no accident that in the 20th century, when, after a period of liberal and rational thought, theology was finding its way back to the biblical and Reformation message, the word 'mediator' became one of the slogans of the new outlook" (4:624). In our estranged generation the message of Christ the Mediator needs to be sounded again and again.

Ransom (2:6)

Christ gave himself as a "ransom" on behalf of all. Only here in the NT do we find the compound *antilytron*.

The simple form *lytron* is found twice, in Matt. 20:28 and Mark 10:45—"For even the Son of man came not to be ministered unto [served], but to minister [serve], and to give his life a ransom for many." The literal meaning of *lytron* was "a price for release." It was used especially for the price paid to free a slave. The noun comes from the verb *lyō*, which means "to loose." Still earlier it was used to designate "the money paid to ransom prisoners of war" (TDNT, 4:340). There does not seem to be any basic difference between *lytron* and *antilytron*. The prefix *anti,* "instead of," follows *lytron* in the saying of Jesus. Here it is incorporated with the simple noun to emphasize the fact that Christ died in our place to ransom us from the slavery of sin. White makes the helpful suggestion: *"Lytron anti* merely implies that the exchange is decidedly a benefit to those on whose behalf it is made" (EGT, 4:105). Bernard says: "Here we have the compound *antilytron* preceding *hyper pantōn,* which suggests that both the elements represented by *anti* 'instead of,' and *hyper* 'on behalf of' must enter into any Scriptural theory of the Atonement" (p. 42).

Doubting or Disputing? (2:8)

The word *dialogismos* occurs eight times in the Gospels—six in Luke, one each in Matthew and Mark—where it is rendered "thought(s)" with the exception of Luke 9:46 ("reasoning"). It occurs five times in Paul's Epistles and is translated five different ways in the KJV! It is found once elsewhere, in Jas. 2:4 ("thoughts").

The noun comes from the verb *dialogizomai*, "to consider, reason," and so means "a thought, reasoning, inward questioning" (A-S). Thayer notes that from the time of Plato it signified "the thinking of a man deliberating with himself" (p. 139).

Schrenk notes that the most common meaning in ancient Greek was "deliberation" or "reflection." He states: "The sense of 'evil thoughts' is predominant in the NT" (TDNT, 2:97). But it can also be used for "anxious reflection" or "doubt." With regard to our passage he writes that the translation "without wrath or disputing" (cf. ASV) "yields good sense." But after pointing out the fact that the idea of contention is not necessarily inherent in the term, he concludes: "We thus do better to follow the linguistic instinct of the Greek exegetes and interpret *dialogismos* as doubt or questioning" (2:98).

Our own inclination, however, follows that of Lock. He says, "probably 'disputing,'" and adds that "the idea of doubt is alien to the context, which emphasizes man's relation to his fellow men" (p. 31). Huther, in Meyer's commentary series, thinks that here it should be taken in the sense of evil deliberations against one's neighbor (p. 102). Bernard prefers "disputation." Likewise E. K. Simpson (*Pastoral Epistles,* p. 45) opts for "controversy," though allowing "the primary Platonic meaning of the word, *cogitation, reasoning."*

Modest Apparel (2:9)

In a day of "undress" this famous passage on how women should dress takes on added significance. We need to find out exactly what the Scripture says here.

The word for "apparel" is *katastolē (ay),* which is found only here in the NT. The latter part of this (cf. English "stole" for a scarf) comes from the verb *stellō,* which meant "to set, place, arrange, fit out" (A-S).

The prefix *kata* means "down." So *katastolē* first meant "a lowering, letting down," and then "a garment let down, dress, attire" (Thayer). In classical Greek it also was used in the sense of "modesty, reserve" (LSJ). Arndt and Gingrich furnish this definition: *"Deportment,* outward, as it expresses itself in *clothing* . . . as well as inward . . . and probably both at the same time" (p. 420). Ellicott says: *"Katastolē* is not simply 'dress' . . . a meaning for which there is not satisfactory authority, but 'deportment,' as exhibited externally, whether in look, manner, or *dress"* (p. 50). Simpson writes: *"Katastolē* can signify *dress;* but usage favours the wider sense of demeanour, so that the entire phrase bespeaks a well-ordered carriage" (p. 46).

However, Abbott-Smith says that in the Septuagint and NT the word means "a garment, dress, attire." As in the case of the NT, the word occurs only once in the Septuagint, in Isa. 61:3, where it is translated "garment" (of praise). This would, of course, be metaphorical.

The adjective "modest" is *cosmios.* It is found only here and in 3:2, where it is translated "of good behaviour." It comes from *cosmos.* This is the regular term for "world"

(186 times in NT), but in the similar passage in 1 Pet. (3: 3) it is rendered "adorning."

The original meaning of *cosmos* was "order" (Homer, Plato, and others). Then it came to be used in the sense of "ornament" or "adornment," especially in relation to women. Only in later writers did it take on the popular usage for "world" or universe, as an ordered system. Finally it came to be used as equivalent to "the earth."

So *cosmios* signifies "well-arranged, seemly, modest" (Thayer). White says: "It means *orderly,* as opposed to disorderliness in appearance" (EGT, 4:108). Perhaps the emphasis here is as much on *neatness* of dress as on *modesty.* The ideal is to combine these two aspects. A good translation here is "becoming attire" (Berk.). The NIV reads: "I also want women to dress modestly."

Adorn (2:9)

The verb is *cosmeō,* which also comes from *cosmos.* Originally it meant "to order, arrange, prepare" (A-S). Homer used it for marshalling armies. In Matt. 25:7 it refers to trimming the wicks on lamps. In Matt. 12:44 and Luke 11:25 it is used for a house "put in order" (RSV). In Rev. 21:2 the New Jerusalem is described as like "a bride adorned for her husband." In contrast to this, a passage in an Oxyrhynchus papyrus speaks of women "adorned for adultery" (AG, p. 445).

Shamefacedness? (2:9)

This unfortunate translation leaves the implication that Christian women should go around in public with heads bowed and eyes averted, as if they were ashamed of themselves. Not so. Actually this rendering appears to be an error. *The Oxford English Dictionary* says that the adjective "shamefaced" was "originally an etymological mis-interpretation of *shamefast*" (9:620) which carries the idea of discreetness. Wycliff's earliest English version of the Bible (1382) has the correct term here, "shamefastness." This is used in the ASV (1901), but, of course, even this word is obsolete today.

The Greek term is *aidos,* found only here in the NT. Bernard says that it implies "(1) a *moral* repugnance to what is base and unseemly, and (2) *self-respect,* as well as restraint imposed on oneself from a sense of what is due to others." He goes on to say: "Thus *aidos* here signifies that modesty which shrinks from overstepping the limits of womanly reserve" (p. 45). In our opinion, that states the case with accuracy and relevance. In this day when many careless women seem to have no sense of shame (cf. Jer. 8:12—"They were not at all ashamed, neither could they blush"), it is refreshing to see a proper "womanly reserve." Here, as in all else in life, it is "the golden mean" which should be sought, something between shamefacedness and boldfacedness. Instead of "shamefacedness and sobriety," the NIV has: "with decency and propriety." That says it.

Broided or Braided? (2:9)

The KJV expression "broided hair" is obviously obsolete. Today we speak of "braided hair" (RSV). The phrase is one word in Greek, *plegmasin,* found only here in the NT (a similar term is found in 1 Pet. 3:3). Literally it means "what is woven or twisted." It is used of baskets and nets.

History goes in strange circles. Women who say that the Bible forbids them to cut their hair wear it long and often braided over their heads. Yet this is apparently condemned here! Long hair used to be considered the sign of a conservative Christian. Now it is the emblem of the hippies.

But what is the correct meaning of the passage? Combining "braided hair" with "gold," TCNT has, "Not with wreaths or gold ornaments for the hair." The NEB reads: "Not with elaborate hairstyles, not decked out with gold." Probably this is what the admonition means.

Costly or Expensive? (2:9)

The adjective "costly" is a strong compound, *polyteleis*. Thayer says it means "requiring great outlay, very costly." Perhaps "expensive" (Moffatt, NIV) conveys the idea best.

Array (2:9)

The Greek word is *himatismos,* not the common NT term for clothing—*himatia.* Trench says: *"Himatismos,* a word of comparatively late appearance . . . is seldom, if ever, used except of garments more or less stately and costly. It is the 'vesture' . . . of kings; thus of Solomon in all his glory . . . is associated with gold and silver, as part of a precious spoil" (p. 185).

The six occurrences of this word in the NT all bear this out. It is used for Christ's expensive seamless tunic, called "vesture," for which the soldiers cast lots (Matt. 27: 35; John 19:24). Luke 7:25 speaks of those who are "gorgeously apparelled" and live in luxury. The "raiment" of Jesus glistened on the Mount of Transfiguration (Luke 9:29). Paul testified that he had coveted "no man's silver, or gold, or apparel" (Acts 20:33). A good translation here is "expensive clothes" (NIV).

Subjection or Submission? (2:11)

The Greek word *hypotagē* occurs only four times in the NT (2 Cor. 9:13; Gal. 2:5; 1 Tim. 2:11; 3:4). It is regularly and correctly translated "subjection." But as applied to women it seems that "submission" (NIV) is less harsh and yet adequate.

Usurp Authority (2:12)

This is one word in Greek, the infinitive *authentein*. The verb occurs only here in the NT. It means "have authority, domineer . . . over someone" (AG). "Usurp" is an over-translation. "Have authority" (NIV) is more accurate.

Man or Husband? (2:12)

The Greek word *anēr* means both. So it is an open question as to whether the primary emphasis here is on the wife's submission to her husband or women's subordination to men—some say to ecclesiastical authorities. Perhaps Paul had both in mind.

In or Through? (2:15)

The KJV says that under certain conditions the woman will be saved "in" childbearing. But the Greek preposition is *dia*, which with the genitive case (as here) signifies "through."

But what does this mean? How can a woman be saved "through childbearing"? The simplest suggestion is that, in spite of Eve's sin, godly women will be preserved through childbirth; that is, as a usual thing. Some think the context may imply that a woman's spiritual salvation is helped by her giving herself to motherly duties in the home, rather than seeking to dominate the church. Since the Greek has the definite article, *tēs teknogonias* (the noun is found only here in NT), others have interpreted *"the* childbearing" as referring to "the childbearing of Mary, which has undone the work of Eve" (Lock, p. 33).

Bishop (3:1)

The first seven verses of chapter 3 are devoted to outlining the qualifications of a bishop. As a leader in the church he must be a man of exemplary character.

"The office of a bishop" is all one word in Greek, *episcopē.* Elsewhere in the NT it is used in this sense only in Acts 1:20, in a quotation from the Septuagint.

In verse 2 "bishop" is *episcopos,* from which comes "episcopal." It occurs only five times in the NT. In Acts 20:28 it is translated "overseers" and applied to the Ephesian elders by Paul. He also refers to the "bishops and deacons" at Philippi (Phil. 1:1). In Titus 1:7 and following, we again find what is required of a "bishop." Finally, in 1 Pet. 2:25, Christ is called "the Shepherd and Bishop of your souls."

The word *episcopos* is made up of *epi,* "upon" or "over," and *scopos,* "watcher." So it literally means "one who watches over." Thayer defines it thus: *"An overseer,* a man charged with the duty of seeing that things to be done by others are done rightly, *any curator, guardian,* or *superintendent. . . .* specifically, the *superintendent, head* or *overseer of any Christian church"* (p. 243).

It will be seen that the basic meaning of *episcopos* is "overseer." The ancient Greeks thought of their gods as *episcopoi.* This usage is found in Homer's *Iliad* and many later writings.

Then it came to be used of men in various functions.

Beyer says: "Protective care, however, is still the heart of the activity which men pursue as *episcopoi*" (TDNT, 2:610). Homer applies the term to ships' captains and merchants, who must be "overseers" of goods.

In the fourth and fifth centuries before Christ *episcopos* was used at Athens as a title for state officials. The same thing was true at Ephesus and in Egypt. But more common was the use of *episcopoi* (plural) for local officials and officers of societies. This brings us closer to the Christian *episcopos*.

In the Septuagint *episcopos* is used both for God, who oversees all things, and for men as supervisors in various fields of activity. The latter usage is found in the earlier, as well as the later, books of the OT.

Turning to the NT, we discover one fact immediately: there is no mention of any diocesan bishop. In the one church at Philippi there were *episcopoi*, "bishops" (Phil. 1:1). The apostles are never given this title. The bishop was a local official, and there were several of these in each congregation.

Furthermore, the "elders" *(presbyteroi)* and "bishops" *(episcopoi)* were the same. This is shown clearly in Acts 20. In verse 17 it says that Paul called for the "elders" *(presbyteroi)* of the church at Ephesus. In verse 28 he refers to them as *episcopoi*—"overseers" (KJV), "guardians" (RSV). The same people are designated by both titles. We shall find this same phenomenon clearly indicated in the Epistle to Titus. In the NT Church each local congregation was supervised by a group of elders or bishops and a group of deacons. It seems likely that the former had oversight of the spiritual concerns of the congregation and the latter of its material business.

When we come to Ignatius early in the second century (about A.D. 115), we find a very different picture. Now there is one bishop over each local church, together with several elders and several deacons. The bishop is supreme in authority. One of the keynotes of Ignatius' seven letters is, "Obey your bishop." To the Trallians he wrote: "For when you are in subjection to the bishop as to Jesus Christ it is clear to me that you are living not after men, but after Jesus Christ. . . . Therefore it is necessary (as is your practice) that you should do nothing without the bishop, but be also in subjection to the presbytery, as to the Apostles of Jesus Christ. . . . And they also who are deacons of the mysteries of Jesus Christ must be in every way pleasing to all men" (*The Apostolic Fathers,* "Loeb Classical Library," 1:213-15). Here we see the beginnings of the episcopal hierarchy that flowered during the second century. But "in the beginning it was not so."

Blameless or Irreproachable? (3:2)

There are six Greek adjectives that are rendered "blameless" in the KJV. At the same time, one of these adjectives, *amōmos,* occurs six times in the NT and is translated six different ways in the KJV. Two of these are incorrect; the other four are acceptable.

The term here is *anepilēmptos* (only here; 5:7; 6:14). It comes from *a* (negative) and the verb *epilambanō,* which means "take hold of." It literally means "not apprehended, that cannot be laid hold of," and so "that cannot be reprehended, not open to censure, irreproachable" (Thayer, p. 44). Trench prefers "irreprehensible" and says the word indicated "affording nothing which an adversary could take hold of, on which he might ground a charge" (pp. 381-82). Arndt and Gingrich give a single definition: "irreproachable." That is the most accurate translation here. No one—not even a bishop—can hope to live without being blamed. But a Christian's conduct must be above reproach. It is important to remember that "bishop" here may indicate any leader in a local church.

Vigilant or Temperate? (3:2)

The Greek term here is *nēphalios*. It occurs only three times in the NT, all of them in the Pastoral Epistles. It is used of bishops (here), of women (v. 11), and of elders (Titus 2:2).

The word was first used literally to describe drink which was "unmixed with wine." The ancient Greeks used to give to the Muses offerings of water, milk, and honey. It was forbidden to mix wine with these. The prohibitions went a step further: the wood burned with the sacrifices must not include the twigs of grapevines. There must not be the slightest contact with that which caused drunkenness.

Applied first to materials, it later referred to persons. The meaning then was "abstaining from wine." Some commentators take the adjective here in this literal sense. But it probably should be taken metaphorically. Bavernfeind writes: "The reference is to the clarity and self-control necessary for sacred ministry in God's work" (TDNT, 4:941). Bernard says: "Primarily having reference to sobriety in the case of wine, it has here the more extended sense of *temperate*" (p. 53).

Sober or Self-controlled? (3:2)

This is another pastoral word, *sōphrōn*. It is found here and three times in Titus (1:8; 2:2, 5). In the KJV it is translated three different ways in the three passages in Titus—"sober," "temperate," "discreet."

It is the adjective related to the noun *sōphrosynē* (2:

9, 15). Basically it means "of sound mind, sane, in one's senses," and then "curbing one's desires and impulses, self-controlled, temperate." The ASV renders it "sober-minded."

There are two objections to "sober." One is that this term is often used as the opposite of "drunk." Much more than that is meant here. The other is that it often suggests a solemn demeanor, such as we find in "Mr. Sobersides." This too often is a denial of that radiant countenance which is the hallmark of the true Christian. "Self-controlled" (NIV) is best here.

Of Good Behaviour or Orderly? (3:2)

This is the adjective *cosmios,* already noted in 2:9, where it is translated "modest." But the basic meaning is "orderly," and that fits well in this context. If a church official does not lead a well-ordered life, the work will suffer. Bernard says of *cosmios:* "This expresses the outward manifestation of the spirit of *sōphrosynē"* (p. 53). That is, inward self-control will be reflected in an outward life that is "orderly."

Given to Hospitality (3:2)

This is a single word in Greek, the adjective *philoxenos* (found also in Titus 1:8 and 1 Pet. 4:9). It is compounded of *philos,* "friend" or "lover," and *xenos,* "stranger." So it means "loving strangers, hospitable" (A-S), or "generous to guests" (Thayer). It's obviously best translated "hospitable," which is all that Arndt and Gingrich give for it.

Apt to Teach (3:2)

This is also one word in Greek, the adjective *didacti-*

cos (cf. *didactic*). It is found only here and in 2 Tim. 2:24. The meaning is "skillful in teaching." It may be rendered "able to teach" (NASB, NIV)—a necessary qualification of bishops.

Not Given to Wine (3:3)

In Greek this is *mē* (may), which means "not," and the adjective *paroinos*—from *para*, "beside," and *oinos*, "wine," which suggests "one who sits long at his wine." It also has the secondary meaning, "quarrelsome over wine" (Thayer). That is why the ASV has "no brawler." Ellicott translates it "violent over wine" and says that it includes "drunkenness and its manifestations" (p. 58). But since "striker" *(plēktēs)* follows immediately, Bernard feels that the more moderate meaning, "given to wine," fits better. These two Greek words are found in the NT only here and in Titus 1:7.

Patient or Gentle? (3:3)

In the best Greek text the words translated "not greedy of filthy lucre" are omitted. So we pass by that phrase and come to the next word, rendered "patient."

The term is *epieikēs*. Simpson bluntly asserts: *"Epieikēs defies exact translation."* He goes on to say: *"Gracious, kindly, forbearing, considerate, magnanimous, genial,* all approximate to its idea" (p. 51).

The earliest meaning (from Homer down) seems to be "seemly, suitable." Thayer thinks that in the NT it means "equitable, fair, mild, gentle." Arndt and Gingrich give "yielding, gentle, kind." Vincent prefers "forbearing" (4:230), as does Bernard (p. 54). In three out of the five occurrences of this word in the NT it is translated "gentle" in KJV. That is the best rendering here (cf. NIV).

Brawler or Contentious? (3:3)

The expression "not a brawler" is one word in Greek, *amachos,* found only here and in Titus 3:2. By Xenophon, the historian, it is used in the sense of "abstaining from fighting, noncombatant." Then it took on the metaphorical sense, "not contentious" (A-S). Perhaps the best translation here is "not quarrelsome."

Covetous or Lover of Money? (3:3)

"Not covetous" is *aphilargyron* (only here and Heb. 13:5). Literally it means "not loving silver (money)." Perhaps the best we can do in English is "not a lover of money" (NIV).

Rule or Manage? (3:4)

The Greek verb *proistēmi* literally means "put before" and so "set over." It can mean "rule" or "govern." But perhaps a more fitting translation here is "manage" (RSV, NASB, NIV) or "preside over." The same applies to "rule" in verse 5 (same word).

Gravity or Respect? (3:4)

This is the same word which is translated "honesty" in 2:2 (see discussion there). The best rendering is probably "respect" (NIV).

Novice or New Convert? (3:6)

The word is *neophytos* (only here in NT), taken over into English as "neophyte." Literally it means "newly planted" and is so used in the Septuagint. In Christian literature alone it is used figuratively in the sense of "new-ly converted." So the most accurate translation is "new convert" (NASB) or "recent convert" (NIV).

Lifted Up with Pride or Puffed Up? (3:6)

This is all one word in the Greek, *typhoō* (found only in the Pastoral Epistles). It comes from *typhos,* "smoke," and so literally means "wrap in smoke." The first meaning given in Liddell-Scott-Jones is "delude," leading to "filled with insane arrogance" (p. 1838). It is used only metaphorically, with the sense of "puffed up" or "conceited" (NIV). This was "the condemnation incurred by the devil" (NASB).

Grave or Dignified? (3:8)

The Greek adjective is *semnos,* from which comes the noun *semnotēs* (2:2; 3:4; Titus 2:7). The adjective is also found three times in the Pastorals (1 Tim. 3:8, 11; Titus 2:2), and only once elsewhere in the NT (Phil. 4:8; see comments there).

Trench says that "the *semnos* has a grace and dignity not lent him from earth; but which he owes to that higher citizenship which is also his" (p. 346). He adds that there is something "majestic and awe-inspiring in *semnos*" (p. 347).

Probably the best discussion of this term is in William Barclay's *More New Testament Words* (Harper, 1958), an exceedingly valuable little book. He says that *semnos* has in it "the majesty of divinity" (p. 141). It is used to express royalty and kingliness, as well as what is stately and dignified in language. The term is found frequently inscribed on tombs as a term of great respect. Barclay devotes nearly two pages to Aristotle's use of this term.

He also mentions an ambassador who described the Roman senate as "an assembly of kings." That, declares Barclay, is what the Christian Church should be. And each believer should manifest in his life "the majesty of Christian living."

It should be noted that this adjective is applied not only to the deacons in our present passage, but also to their wives in verse 11 and to elderly men in Titus 2:2. It carries with it the suggestion of the dignity and seriousness which should characterize leaders and older Christians.

Doubletongued or Double Talkers? (3:8)

The term *dilogos* (only here in NT) literally means "saying the same thing twice." And so it has the sense *"doubletongued, double in speech, saying one thing with one person, another with another* (with intent to deceive)" (Thayer, p. 152). Arndt and Gingrich suggest the translation "insincere," which is probably too general. The idea is conveyed well by "indulging in double talk" (NEB).

Greedy of Filthy Lucre (3:8)

This is all one word in Greek, *aischrokerdēs*, occurring only here and in Titus 1:7—in relation to a bishop there, to a deacon here. It means "eager for base gain" (Thayer) or "fond of dishonest gain" (AG).

Proved or Tested? (3:10)

The verb *dokimazō* is used for three stages. Basically it means "test." But it also can mean "prove" by testing and even "approve" as the result of being tested. Perhaps all three ideas are included here.

The Office of a Deacon (3:10)

Again it is one word, the verb *diaconeō*. It is from *diaconos*, a "servant," especially one who waits on table. So *diaconeō* means "serve." But in the Christian Church *diaconos* finally took on the technical connotation "deacon." So here and in verse 13 (nowhere else in NT) the verb means "serve as deacons" (NIV).

Slanderers or Gossips? (3:11)

The Greek is *diabolous* (v. 11), plural of *diabolos*, "devil." In fact, the word is translated "devil" 35 out of the 38 times it occurs in the NT. It is rendered "false accuser" in 2 Tim. 3:3 and Titus 2:3—both times of human beings who engage in slander. Perhaps the modern equivalent would be "gossips" (Goodspeed; cf. "malicious gossips," NASB). This suggests the idea that those who indulge in gossip or slander are doing the devil's business!

Degree or Standing? (3:13)

Today we think of obtaining a "degree" in academic circles. But the Greek word *bathmos* (only here in NT) means something a little different. Originally meaning "step," it is here used for "a grade of dignity and wholesome influence in the church" (Thayer, p. 129). Arndt and Gingrich say that the entire phrase here means "win a good standing (or rank) for oneself" (p. 92).

House or Household? (3:15)

The Greek word is *oikos*, the common term for "house." But since "the house of God" might be taken as referring to the church building, it is better to use "household" (NIV). *Oikos* here means the family, not the home.

Ground or Bulwark? (3:15)

The word *hedraiōma* (only here in NT) is an ecclesiastical term. It means "a support," "bulwark." Either of these is a good translation. The church is to protect and defend the truth.

Expressly or Explicitly? (4:1)

The noun *rhēma* means something said or spoken. So the adverb here, *rhētōs,* is well translated "expressly." But "explicitly" is a more contemporary term.

Latter Times or Last Times? (4:1)

The Greek literally says "later seasons." But Arndt and Gingrich suggest for this passage "in the last times." It would thus be equivalent to "the last days" (2 Tim. 3:1).

Seared with a Hot Iron (4:2)

This is all one word in the Greek, the perfect passive participle *kekaustēriasmenōn.* The verb *kaustēriazō* (only here in NT) means "to mark by branding, brand" (A-S), or "to burn in with a branding iron" (Thayer). Schneider develops this point further. He sees a reference to the custom of branding slaves and criminals. "Among the Greeks branding was mainly a punishment for runaway slaves. . . . The mark was usually put on the forehead with an iron" (TDNT, 3:644-45). So these false teachers bear the mark of slaves.

Bernard translates the whole phrase "branded in their own conscience." It is more than "seared," that is, made insensitive. He comments: "But the metaphor more probably has reference to the *penal branding* of criminals . . .

these hypocrites, with their outward show of holiness and of extreme asceticism . . . have the brand of sin on their own consciences" (p. 65). Similarly Schneider writes: "The meaning is that they are in bondage to secret sin" (p. 644).

Sanctified or Consecrated? (4:5)

When applied to things, not persons, the verb *hagiazō* usually means "to set apart for sacred use, consecrate." But that idea hardly seems to fit here. Lock comments: "It becomes holy to the eater; not that it was unclean by itself, but that his scruples or thanklessness might make it so" (p. 48). Probably the best translation here is "sanctified."

The Word of God and Prayer (4:5)

The custom of saying grace before meals was practiced by the Jews and taken over by the early Christians. Often phrases of Scripture were used in this prayer of thanksgiving for the food, as is indicated in the *Apostolic Constitutions* (7:49). "The word of God and prayer" could suggest the reading of a brief biblical passage, followed by a prayer of thanks. This custom is observed at the breakfast table in many Christian homes today. White ties the two expressions together. He thinks it means "a scriptural prayer; a prayer in harmony with God's revealed truth" (EGT, 4:122). All of these suggestions may be employed in "asking the blessing" before meals.

Put in Remembrance or Point Out? (4:6)

In the active, the verb *hypotithēmi* means "place under" or "lay down." This is the way it is used in the only other place where it occurs in the NT (Rom. 16:4). But here it is in the middle voice and means "to suggest" (A-S) or "point out" (AG). It refers to teaching the truth.

Attained or Followed? (4:6)

The verb is *parakoloutheō*, from *akoloutheō*, which means "follow," and *para*, "beside." So it means "follow closely." Here and in 2 Tim. 3:10 it suggests "follow faithfully" a rule or standard (Thayer). Timothy had faithfully followed the good teaching ("doctrine," KJV) of Paul. Now he was to pass this on to those to whom he ministered.

Paul belonged to the first generation of Christians, Timothy to the second. The continuance of Christianity depended on the faithfulness of the new generations of believers. This puts a heavy responsibility on us today, if the faith is to survive.

Profane or Worldly? (4:7)

The adjective *bebēlos* occurs five times in the NT. Twice it is applied to persons (1 Tim. 1:9; Heb. 12:16). Three times it describes things (1 Tim. 4:7; 6:20; 2 Tim. 2:16). In every case it is translated "profane" in KJV. Arndt and Gingrich suggest "worldly" for our passage here, but "profane" for the other two applications to things. With regard to persons, they prefer "godless" for 1 Tim. 1:9 and "irreligious" for Heb. 12:16 (as a description of Esau).

J. C. Lambert points out the origin of the word. He writes:

> *Bebēlos* is the almost exact equivalent of Latin *profanus*, whence English "profane." *Profanus* (from *pro*—"before," and *fanum*—"temple") means "without the temple," and so "unconsecrated," as opposed

to *sacer. Bebēlos* (from *baino*—"to go," whence *bēlos*
—"threshold") denotes that which is "trodden," "open
to access," and so again "unconsecrated" in contrast to
hieros (sacred) *(HDCG, 2:422).*

Arndt and Gingrich point out the fact that while
bebēlos is used in the OT in a ritualistic sense, it occurs in
the NT always as an ethical and religious term. That is
"profane" which is secular, not sacred, which leaves God
out of account.

Hauck says this about *bebēlos* in our passage: "As
applied to material things in the Pastorals, the word refers
to Gnostic teachings which are scornfully described as profane and unholy *mythoi* (1 Tim. 4:7)" (TDNT, 1:604). It
would seem that "worldly" (Goodspeed, NASB) fits well
here.

Exercise or Training? (4:8)

The noun (only here in NT) is *gymnasia,* from which
obviously comes *gymnasium.* The verb is *gymnazō* (v. 7,
"exercise"), which comes from *gymnos,* "naked." This
calls attention to the fact that Greek athletes customarily
wore no clothes when exercising. Since the idea of athletic
training is inherent here, it would seem that "training"
(NIV) is a more adequate translation than "exercise."

This gives a bit of added thrust to the verb "exercise"
in verse 7. We are to "train" (AG) ourselves daily in spiritual things, if we wish to maintain good health spiritually.

Suffer Reproach or Strive? (4:10)

This is a matter of textual criticism. The bulk of the
medieval manuscripts have *oneidizometha.* But the original reading seems to have been *agōnizometha.* The verb
agōnizō literally means "compete in an athletic contest"

(cf. Col. 1:29). The best translation of this passage is either "toil and struggle" (Goodspeed) or "labor and strive" (NASB, NIV).

Trust or Hope? (4:10)

These two words do not mean exactly the same thing. The Greek clearly has "hope"; literally, "have set our hope."

Conversation or Conduct? (4:12)

We have already met the Greek word *anastrophē* and noted that it refers to the whole "manner of life." "In word, in conversation" is obviously redundant. The Greek has two distinct items: "in word, in conduct."

Doctrine or Teaching? (4:13)

The Greek word *didaskalia* has no theological overtones, such as attach to our word "doctrine." What this verse says is that Timothy is to perform three essential functions as pastor: (1) the public reading of the Scriptures; (2) exhorting the people to walk in the light of God's Word; (3) teaching them what the Word means.

The Presbytery (4:14)

This comes directly from the Greek word *presbyterion*. Elsewhere in the NT the term occurs only in Luke 22:66 and Acts 22:5. In both those places it refers to the Jewish Sanhedrin. Here it means the group of elders who laid their hands on Timothy, evidently at the time of his ordination into the Christian ministry.

Meditate or Be Diligent? (4:15)

The verb is *meletaō*. It comes from *meletē*, "care," and so means "to care for," "to attend to" (A-S). It is from the stem of the verb *melō*, "to care for." In verse 14 "neglect" is the verb *amelō, melō* with the *a*-negative. There is thus a play on words in the Greek which is lost in English. In verse 14, Paul says to Timothy, "Don't be careless about the gift you received at your ordination"—perhaps the "gift" (Greek, *charisma*) of prophecy, or prophetic preaching. In verse 15 he says, "Be constantly careful about these things."

In Greek the second clause, "Give thyself wholly to them," literally reads, "Be in these things."

Profiting or Progress? (4:15)

The word *prokopē* means "a cutting forward," "an advance." Its clear and simple meaning is "progress." Aside from this passage it occurs only in Phil. 1:12, 25, where it is rendered "furtherance." It should be "progress" in all three places (cf. NIV).

The NASB has properly caught the meaning of this verse. It reads: "Take pains with these things; be *absorbed* in them, so that your progress may be evident to all."

Rebuke (5:1)

The verb *epiplēssō* is a strong compound (cf. NASB, "sharply rebuke"), occurring only here in the NT. Literally it means "strike at" or "beat upon." Paul warns young Timothy not to strike at an older man in the church. (The reference to "elder women" in verse 2 suggests that "elder" here is not used in an official sense.)

Incidentally, we must not think of this "youth" (cf.

4:12) as a teenager or even a young man in his twenties. Probably he was around 20 years old when Paul, at Lystra on his second missionary journey, took on Timothy as an associate. That was at least 15 years before this Epistle was written. By now Timothy would have been in his upper thirties. But in the Roman Empire one was referred to as a "young man" until he was 45.

Nephews or Grandchildren? (5:4)

The word *ekgona* is found only here in the NT. All lexicons are agreed that the proper translation is "grandchildren," which also fits the context better.

Requite or Repay? (5:4)

The one word in English represents two in Greek. The first is a verb which literally means "return," "render what is due," or simply "pay." The second is the noun *amoibē* (only here in NT), which means a "return" or "recompense." Arndt and Gingrich translate the passage: "Make a return to those who brought them up" (p. 46). The idea is that children and grandchildren should repay the care that was given them when they were growing up.

Desolate or Left Alone? (5:5)

The Greek has *memonōmenē*, the perfect passive participle of *monoō* (only here in NT). This comes from the adjective *monos*, "alone," and so means "leave alone." The best rendering here is "left alone" or "all alone" (NIV).

Pleasure or Indulgence? (5:6)

Lock suggests that the word *spatalōsa* is "probably

akin to *spaō,* to suck down, hence to live luxuriously, self-indulgently" (p. 58). Moffatt writes: "The modern term *fast,* in which the notion of prodigality and wastefulness is more prominent than that of sensual indulgence, exactly expresses the significance of this word" (EGT, 4:129). But in his translation of the New Testament he has: "The widow who plunges into dissipation."

Infidel or Unbeliever? (5:8)

The Greek has the adjective *apistos,* which simply means "unbelieving." It is used frequently in the Corinthian letters for "unbelievers," as opposed to Christians. What Paul is saying here is that a professing Christian who does not take care of his family is worse than a non-Christian.

Taken into the Number or Enrolled? (5:9)

"Let . . . be taken into the number" is all one word in Greek, *katalegesthō.* This verb (only here in NT) is used by ancient writers for enrolling soldiers. The correct translation here is "enrolled."

There has been a great deal of discussion as to whether there was an official "order" of widows in the NT Church. Vincent writes: "The Fathers, from the end of the second century to the fourth, recognized a class known as *presbytidēs, aged women* (Titus ii. 3), who had oversight of the female church-members and a separate seat in the congregation. The council of Laodicea abolished this institution, or so modified it that widows no longer held an official relation to the church" (4:257).

Somewhat different is the opinion of Moffatt. He says: "In the references to widows in the earliest Christian literature outside the N.T. (with the exception of Ignatius

Smyrn. 13) they are mentioned as objects of charity along with orphans, etc. . . . None of these places hints at an order of widows" (EGT, 4:130).

At any rate, we know that widows, especially elderly ones, were cared for by the church (Acts 6:1). But they must be widows in real need.

Afflicted or Distressed? (5:10)

"She have brought up children" and "she have lodged strangers" are each one word in Greek—two compound verbs found only here in the NT. The second is more accurately rendered "shown hospitality to strangers."

"Afflicted" is a participle of the verb *thlibō,* which means "to press." It includes all those who are suffering from the various pressures of life. Today "afflicted" generally suggests one who is ill. The term here has a wider application. Probably "distressed" or "oppressed" gives the idea better.

Wax Wanton (5:11)

The verb is *katastrēniaō* (only here in NT). It literally means "to feel the impulses of sexual desire" (Thayer, p. 337). Arndt and Gingrich translate the clause, "when they feel sensuous impulses that alienate them from Christ" (p. 420). Lock suggests that the meaning here is "to grow physically restless and so restive against the limitations of Christian widowhood" (p. 60). Bernard says, "The metaphor is that of a young animal trying to free itself from the yoke" (p. 82). Schneider says the meaning is that "they become lascivious against Christ" or that "they burn with sensual desire in opposition to Christ" (TDNT, 3:631).

Hendriksen (pp. 175-76) thinks that evil desire is not

necessarily indicated here. It is natural for young widows to wish to remarry. For that very reason they should not be put on the official list of widows, lest they be more concerned with finding a husband than serving the Lord in the church. Hendriksen suggests "grow restless with desire." Unfortunately we have no secular example of this verb—this is the only passage cited in the two-volume *Lexicon* of Liddell-Scott-Jones—so that the meaning is not completely clear. Goodspeed has, "When their youthful vigor comes between them and Christ," which is a minimum rendering. The NEB puts it more strongly: "For when their passions draw them away from Christ" (cf. NIV).

Damnation or Condemnation? (5:12)

The term "damnation" occurs about a dozen times in the KJV (all in NT). This is considered by most to be an over-translation. The word here literally means "judgment." The strongest rendering it can properly be given is "condemnation."

Faith or Pledge? (5:12)

The Greek word is *pistis,* which in the KJV is translated "faith" 239 of the 244 times it occurs in the NT. But the original classical connotation was "faithfulness, reliability" (AG). Then it means "solemn promise, oath." Thirdly, it signified "proof, pledge." Finally it came to have the religious signification of "trust, confidence," or "faith" in the active sense of believing.

The context indicates that here it clearly means "pledge"; that is, the pledge they made to give full loyalty to Christ (cf. NIV: "they have broken their first pledge").

Tattlers or Gossips? (5:13)

The term *phluaros* is found only here in the NT. It comes from the verb *phluō*, which means "to boil up" or "throw up bubbles" of water, and so "to indulge in empty and foolish talk" (Thayer). Actually the word here is an adjective, meaning "gossipy" (AG). The best translation here is "gossips" (NIV) which is used more today than "tattlers."

Guide or Rule? (5:14)

Paul advises younger women to marry, bear children, and "guide the house." This is one word in Greek, compounded of *oikos*, "house" or "household," and *despotēs*, "master" or "lord" (cf. our "despot"). So the verb (only here in NT) literally means "to rule a household" (A-S) and is translated that way in the ASV. But since the NT suggests that the husband should be the head of the house, "manage their homes" (NIV) is the basic idea. The NEB expresses it well: "preside over a home." That is what the wife and mother should do.

Charged or Burdened? (5:16)

The Greek verb is *bareō*. It comes from *baros*, which means a "weight" or "burden." So the verb means "weigh down" or "burden." In the passive, as here, it signifies "be burdened." The church was not to be burdened with the care of widows who had relatives that could provide for them. Only those who were widows without support should be on the rolls.

Donald MacKenzie says:

> The Apostle makes it clear that no widows were to be relieved who had children or grandchildren able to support them. This was not simply to save the scanty

finances of the Church, but much more in order to enforce a binding moral principle. There is every reason to believe that there were families who tried to evade what was a cardinal obligation of piety by attempting to get their widowed mothers or grandmothers to be supported by the Church. Possibly some widows were themselves eager to do so, so as to gain thus greater personal liberty. Against this St. Paul is emphatic in declaring that descendants ought to support their widowed relatives. He repeats this duty thrice. . . . Church support is not a substitute for filial indifference or neglect *(HDAC, 3:676)*.

The Early Church gave much attention to the care of widows. Polycarp speaks of widows as an "altar of sacrifice," on which Christians should lavish their offerings. Hermas urges believers to buy "oppressed souls" instead of more fields. Ignatius criticizes the heretics for failing to care for their widows and orphans. Aristides in his *Apology* says that Christians "do not turn away their countenance" from widows.

It was the Church of Jesus Christ which set the pattern for the care of the needy, providing orphanages, hospitals, and schools. Today the state has taken over many of these functions. But as Christians still need to feel a personal compassion for those who are in need. It is a part of our Christian duty.

Honour or Honorarium? (5:17)

The Greek word is *timē* (tee-*may*). Originally it signified *"a valuing by which the price is fixed;* hence *the price* itself: of the price paid or received for a person or thing bought or sold"* (Thayer, p. 624). It is used that way several times in the NT and is translated "price" (Matt. 27:6, 9; Acts 4:34; 5:2-3; 19:19; 1 Cor. 6:20; 7:23). On the other hand, it is translated "honour" (KJV) 33 times. Moulton and Milligan cite clear examples of both meanings in the papyri. The word was used for the "price" of oil, wheat, hay, and medicine. As one of the meanings of *timē*, Arndt and Gingrich give "honorarium, compensation" and suggest that this is "perhaps" the sense here. Under *diplous* ("double") they cite the case of an emperor giving double wages to a prophet for his services.

Most of the versions have "honor" in this passage. However, the NEB reads, "Elders who do well as leaders should be reckoned worthy of a double stipend." And the *Jerusalem Bible* has "double consideration," with the marginal suggestion "doubly paid." Pastors will appreciate the way Charles B. Williams renders it: "should be considered as deserving twice the salary they get." N. J. D. White says: *"Remuneration* is a better rendering of *timē* than pay, as less directly expressive of merely monetary reward." Liddon suggests the rendering *"honorarium"* (EGT, 4:134). That this is the meaning of *timē* here is clearly indicated by the fact that Paul has just been talking about the church's support of needy widows and that he goes on (v. 18) to say, "The worker deserves his wages" (NIV).

Doctrine or Teaching? (5:17)

The word *didaskalia* occurs 21 times in the NT. In the KJV it is rendered "doctrine" 19 times and "teaching" only once. This order should be reversed. Paul is not talking about doctrine in the sense of theology. "The word and doctrine" simply means "preaching and teaching" (NIV).

Before or On the Basis of? (5:19)

The Greek word translated "before" is *epi*, which means "upon." By extension it means "on the basis of," and that is the correct idea here (cf. NASB).

Rebuke or Reprove? (5:20)

The word *elenchō* first meant *"to convict . . .* generally with a suggestion of the shame of the person convicted" and here means *"to reprehend severely, chide, admonish, reprove"* (Thayer, p. 203). For this passage Arndt and Gingrich suggest "reprove, correct." The NEB has "expose publicly." It appears that either "rebuke" or "reprove" fits well here.

Prejudice and Partiality (5:21)

We find two Greek words that occur only here in the NT. The first, *prokrima,* is rendered in the KJV "preferring one before another." The word literally means "prejudging," and so "prejudice." That is perhaps the best translation here. Arndt and Gingrich suggest "discrimination," which sounds contemporary.

The second word is *prosklisis,* which means "inclination, partiality" (A-S). Cremer writes: *"Prokrima* includes an unfavourable *prejudgment* against one; *prosklesis,* nothing but positive *favour, partiality"* (p. 378).

Suddenly or Hastily? (5:22)

The word is *tacheōs,* which means "quickly, hastily." Abbott-Smith goes on to say that here, in Gal. 1:6, and in 2 Thess. 2:2 it carries the "suggestion of rashness." Arndt and Gingrich give for these same passages: "too quickly, too easily, hastily." The thought of the command is expressed well in the NEB: "Do not be over-hasty in laying on hands in ordination."

Water and Wine (5:23)

This verse has posed a problem for many Christians,

particularly in the United States. Why would the Apostle Paul tell his young associate Timothy no longer to drink water, but to use a little wine because of his stomach (Greek, *stomachon*) and his frequent "infirmities" (lit., "weaknesses," or "illnesses")?

Some have tried to dissolve the difficulty by saying that there are two Greek words for *wine. Gleukos* (cf. *glucose*) means "sweet new wine," that is, unfermented grape juice. *Oinos* simply means "wine." True. But the problem is that *oinos* is the word used here and in the story of Jesus turning the water into wine (John 2:9). So this suggestion is of no help at all.

The important thing to note is that *oinos* is used in the Septuagint for both fermented and unfermented grape juice. Since it can mean either one, it is valid to insist that in some cases it may simply mean grape juice and not fermented wine.

It has often been objected that in those days of no refrigeration it would have been impossible to keep grape juice from fermenting. But the Roman writer Cato, in his treatise *On Agriculture,* gave this prescription: "If you wish to keep new wine sweet the whole year round, put new wine in a jar, cover the stopper with pitch, place the jar in a fishpond, take it out after the thirtieth day; you will have sweet wine all the year round."

Probably the question cannot be settled on the basis of Greek words, but rather on moral and scientific principles. Does fermented wine have medicinal value? The present writer once put this question to a noted surgeon, the head of a department in a university medical school. His answer was an emphatic no.

One thing, of course, must be insisted on: Paul was not advocating the general use of wine as a beverage. The most that can be said is that he was suggesting that Timothy, because of frequent stomach illness, should take "a little wine" as medicine. And the possibility is still open that the apostle referred to unfermented grape juice, which of course is good for a weak stomach.

Open (Manifest) Beforehand (5:24-25)

The expression "open beforehand" (v. 24) and "manifest beforehand" (v. 25) are both translations of the same Greek adjective, *prodēlos* (only here and Heb. 7:14). It means "evident beforehand" or "clearly evident" (A-S). Thayer defines the term as "openly evident, known to all, manifest." White comments: "Not *open beforehand* (AV), but *evident* (RV). . . . The *pro* is not indicative of antecedence in time, but of publicity" (EGT, 4:139). "Going before" (v. 24) is literally "leading the way." Men's evident sins lead them to the judgment.

Masters (6:1)

Elsewhere in his Epistles, Paul uses the word *kyrios* for masters of slaves. But in the first two verses of this chapter and in Titus 2:9 we find the term *despotēs*. The only other place in the NT where this usage occurs is in 1 Pet. 2:18. The other six times that the word is found in the NT it applies to God as the sovereign Lord of all. Thayer says the term "denoted absolute ownership and uncontrolled power." Similarly Trench says that "the *despotēs* exercises a more unrestricted power and absolute domination" (p. 96). That is why the ancient Greeks applied this word only to their gods. It was when the slave-masters became more autocratic that the term was used for them. Originally the word carried none of the opprobium attached to the modern English derivative *despot*.

Luke is the only one of the Evangelists to use *despotēs*, once in his Gospel (2:29) and once in Acts (4:24). It has been suggested that Luke may have actually composed the Pastoral Epistles for Paul, under his direction, when the apostle was elderly and needed the care of his physician and secretary.

From this passage, and many others, it is clear that the NT did not directly attack the institution of slavery. It is claimed that half the population of the Roman Empire in Paul's day consisted of slaves. To have launched a frontal assault on slavery would probably have resulted in the extinction of Christianity. What the NT does do is to lay down the principles of love and justice which finally brought about the abolition of this accursed custom of long standing.

Wholesome or Sound? (6:3)

The heterodox teacher does not consent to the use of "wholesome" words. The adjective is actually a participial form of the verb *hygiainō,* from which comes *hygienic.* Elsewhere in the Pastoral Epistles it is regularly translated "sound" (cf. 1:10).

Aside from the Gospel of Luke (three times) and the Pastorals (eight times), the word is found only in 3 John 2, where it conforms to the customary greeting of those days. This fact also suggests that Luke may have had a considerable part in the composition of the Pastoral Epistles. We know that he was the amanuensis for 2 Timothy, for Paul says, "Only Luke is with me" (4:11).

Doting or Morbid? (6:4)

"Doting" is the present participle of *noseō* (only here in NT). Literally the verb means "to be sick." In classical Greek it was used metaphorically for mental illness. Thayer says that here it means "to be taken with such an interest in a thing as amounts to a disease, to have a morbid fondness for" (p. 429). Arndt and Gingrich suggest the translation "have a morbid craving for" (cf. Goodspeed). White says of the person described here: "His disease is intellectual curiosity about trifles" (EGT, 4:141).

Word Battles (6:4)

This is the literal meaning of the compound *logomachias* (only here in NT). It is rendered in the KJV "strifes of words." A good translation for this section of the verse is: "He has a morbid interest in controversial questions and disputes about words" (NASB). This is a form of illness that is not only psychological and social; it is also a spiritual sickness. Too many church members are afflicted with it.

Surmisings or Suspicions? (6:4)

The term *hyponoiai* (only here in NT) is best translated "suspicions" (NIV). Moulton and Milligan give several examples of this meaning in the papyri. White defines the phrase here: *"Malicious suspicions* as to the honesty of those who differ from them" (EGT, 4:142). This is a serious judgment for people to make, but it is often done.

Perverse Disputings (6:5)

The double compound *diaparatribai* (only here in NT) has basically the idea of friction or irritation. Thayer says it means "constant contention, incessant wrangling or strife." Bernard comments that "the first of two prepositions in a composite word governs the meaning, and thus *dia* is emphatic, signifying the persistency and obstinacy of the disputes" (p. 94). White agrees. He says that it "denotes *protracted* quarrelings."

Destitute or Deprived? (6:5)

The form here is the perfect passive participle of *apo-stereō*. Abbott-Smith gives this definition for the verb: *"To defraud, deprive of, despoil* (in classics chiefly of the misappropriation of trust funds)" (p. 54). For this passage he suggests "bereft of" (cf. RSV). White comments: *"Apo-stereō* conveys the notion of a person being deprived of a thing to which he has a right. . . . This is expressed in R.V., *bereft of.* The truth was once theirs; they have disinherited themselves. The A.V., *destitute of,* does not assume that they ever had it" (EGT, 4:142). The best translation is "deprived of" (NASB).

Gain Is Godliness (6:5)

This is obviously an incorrect rendering. The word for "godliness" is clearly the subject, for it has the article, while "gain" does not. The correct translation is: "supposing godliness to be a means of gain." The word for "means of gain," *porismos* ("a gainful trade"), is found in the NT only in this passage (vv. 5-6).

Contentment (6:6)

The first meaning of *autarkeia* is "sufficiency" or "competence." Then it came to mean "contentment" or "self-sufficiency" (AG). This was a favorite virtue of the Stoics. Bernard comments: "That riches are not essential to true well-being was a commonplace of pre-Christian philosophy, which laid great emphasis on *autarkeia* or the 'self-sufficiency' of the wise man. . . . St. Paul's words go deeper, inasmuch as they lay stress on *eusebeia* (godliness) as a chief condition of happiness, and recognize the proper place of *autarkeia,* as *contentment,* not *self-sufficiency"*

(p. 95). The word occurs elsewhere in the NT only in 2 Cor. 9:8, where it carries the original meaning, "sufficiency."

White feels that "contentment" is not strong enough here. He writes: "*Autarkeia* is more profound, and denotes independence of, and indifference to, any lot; as man's finding not only his resources in himself, but being indifferent to everything else besides. This was St. Paul's condition when he had learnt to be *autarkes,* Phil. iv. 11" (EGT, 4:142).

Food and Raiment (6:8)

Both of these terms in Greek are found only here in the NT. The first, *diatrophas,* signifies "means of subsistence," and so may have a broader connotation than simply food, though the primary reference is to that which nourishes or sustains. In a payrus contract of apprenticeship from Oxyrhynchus, Egypt, and dated A.D. 66—perhaps the very year that 1 Timothy was written—this word occurs in the sense of board and room. Five drachmas was to be paid for the boy's "keep" (VGT, p. 156).

The second term is *skepasma.* Literally it means a "covering." Though used mainly for clothing, it sometimes referred to a house (as in Aristotle's *Metaphysics*). In the broadest sense it means "protection." So these two terms taken together would cover the necessities of life, which we refer to today as "food, clothing, and shelter."

Hurtful or Harmful? (6:9)

This is another word found only here in the NT. *Blaberos* comes from the verb *blaptō,* which means hurt, harm, injure, or damage. Probably "harmful" (NIV) is a more contemporary translation than "hurtful."

All Evil or All Kinds of Evil? (6:10)

The Greek says "all evils." Most modern versions have either "all kinds of evil" (ASV, NIV) or "all sorts of evil" (NASB). As Patrick Fairbairn says, "There is no kind of evil to which the love of money may not lead men, when it once fairly takes hold of them" (*Pastoral Epistles,* p. 239).

Sorrows or Pangs? (6:10)

The word *odynē* occurs scores of times in the Septuagint, translating no less than 26 different Hebrew words. But in the NT it is found only twice. In Rom. 9:2, Paul uses it to express his mental distress over the unbelief of his fellow Jews. Here it is used for the remorse of conscience. Moffatt has "many a pang of remorse."

The verb *peripeirō,* "pierced . . . through," occurs only here in the NT. "Erred from the faith" is literally "have been led astray from the faith." That is, they have forsaken the straight path of truth. Bernard comments: "Struggling out of this they get entrapped among the briars and thorns of the world, and pierce themselves" (p. 97). This is what always happens to those who go astray.

Meekness or Gentleness? (6:11)

The word *praupothia* is found only here in the NT. The cognate adjective means "gentle," and "gentleness" (NIV) is the best translation for this noun. Michaelis writes: "The meaning is not so much 'meekness' in the sense of 'tractability' but 'composure' . . . which can take wrongs calmly" (TDNT, 5:939).

Fight or Contest? (6:12)

The verb is *agōnizomai.* The noun is *agōn.* They come

from the verb *agō,* which means "lead." So the basic idea of *agōn* was a gathering. But since the largest gatherings of the first century, as usually also of the twentieth century, were for athletic contests, the term came to be used for such events. The verb signified "to compete in an athletic contest." So Goodspeed translates this passage, "Enter the great contest of faith!" Since the leading event in the ancient contests was the long-distance race (e.g., the Marathon race), *The New English Bible* has, "Run the great race of faith." White thinks that "the metaphor has its full force here . . . *Engage in the contest which profession of the faith entails"* (EGT, 4:145).

Bernard agrees with this. He writes: "The metaphor of life as a gymnastic contest was one which naturally suggested itself to those who had witnessed the Olympian or Isthmian games which played, even as late as the Apostolic age, so important a part in Greek national life. Philo uses the illustration again and again" (pp. 97-98). It is reflected in Heb. 12:1. It was a favorite figure with Paul (cf. 1 Cor. 9:24; Phil. 3:12, 14; 2 Tim. 4:7).

Though the original meaning of the noun and verb was that of "contest" in an athletic sense, the words came to be used generally in the sense of "struggle" or "fight." But it should be remembered that the primary reference is athletic rather than military.

Profession or Confession? (6:12-13)

"Profession" (v. 12) and "confession" (v. 13) are exactly the same in Greek. Consistency would seem to suggest that we use the same translation in both cases, but which is better?

The word is *homologia.* In the KJV it is translated "profession" everywhere else in the NT (Heb. 3:1; 4:14; 10:23; cf. 2 Cor. 9:13). The cognate verb *homologeō* ("professed," v. 12) occurs 23 times in the NT. In the KJV it is rendered "confess" 17 times, "profess" 3 times, and once each "promise" (Matt. 14:7), "give thanks" (Heb. 13:15), and "confession is made" (Rom. 10:10).

The literal meaning of the verb is "say the same thing" *(legō-homos)*, and so means not to deny but "to declare." In Matt. 14:7 it suggests "not to refuse," and so "to promise."

Thayer points out the basic difference between "confess" and "profess" by calling attention to their roots in Latin. *Profiteor* means "to declare openly and voluntarily," *confiteor* "to declare fully"—"implying the yielding or change of one's conviction" (p. 446). So one professes his faith but confesses his sin. Arndt and Gingrich think that the meaning here is "bear testimony to a conviction." They would translate the combination of verb and noun in verse 12, "make the good profession of faith." They go on to say, "Jesus, the first Christian martyr . . . bore witness to the same *good profession of faith* vs. 13" (p. 571).

Michel notes that the Greek sense of the verb is "to state solemnly," "to affirm," "to attest." He says that it signifies "a solemn declaration of faith in the Christian sense of proclamation" (TDNT, 5:207).

Michel also has some helpful observations about the noun. He writes: *"Homologia* implies consent to some thing felt to be valid, and in such a way that it is followed by definite resolve and action, by ready attachment to a cause. The aim in *homologia* is not a theoretical agreement which does not commit us, but acceptance of a common cause" (p. 200). With regard to our passage he comments: "Just because Timothy has made this binding confession he is committed to passing on the proclamation, keeping the commandment and walking without blame until Christ is manifested" (p. 211). He also holds that the reference here is to Timothy's ordination, when the young preacher made a good confession before the congregation (p. 216). Others think it refers to the time of his baptism.

Which shall it be, "confession" or "profession"? The choice is difficult. Weymouth and Moffatt have "confession," but Goodspeed has "profession." However, most of the recent versions agree on "confession" (ASV, RSV, NASB, NEB, NIV). The majority of the best commentators support this.

Potentate or Sovereign? (6:15)

The Greek word is *dynastēs,* from which we get *dynasty.* Literally it means "the one who can do something" (from *dynamai,* "I am able"). Grundmann writes: "It was used from an early period for 'ruler,' 'the one who is powerful,' 'the one who exercises authority and rule'" (TDNT, 2:286).

The word occurs only three times in the NT, with three different connotations. In Luke 1:52 it is used for "rulers." In Acts 8:27 it describes a court official. But here it clearly refers to God, who is the "Sovereign" of the universe.

Immortality (6:16)

Two Greek words are translated "immortality" in the NT. In this passage it is *athanasia,* which literally means "deathlessness." It occurs only here and in 1 Cor. 15:53-54.

The other word is *aphtharsia,* "incorruptibility." Only twice is it translated "immortality" (Rom. 2:7; 2 Tim. 1:10). Four times it is rendered "incorruption" and twice "sincerity." The English adjective "immortal" is found only once (1 Tim. 1:17), though the Greek original, *aphthartos,* is given its more literal translation in half a dozen other passages. The two nouns seem to be used interchangeably by Paul in his great treatise on the Resurrection (1 Corinthians 15). There *athanasia* is found in verses 53 and 54, *aphtharsia* in verses 42, 50, 53, and 54.

Unapproachable (6:16)

"Which no man can approach unto" is all one word in Greek, *aprositos*. It simply means "unapproachable" (NIV). Paul probably had in mind the experience of Moses (Exod. 33:20).

Highminded (6:17)

The compound verb *hypsēlophroneō* is found only here in the NT. E. K. Simpson (*Pastoral Epistles,* p. 90) calls it "a compound probably of Pauline mintage." The more common Greek term of that day was *megalophroneō.* Both mean "haughty, arrogant, proud." Bernard comments: "The pride of purse is not only vulgar, it is sinful" (p. 101).

Trust in Uncertain Riches (6:17)

The Greek says, "Set their hope on the uncertainty of riches." The word for "uncertainty," *adēlotēs,* occurs only here in the NT. There is nothing in this life more uncertain than riches, as many men have found to their sorrow.

Distribute . . . Communicate (6:18)

Both the Greek words are found only here in the NT. They are adjectives, introduced by *einai,* "to be." The first, *eumetadotos,* "is best rendered 'ready to impart'" (VGT, p. 263). Thayer adds to this "liberal," whereas

Arndt and Gingrich simply give "generous." The second, *koinōnokos,* comes from *koinos,* "common." It is related to *koinōnia,* "fellowship." In classical Greek it first meant "sociable, ready and apt to form and maintain communion and fellowship," and then "inclined to make others sharers in one's possessions, inclined to impart, free in giving, liberal" (Thayer, p. 352).

Bernard suggests that the second adjective "seems to express a wider idea" than the first, and adds: "As is often the case, the larger word is placed second, by way of explanation; a kind heart as well as a generous hand is demanded of the rich" (p. 102). Lock spells it out a little more fully. He says that the distinction between the adjectives is either "quick to give away to others in charity . . . and ready to share with one's friends that which is one's own," or *"eumetadotos,* of action, 'open-handed' . . . *koinōnikos,* of demeanour and temper, 'gracious,' with true sense of human fellowship, the antithesis of *hypsē-lophronein"* (pp. 74-75). Since God is so rich toward us (v. 17), we should be rich toward others.

Probably the best translation of the latter half of verse 18 is "to be generous and willing to share" (NIV).

Laying Up in Store (6:19)

This is all one word in Greek—the participle *apothē-saurizontas.* It comes from *thēsauros,* which first meant "a treasury" and then "a treasure." The idea here is evidently that by giving generously people will be "storing up for themselves the treasure of a good foundation for the future" (NASB).

Eternal or Indeed? (6:19)

The best Greek text has "that which is life indeed"

rather than "eternal life." The correct wording obviously has great homiletical possibilities.

Guard the Deposit (6:20)

That is the simple Greek for "Keep that which is committed to thy trust." The expression is found again in 2 Tim. 1:12, 14 (the only other places where *parathēkē*, "deposit," occurs in NT). This deposit was the truth of the gospel, to be guarded against heresies.

Science Falsely So Called (6:20)

The use of the word "science" here is obviously incorrect. The Greek has *gnōsis*, "knowledge." Science is only a part of human knowledge. Paul was not antiscientific!

"Falsely so called" is one word in Greek, *pseudonymos* (cf. *pseudonym*), found only here in the NT. It literally means "falsely named." The reference is probably to the false claims of the Gnostics that they had the true *gnōsis*. With them "knowledge" was the key word. They found contradictions between the OT and the NT, as elaborated in Marcion's famous second-century work, *Antitheses*. But this does not mean, as some older critics claimed, that the Pastoral Epistles were written later than Marcion's time. Now we know that Gnosticism had already penetrated Judaism before the time of Christ.

Hort, however, feels that the primary reference here is to "the endless contrast of decisions, founded on endless distinctions, which played so large a part in the casuistry of the scribes as interpreters of the law" (*Judaistic Christianity*, p. 140, quoted approvingly by both Bernard and Lock).

SECOND TIMOTHY

❧⊙❧

Forefathers (1:3)

The Greek word *progonos* is an adjective meaning "born before." But in the plural it is used as a substantive. It occurs (in NT) only here and in 1 Tim. 5:4. There it refers to living parents or grandparents. Here it means "ancestors."

Stir Up or Stir into Flame? (1:6)

Found only here in the NT, the verb is *anazōpyreō*. The prepositional prefix *ana* has two meanings, "up" and "again." The middle item, *zō*, means "life." The last root, *pyr*, is "fire." If we take *ana* as "again," the full translation would be "stir alive again into a flame." Arndt and Gingrich give here the simple rendering "rekindle" (cf. NASB, "kindle afresh").

But probably a majority of the best commentators agree that *ana* here means "up" rather than "again" (re-). Ellicott writes: "The simple form *zōpyrein* is 'to kindle to flame,' the compound *anazōpyrein* is either (a) to 're-kindle' . . . or (b) as here, 'to kindle *up*,' 'to fan into a flame,' without, however, involving any *necessary* reference to a *previous* state of higher ardor or of fuller glow" (p. 124). Lock says that the verb properly means "to stir up smouldering embers into a living flame," or "to keep at white heat" (p. 85). In line with this, Donald Guthrie comments: "There is no necessary suggestion, therefore, that Timothy had lost his early fire, although undoubtedly, like every Christian, he needed an incentive to keep the fire burning at full flame" ("The Pastoral Epistles," *Tyndale New Testament Commentaries*, p. 126). In a similar vein Hendriksen writes: "The flame had not gone out, but it was burning slowly and had to be agitated to white heat" (*New Testament Commentary: Pastoral Epistles*, p. 229). The best translation here is "fan into flame" (NIV).

General Booth of the Salvation Army once made this pertinent observation: "The tendency of fire is to go out; watch the fire on the altar of your heart." Anyone who has burned wood in a fireplace knows that periodically it is necessary to add fresh fuel and sometimes to fan the embers into a flame. We need to keep alive the inner flame by adding the fuel of the Word of God and fanning it with prayer.

Charisma (1:6)

That is the Greek word here translated "gift." Paul reminds Timothy that he had received this gift "by the putting on of my hands." In 1 Tim. 4:14 it was "the hands of the presbytery," a rather clear reference to ordination. Here it may refer to the time when Paul chose to take Timothy along with him as a helper. Bernard comments: "The *charisma* is not an ordinary gift of God's grace, such as every Christian may seek and obtain according to his need; but is the special grace received by Timothy to fit him for his ministerial functions" (p. 109).

Fear or Cowardice? (1:7)

Three Greek nouns are translated as "fear" in the NT (KJV). *Deilia* is found only here. The most frequent one is *phobos* (47 times). *Eulobeia* occurs twice (Heb. 5:7; 12:28). Trench points out these differences between them: "Of these three words the first, *deilia,* is used always in a bad sense; the second, *phobos,* is a middle term, capable of a good interpretation, capable of an evil, and lying indifferently between the two; the third, *eulobeia,* is quite predominantly used in a good sense" (pp. 34-35). In Heb. 12:28 it is translated "godly fear."

Thayer defines *deilia* as meaning "timidity, fearfulness, cowardice." The last of these is what Arndt and Gingrich suggest for the passage here. Bernard comments: "Of the gifts of the Holy Spirit cowardice is not one; a Christian man, a Christian minister, has no right to be a coward, for God has given him the spirit of *power*" (p. 109).

Sound Mind or Self-discipline? (1:7)

The noun *sōphronismos* is found only here in the NT. Lock says it suggests "the power to make *sōphrōn* (sane, sensible, self-controlled); whether to discipline others . . . or to discipline oneself, to keep oneself in hand, free from all excitement or hesitation; it is 'the sanity of saintliness,' cf. Bishop Paget, *Studies in the Christian Character,* pp. 64-67. The context probably limits the reference here to self-discipline. . . . The Christian minister must be strong, efficient, courageous, but never forget personal tenderness for others . . . or control of his own temper" (p. 86).

N. J. D. White discusses the relevance of this exhortation. He writes: "There was an element of *deilia* in Timothy's natural disposition which must have been prejudicial to his efficiency as a Church ruler. For that position is needed (a) force of character, which if not natural may be inspired by consciousness of a divine appointment, (b) love, which is not softness, and (c) self-discipline, which is opposed to all easy self-indulgence which issues in laxity of administration" (EGT, 4:155).

Timothy had been brought up by his mother and grandmother (v. 5), two devout Jewish Christians. His Greek father (Acts 16:1), who was probably a pagan, evidently left the religious training of his son to the two women. These factors may have contributed to the fact that Timothy's personality was more gentle than rugged. Throughout Paul's two letters to Timothy he exhorts his young associate to be firm, and even stern (cf. 2:1; 4:2). From Paul's correspondence with the Corinthians we gather that the apostle sent Timothy to try to straighten out the sad state of affairs among them. But the gentle-hearted young man was no match for Paul's harsh opponents in Corinth. Soon afterward, Titus succeeded where Timothy had failed.

It has been suggested that the "love" and the "self-discipline" must be present to control the "power." One might use the automobile for an analogy. The higher the horsepower of the engine, the more one needs power brakes and power steering. And the man behind the wheel must be in control at all times.

Sharing Suffering (1:8)

"Be thou partaker of the afflictions" is all one word in Greek, *synkakopotheō* (only here and 2:3 in NT). It literally means "suffer evil with," and so "suffer hardship together with." Arndt and Gingrich suggest here: "Join with me in suffering for the gospel." That is evidently the idea. It is thought that Paul coined this term.

Before Times Eternal (1:9)

This is the literal meaning of *pro chronōn aiōniōn,* which in the KJV is translated "before the world began" (v. 9). It probably means "long ages ago," or "from eternity."

My Deposit (1:12)

"That which I have committed unto him" is *tēn parathēkēn mou,* "my deposit." It may also be translated "what has been entrusted to me" (RSV; cf. NEB). Obviously "my deposit" is somewhat ambiguous. White says that the Greek expression is best taken as "that which I have deposited for safe keeping." He adds: "Here it means 'my soul' or 'myself' (EGT, 4:157-58).

E. K. Simpson agrees with this. He writes: "The apostle is looking at home. Philo applies the term to the soul (ii. 37), our costliest treasure, and it is that entrustment the saints, especially in prospect of taking flight, commit into Immanuel's steadfast hands" (p. 127).

Lock also favors this interpretation. He says that the Greek phrase means "that which I have deposited with Him . . . all my precious things which I have put under His care. He does not define or limit; it will include his teaching . . . his apostolic work, his converts . . . his life which has been already in God's keeping and which will remain safe there even through death. . . . The last is perhaps the primary thought" (p. 88).

Bernard takes a different view. He comments: "In I Tim. vi. 20 and 2 Tim. i. 14 *parathēkē* plainly means the doctrine delivered to Timothy to preach; and hence it appears that here *tēn parathēkēn mou* = the doctrine delivered to Paul by God" (p. 111). He notes that this also ties in more closely with the admonition of the next verse: "Hold fast the form of sound words."

In an extended note, Lock observes that "*paratheke* . . . always implies the situation of one who has to take a long journey and who deposits his money and other valuables with a friend, entrusting him to restore it on his return" (p. 90). He goes on to say: "In the N. T. the substantive is only used in the Pastoral Epistles: it comes naturally from one who is preparing for his last long journey, but the verb occurs elsewhere, and the word was used metaphorically in many applications. *(a)* Of the body of truth which Christ deposits with the Apostle and the Apostle with Timothy, cf. 2 T 1:18 . . . 6:20 . . . 2 T 1:14, and which Timothy has to hand on to others when he takes his journey to Rome, 2 T 2:2 . . . *(b)* Of our true self which the Creator has handed over to us to keep safe. . . . *(c)* Of good works deposited with God in heaven: a very common Jewish thought. . . . *(d)* Of persons entrusted to the care of others. . . . *(e)* Of our life deposited with God at death. . . . The life which at first was God's deposit with us becomes our deposit with God" (pp. 91-92). The NIV has "what I have entrusted to him."

Form or Pattern? (1:13)

The word *hypotyposis* occurs only here and in 1 Tim. 1:16. In that place it is best rendered "example"—the example of Paul's life. But here it means "the pattern placed before one to be held fast and copied" (Thayer). Lock suggests that "the signification of a *summary, outline,* which Galen assigns the word, best tallies with this context" (p. 127). Timothy was to hold fast the summary or outline of the gospel as expressed in sound words. This suggests the beginnings of a Christian creed.

Once more Timothy is admonished, "Guard the good deposit" (v. 14). He can do this only "by the Holy Spirit," who is the great Conservator of orthodoxy.

Asia (1:15)

In view of the current use of "Asia" it is important to note that in the NT the term never refers to a continent. It designates the Roman province of Asia, on the western end of the peninsula which we now call Asia Minor (modern Turkey). It was only one of half a dozen Roman provinces in that area.

The main city in that province was Ephesus, where Timothy was in charge of the Christian work (1 Tim. 1:3). It is a pathetic report that the apostle gives here. Lock suggests: "Possibly all the Asiatic Christians who were in Rome at the time, cf. 4:6, failed to support him at his trial and had now returned to Asia"—they were now "in Asia" and known to Timothy—"or all the Christians in Asia at the time when he was arrested there failed to help him or come with him to Rome" (p. 89).

Refreshed (1:16)

The verb is *anapsychō,* found only here in the NT. It comes from *psychō,* which meant "to breathe, to blow," and so "to cool, to make cool" (Cremer, p. 588). The compound then means "to make cool, to refresh" *(ibid.).* The Latin Vulgate has *refrigeravit.* When Onesiphorus came to see Paul in the stuffy dungeon, it was as if the air conditioning had been turned on!

Enlistment in God's Army (2:4)

"Him who hath chosen him to be a soldier" is in Greek simply the definite article with the participle *stratologē-santi.* Literally it means "the one who enlisted him."

Today we generally use "enlist" in the intransitive sense. A man enlists in the army or navy; that is, he enters voluntarily, is not drafted. But the first meaning of "enlist" is transitive, "to persuade to enter the armed forces."

Actually, there are three steps involved. First, God invites us to enlist, seeks to persuade us to do so. Second, in response to this we volunteer to join. Third, God then enlists us; that is, records us as soldiers in His army. And enlistment is not for a short term of three or four years; it is for life! Our duty and pleasure are to please our Commander in Chief. We should beware of absenteeism or going AWOL.

Strive or Compete? (2:5)

"Strive for masteries" is one word in Greek—*athlei,* from which we get *athlete.* The verb is found only here in the NT (twice in this verse). It means "to compete in an athletic contest." The adverb *nomimōs,* "lawfully," means "according to the rules." The one who does not keep the rules is disqualified from the contest. We need to study the Bible in order that we may be familiar with the rules of the game.

Typically, Paul uses three figures here to illustrate the life of the Christian. The follower of Christ is to be a soldier (vv. 3-4), an athlete (v. 5), and a farmer (v. 6). These could well be used for the three points of a sermon, or, better still, for a series of three sermons on the Christian life.

An Innocent Sufferer (2:9)

Paul says, "I suffer trouble," as though I were "an evildoer." The compound verb is *kakopatheō,* literally, "suffer evil." The compound noun is *kakourgos.* It is used elsewhere in NT only for the "malefactors" crucified on either side of Jesus (Luke 23:32-33, 39). The righteous Paul was being treated like one of them. In this way, as in many others, the apostle was being identified with his Lord.

Patient Endurance (2:10, 12)

"Endure" has no direct relation to "endure" in verse 3. There it is a double compound, *synkakopatheō,* "suffer evil together," and is found elsewhere only in 1:8—"Be thou partaker of the afflictions."

But here the verb is *hypomenō,* literally, "remain under." Of itself it does not suggest suffering, but "I am patiently enduring."

The same verb, *hypomenō,* is found in verse 12, where it is wrongly translated "suffer." The passage should read: "If we patiently endure [keep steadfast to the end], we shall also reign with him."

Catastrophē (2:14)

That is exactly the Greek word translated "sub-verting." It means "ruin" or "destruction." That is what Paul declares results when people "strive about words." The verb *logomacheō* means to "fight with words." It is found only here in the NT. The corresponding noun, *logomachia,* occurs only in 1 Tim. 6:4. Word battles bring catastrophe wherever they occur.

Study or Endeavor? (2:15)

In contemporary language the verb *study* is used mostly for reading books. While this occupation is commendable, the word thus translated in verse 15 has no direct reference to reading. It is the verb *spoudazō.* It means *"to make haste;* hence, *to be zealous* or *eager, to give diligence"* (A-S). Arndt and Gingrich define it as *"be zealous* or *eager, take pains, make every effort."* It is obvious that it takes in a lot more territory than "study."

Approved (2:15)

This English word is based on the root *prove.* But it is doubtful if the average person is aware of this when he uses the term.

The Greeks were probably more conscious of the connection. They realized that the adjective here, *dokimos,* was related to the verb *dokimazō,* which meant "test, try, prove." So *dokimos* was used primarily of metals, in the sense "tested, accepted, approved" (A-S). In other words, a thing or person must first be "proved" before being "approved." Arndt and Gingrich define *dokimos* as follows: *"approved* (by test), *tried and true, genuine."* God can approve only those who have proved themselves true in the tests of life.

Rightly Dividing? (2:15)

This KJV translation has caused much confusion in biblical interpretation. To many people this phrase is the key to understanding the Bible, and so they have gone down the dead-end street of extreme dispensationalism— which holds, for instance, that the Sermon on the Mount does not apply to us today; it applies to the millennium. So we Christians are robbed of some of the most important teachings of Jesus for daily living.

"Rightly dividing" is one word in Greek, *orthotomounta.* It comes from *orthos,* "straight," and *temnō,* "cut." So the verb *orthotomeō* (only here in NT) means "cut in a straight line." The Liddell-Scott-Jones *Lexicon* gives for this passage: "teach aright" (p. 1250). It was used for cutting a straight furrow in a field, or laying out a straight road. In the Septuagint it is used in the sense of "direct, make straight, make plain."

N. J. D. White says: "This use of the word suggests that the metaphor passes from the general idea of a workman to the particular notion of the minister as one who 'makes straight paths' for the feet of his people to tread in (Heb. xii. 13)" (EGT, 4:165). In a similar vein Vincent writes: "The thought is that the minister of the gospel is to present the truth rightly, not abridging it, not handling it as a charlatan . . . not making it a matter of wordy strife (ver. 14), but treating it honestly and fully, in a straightforward manner" (4:302). E. K. Simpson prefers the idea of "cut a road," and adds the observation: "It enjoins on every teacher of the Word straightforward exegesis" (p. 137).

The translation we prefer is that found in the margin of the Revised Version: "holding a straight course in the word of truth." Instead of detouring on devious and crooked ways, or going recklessly down side roads, the preacher should "hold a straight course" in the middle of the road, offering a sane, sensible interpretation of Scripture. This is the kind of preaching that will build up people in the most holy faith.

Vain Babblings or Empty Chatter? (2:16)

The noun *kenophōnia* occurs only here and in 1 Tim. 1:16. It is compounded of *kenos*, "empty," and *phōnē*, "sound." So it literally means "empty sounds." Perhaps the best translation is "empty chatter" (NASB).

In both passages where the word is found it is preceded by *bebēlos*, "profane." Arndt and Gingrich would combine this adjective with the compound noun and translate the whole expression as "godless chatter" (NIV). This is what we are told to avoid.

Canker or Gangrene? (2:17)

The word *gangraina* is found only here in the NT. Thayer defines it as follows: "*A gangrene,* a disease by which any part of the body suffering from inflammation becomes so corrupted that, unless a remedy be seasonably applied, the evil continually spreads, attacks other parts, and at last eats away the bones" (p. 107). Abbott-Smith calls it "a gangrene, an eating sore." Arndt and Gingrich say, "*Gangrene, cancer* of spreading ulcers, etc. (medical term since Hippocrates)." They note that it is used figuratively here, as in Plutarch. The one-volume Hastings *Dictionary of the Bible* (rev. ed., 1963) defines *gangraina* as "a medical term for spreading ulcers." Since it is not a doctrinal term, it is not discussed in TDNT.

The root question is: Can we translate this term as "cancer"? In spite of Arndt and Gingrich's use of that word, it seems that the safer rendering is "gangrene" (NIV). This appears to be the correct medical term today.

Sure or Solid? (2:19)

The word is *stereos,* which has been taken over into English for stereo records and record players. The original meaning is "firm, solid, compact, hard, rigid," and as used here to describe a foundation it means "strong, firm, immovable" (Thayer). The correct translation here is "firm" (NIV) or "solid."

Earth or Earthenware? (2:20)

The adjective ("of earth") is *ostrakinos,* found only here and in 2 Cor. 4:7. It means "made of clay." Today we speak of "earthenware" dishes. The plural noun *ostraca* has been taken directly over into English for potsherds, or broken pieces of pottery that are found in archaeological excavations. The last clause of this verse is best translated, "some for great occasions and some for ordinary use" (Goodspeed).

Meet for Use or Useful? (2:21)

The adjective *euchrēstos* occurs only here, in 4:11, and in the eleventh verse of Philemon. It means "useful" (NIV) or "serviceable."

Follow or Pursue? (2:22)

Timothy is admonished to flee from youthful lusts but to "follow" good things. The Greek word *diōkō* literally means "pursue" (NIV). Furthermore, it is in the continuous present. So it means "keep on pursuing."

Unlearned or Ignorant? (2:23)

The adjective *apaideutos* is found only here in the NT. It comes from *a*-negative, and the verb *paideuō*, which means "train a child" *(pais)*. So the adjective means "without instruction and discipline, uneducated, ignorant, rude" and here indicates "stupid questions" (Thayer, p. 53). Arndt and Gingrich translate this phrase "stupid speculations." Probably "ignorant" (ASV, NASB, NEB) is better than "unlearned."

Gender Strifes or Breed Quarrels? (2:23)

The KJV rendering of *gennōsin machas* is certainly correct. But "breed quarrels" would be more contemporary. The KJV is also right in using "strive" in verse 24 for *machesthai,* since the noun and verb have the same root. "Quarrel" (v. 24, NIV) would fit better now.

Patient or Forbearing? (2:24)

Paul says that the Lord's servant must not be quarrelsome, but "gentle" (or "kind") and "apt to teach" (or "skillful in teaching"; see 1 Tim. 3:2), and "patient."

The last word is the rendering of *anexikakos,* found only here in the NT. It is compounded of *anechō,* "hold up," and *kakos,* "bad" or "evil." So it means "holding up under wrong." That is something more than just being patient. Thayer defines it as "patient of ills and wrongs, forbearing" (cf. RSV). Arndt and Gingrich suggest "bearing evil without resentment" (cf. Goodspeed, "unresentful"). Grundmann (TDNT, 3:487) says it means "tolerant of evil or calamity" (cf. NEB, "tolerant"). The NASB uses a phrase, "patient when wronged." This is needed, perhaps, to convey the full sense of the compound term in Greek (cf. NIV: "not resentful").

Instructing or Correcting? (2:25)

The verb *paideuō* literally means to "train children." But it is also used in the Septuagint and in the papyri in the sense of "correct." That is the meaning given for it here by Thayer, as well as Arndt and Gingrich.

Those That Oppose Themselves (2:25)

In the Greek this is simply the definite article with the participle *antidiatithemenous* (only here in NT). The verb is a double compound, composed of *anti,* "against," *dia,* "through," and *tithēmi,* "place." So it means "place oneself in opposition" (Thayer). Arndt and Gingrich would translate the article and participle "his opponents."

Acknowledging or Knowledge? (2:25)

The term *epignōsis* is a compound of *gnōsis*, "knowledge." It means "precise and correct knowledge" (Thayer). For this passage Arndt and Gingrich give "knowledge" or "recognition." Actually, the phrase here in the Greek, *epignōsin alētheias*, "the acknowledging of the truth," is exactly the same as in 1 Tim. 2:4 and 2 Tim. 3:7, where it is translated as "the knowledge of the truth." That is the best translation here. It must be admitted that Paul seems to use *gnōsis* and *epignōsis* interchangeably.

Recover or Come to Their Senses? (2:26)

The verb *ananēphō* occurs only here in the NT. It literally means "return to soberness." Thayer (p. 40) suggests that the meaning of the passage here is: "To be set free from the snare of the devil and to return to a sound mind ('one's sober senses')." Arndt and Gingrich (p. 57) say the compound verb means "come to one's senses again" and offer this translation: "Come to one's senses and escape from the snare of the devil" (cf. NASB). The addition of "escape" seems necessary for smooth English. However, Bernard offers this translation: "And may return to soberness out of the snare of the devil" (p. 127).

Taken Captive or Held Captive? (2:26)

The verb *zōgreō* is found only here and in Luke 5:10. It is compounded of *zōos*, "alive," and *agreuō*, which means "*to catch* or *take* by hunting or fishing" (A-S). So it literally means "to take alive." Then it came to have the more general sense of "catch" or "capture." But Bernard writes: "*Zōgrein* only occurs elsewhere in N.T. at Luke v. 10 where it means 'to catch alive,' as it does here" (p. 128).

Both Bernard and Ellicott (on Greek text) think that "his will" means "God's will." But we prefer the interpretation of Arndt and Gingrich: "*Held captive by him* (the devil) *to perform his* (the devil's) *will*" (p. 340). The fact that the verb *sōgreō* is here in the perfect passive participle suggests that "held captive" is more accurate than "taken captive." The devil holds as captive everyone he can.

Perilous or Difficult? (3:1)

The basic meaning of *chalepos* is "hard." Abbott-Smith defines it thus: "(a) *hard to do or deal with, difficult;* (b) *hard to bear, painful* . . . 2 Tim. 3:1; (c) of persons, *hard to deal with, harsh, fierce, savage:* Mt. 8:28" (p. 478). These are the only two times that the word occurs in the NT. For this passage Arndt and Gingrich suggest "hard times, times of stress" (p. 882).

Bad Lovers (3:2-4)

In verses 2-4 Paul lists 18 characteristics of men in the last days. Five terms here have the prefix *phil*, which means "friend" or "lover." There are no less than 35 words in the NT beginning with *phil*.

The first term here is *philautoi*, "lovers of self" or "selfish." Bernard comments: "In Greek thought of an earlier age *philautia* had a good sense, and was expressive of the self-respect which a good man has for himself. . . . But a deeper philosophy, recognizing the fact of man's Fall, transferred the moral centre of gravity from self to God; once the sense of sin is truly felt, self-respect becomes an inadequate basis for moral theology" (p. 129).

The second term is *philargyroi*, "lovers of money" (KJV, covetous). The phrase, "despisers of those that are good" is one word in Greek, "*aphilagathoi.*" Literally it means "not loving good people." (This word has not been found anywhere else in Greek literature.) The fourth term is *philēdonoi*, "lovers of pleasure." The last is *philotheoi*, "lovers of God." Probably no one would dare deny that the majority of people in modern society are "lovers of pleasure more than lovers of God." Hedonism is one of the main characteristics of our day.

Boasters (3:2)

The word *alazōn* is found only here and Rom. 1:30. It likewise occurs twice in the Septuagint. Coming from *alē*, "wandering," it first meant "a vagabond." It was used for those who were "full of empty and boastful professions of cures and other feats which they could accomplish" (Trench, p. 98). Then it was applied to any braggart or boaster. Phillips translates it, "full of big words." (For "proud" see Rom. 1:30.)

Blasphemers (3:2)

This is an adjective *lasphēmos*, used here for persons as in 1 Tim. 1:3. In Acts 6:11 it describes words. In its only other occurrence in the NT it refers to "railing" accusation (2 Pet. 2:11). It sometimes means "speaking evil, slanderous, reproachful, railing, abusive" (Thayer, p. 103). Bernard writes: "*railers,* or evil-speakers, in reference to their fellow men rather than to God. This is the regular force of *blasphemos* and the cognate words in the Pastoral Epistles" (p. 130).

Unthankful or Ungracious? (3:2)

The adjective *acharistos* is found only here and in Luke 6:35. It is compounded of *a*-negative and *charis* ("grace"). So its earliest meaning was "ungracious." Homer uses it in the sense of "unpleasing." But beginning with Herodotus it took on the meaning "unthankful." Probably the best translation here is "ungrateful" (NIV), the only meaning given by Arndt and Gingrich. Bernard says: "*Without gratitude.* This follows naturally from the last mentioned characteristic (disobedient to parents), for the blackest form of ingratitude is that which repudiates the claim of parents to respect and obedience" (p. 130). Though written in the nineteenth century, this observation is particularly relevant right now.

Unholy (3:2)

Of the term *anosios,* Hauck writes: "In the NT it occurs twice in the Pastorals for 'impious' persons who impiously reject sacred obligations. In 1 Tim. 1:9 . . . it seems to have the sense of 'ungodly,' but in II Tim. 3:2 the sequence . . . suggests the sense of 'impious,' 'devoid of piety'" (TDNT, 5:492).

Without Natural Affection (3:3)

This is all one word in Greek, *astorgoi.* It is composed of *a*-negative and *storgē,* "family affection." The word occurs only here and in Rom. 1:31. Arndt and Gingrich suggest "unloving." The NIV has "without love."

Trucebreakers (3:3)

The term *aspondos* is found only here in the NT. Like one-third of the adjectives in this list (vv. 2-4) it begins with *a*-negative. The noun *spondē* meant "a libation, which, as a kind of sacrifice, accompanied the making of treaties and compacts" (Thayer, p. 81). So the adjective here means "that cannot be persuaded to enter into a covenant, implacable" *(ibid.).* Perhaps the best translation is "irreconcilable" (AG). (For "false accusers" see 1 Tim. 3:11.)

Incontinent (3:3)

The basic meaning of *akrateis* (only here in NT) is *"without self-control, intemperate"* (Thayer). Arndt and Gingrich add to this: "dissolute." Bernard says that it means "without self-control, in the widest sense, but more particularly in regard to bodily lusts" (p. 130).

Fierce or Brutal? (3:3)

This adjective, *anēmeros,* also occurs only here in the NT. It literally means "untamed," and so "savage" or "brutal." It would seem that "brutal" (NIV) conveys the idea correctly.

Traitors or Treacherous? (3:4)

The noun is *prodotēs,* which occurs also in Luke 6:16 (of Judas Iscariot) and Acts 7:22. It means "betrayer" or "traitor." It describes those who are "treacherous in their dealings with their fellows." Perhaps "treacherous" (NIV) is the best rendering.

Heady or Headstrong? (3:4)

The adjective *propetēs* occurs only here and in Acts 19:36. It literally means "falling forwards, headlong" and metaphorically "precipitate, rash, reckless" (A-S). Probably "headstrong" is the term we would use today. (For "highminded" see "lifted up with pride," 1 Tim. 3:6.)

Creep or Enter? (3:6)

The verb is *endynō,* elsewhere in the NT spelled *endyō.* The latter is used literally for putting on clothes, or figuratively for clothing oneself with certain virtues or with Christ (Rom. 13:14).

But since *dynō* means to "enter, sink into," so *endynō* can mean "to enter, press into" (A-S). Only here in the NT does it have that meaning. Thayer suggests for this passage: "to creep into, insinuate one's self into; to enter" (p. 214). Arndt and Gingrich have "worm their way into houses" (p. 263). Since *oikia* means "household" as well as "house," Moffatt reads, "worm their way into families" (cf. NIV). The *Jerusalem Bible* has "insinuate themselves into families." The NASB says, "enter into households." A. T. Robertson thinks that "slip into by insinuation" is the meaning here. In the light of the context this unfavorable sense is probably justified.

Silly Women (3:6)

This is one word in the Greek, *gynaikaria* (only here in NT), the diminutive of *gynē,* "woman." So it literally means "little women." As Vincent remarks, *"Silly* is expressed by the contemptuous diminutive" (4:312).

Laden or Loaded? (3:6)

The perfect passive participle of *soreuō* (only here and Rom. 12:20) means "heap together," and so "to overwhelm one with a heap of anything"; here, "to load one with the consciousness of many sins" (Thayer, p. 612). "Loaded down with sins" (NIV) gives the correct idea.

Divers or Various? (3:6)

The word *poikilos* occurs 10 times in the NT. In 1 Pet.

1:6; 4:10 it is translated "manifold." The rest of the time it is rendered "divers," the Middle English form of "diverse." The Greek word literally means "many-colored, variegated," and so "of various kinds, diversified." Both meanings are found as early as Homer. The correct translation is "various."

Corrupt Minds (3:8)

The Greek phrase is a strong one, carrying the sense "utterly corrupted in their minds." The verb *kataphtheirō* (only here in NT) literally means "destroy entirely," and so in a moral sense, "deprave, corrupt" (A-S). The form here is the perfect passive participle, indicating a thoroughly depraved state of mind. The NIV translates this, "men of depraved minds."

Folly (3:9)

The term *anoia* occurs only here and in Luke 6:11, where it is translated "madness." It is compounded of *a*-negative and *nous,* "mind." So it literally means "mindlessness" or "want of sense."

Manifest (3:9)

The compound *ekdēlos* (only here in NT) is a strengthened form of *dēlos,* which means "*clear* to the mind." So this word means "quite clear, evident" (A-S).

Fully Known (3:10)

This is the same verb *parakoloutheō* which is found in 1 Tim. 4:6. There it means "follow faithfully." But here the thought seems to be "followed closely"; that is, you are familiar with what happened to me. Elsewhere in the NT it is found in Luke 1:3, where it means "investigate" or "trace carefully."

Manner of Life (3:10)

The noun *agōgē* (only here in NT) comes from the verb *agō*, meaning "lead." Properly it means "a leading." But it was used figuratively in the sense of "education" or "discipline," and then more generally for "the life led" or "the course of life." Since "doctrine" should definitely be "teaching," a helpful translation here is that of Moffatt: "my teaching, my practice."

Godly (3:12)

The adverb *eusebōs* is found only here and in Titus 2:12. Since "godly" is properly an adjective, the best translation is "live a godly life" (RSV, NIV).

Seducers or Impostors? (3:13)

The noun *goēs* (only here in NT) comes from *goaō*, "wail" or "howl." So it originally meant a wailer or howler. Then it signified a wizard or enchanter, "because incantations used to be uttered in a kind of howl" (Thayer, p. 120). Here the correct meaning is "impostors" (NIV).

Been Assured of (3:14)

Whereas the verb *pisteuō*, "believe," occurs 248 times in the NT, the cognate verb *pistoō* is found only here. It meant "to make faithful, render trustworthy," and then "make firm, establish." In the passive, as here, it means "to be firmly persuaded of; to be assured of" (Thayer, p. 514).

Given by Inspiration (3:16)

This is one word in Greek, *theopneustos* (only here in NT). It literally means "God-breathed"—*theos,* "God," and *pneō,* "breathe." That is, God breathed His truth into the hearts and minds of the writers of Scripture. The best translation is "God-breathed" (NIV).

Reproof or Conviction? (3:16)

The noun *elegmos* is found only here in the NT. In the Septuagint it is used for the "conviction" of a sinner, for "reproof," and even for "punishment." Thayer says it means "correction, reproof, censure." While "reproof" is the popular translation, the idea of "conviction" should not be ruled out.

Correction (3:16)

The word (only here in NT) is *epanorthōsis* (*orthos* means "straight"). The term suggests "restoration to an upright or a right state; correction, improvement" (Thayer, p. 228). Arndt and Gingrich prefer the last of these, "improvement," for this passage. Trench says it means "rectification" (p. 111).

Instruction or Training? (3:16)

The noun *paideia* comes from *pais,* "child," and the verb *paideuō,* which in classical Greek meant "to train children." So the literal meaning of *paideia* is "child training." Thayer says it refers to "whatever in adults also cultivates the soul, especially by correcting mistakes and curbing the passions" (p. 473). Trench writes: "*Paideia* is one among the many words, into which revealed religion has put a deeper meaning than it knew of, till this took possession of it. . . . For the Greek, *paideia* was simply 'education.'" But biblical writers "felt and understood that all effectual instruction for the sinful children of men, includes and implies chastening" (p. 111). Since "instruction" is thought of as mainly intellectual, "training" is a more adequate translation.

Perfect or Complete? (3:17)

In the Greek there is a play on words that is lost in English translation. The adjective "perfect" is *artios* (only here in NT), and "throughly furnished" is the perfect passive participle of the verb *exartizō,* based on the adjective. The verb is found here and in Acts 21:5 ("accomplished"; that is, "finished").

The basic meaning of *artios* is "fitted" or "complete." Trench comments: "If we ask ourselves under what special aspects completeness is contemplated in *artios,* it would be safe to answer that it is not as the presence only of all the parts which are necessary for that completeness, but involves further the adaptation and aptitude of these parts for the ends which they were designed to serve. The man of God, St. Paul would say (2 Tim. iii. 17), should be furnished and accomplished with all which is necessary for the carrying out of the work to which he is appointed" (p. 77).

Delling writes: "At 2 Tim. 3:17 *artios* is used . . . to denote what is right or proper, and more particularly what is becoming to a Christian, obviously with a moral accent, as shown by what follows. At 2 Tim. 3:17 *exartizō* means to bring to a suitable state for Christian moral action" (TDNT, 1:476).

The meaning of the passage is "that the man of God may be complete, equipped for every good work" (RSV).

Quick or Living? (4:1)

The Oxford English Dictionary has no less than nine long columns on the use of "quick" in our language. Its original meaning was "living," and that is all the Greek word here, *zōntas,* means. It has no relation to our modern concept of "quick." The archaic use of "quick" for "living" in the KJV is found four times in the NT (Acts 10:42; 2 Tim. 4:1; Heb. 4:12; 1 Pet. 4:5).

Instant or Ready? (4:2)

The verb *ephistēmi* is translated "be instant" in verse 2 and "is at hand" in verse 6. It literally means "be on hand" and so "be ready." The former sense fits verse 6; the latter, verse 2.

"In season, out of season" is *eukairōs akairōs.* Lock has an excellent comment on this for preachers: *"Both* whether or no the moment seems to fit your hearers, 'welcome or not welcome,' and 'whether or no it is convenient to you,' 'on duty or off duty,' 'in the pulpit or out of it,' 'take or make your opportunity'" (p. 113). That is the way Paul preached.

Itching (4:3)

The verb *knēthō* (only here in NT) literally means "scratch" or "tickle." In the passive (as here) it means "itch." Arndt and Gingrich remark that the word is here used "figuratively of curiosity, that looks for interesting and spicy bits of information" (p. 438). Weymouth puts it well: "wanting to have their ears tickled."

Offered or Poured Out? (4:6)

The statement "I am now ready to be offered" is much

stronger in the Greek: "I am already being poured out as a drink offering." The whole of Paul's life of service was a sacrifice. But as it came to a close, his lifeblood was being poured out on the altar as a final act of dedication. The verb *spendō* is found only here and in Phil. 2:17. Michel writes: "The LXX uses the verb *spendō* . . . in the sense 'to pour out a drink offering'" (TDNT, 7:531).

Fight or Contest? (4:7)

For the first clause almost all translations have, "I have fought a [the] good fight." But in the Greek the verb is *agōnizō* and the noun is *agōn*, from which we get *agonize* and *agony*.

These words came from the verb *agō*, which means "lead." An *agōn* was a gathering. But since the largest gatherings, then as now, were for athletic contests, it came to be used for the contest itself. So Paul's meaning here is probably, "I have competed well in the great contest of life."

The climax of all the contests of that day was the marathon race (26 miles). The winner of this was given the highest honors. He was greeted as a great hero. He had "agonized" and won the *agōna*.

This fits in perfectly with the second clause, "I have finished my course." The Greek word for "course" is *dromon*, which comes from the verb meaning "to run" (second aorist, *edramon*). So it definitely refers to a race-course. TDNT has correctly captured the thought: "I have run the great Race, I have completed the Course."

The third clause, "I have kept the faith," could possibly suggest: "I have kept the rules; I have not been disqualified." It may well be that Paul, who was especially fond of athletic metaphors, thus intended that all three of these clauses be taken as referring to the Christian life as a long-distance race. This is the figure which is clearly used in Heb. 12:1-2.

Verse 8 also fits into this pattern. The "crown" which Paul knew was awaiting him was not the royal diadem (Greek, *diadēma*) but the victor's wreath *(stephanos)*. It would be given him by the Lord, who is the righteous "judge," or Umpire. He stands at the end of each Christian's race, waiting to give him the victor's crown and welcome him into his eternal home. What an encouragement to all of us to keep pressing on to the end! This is the apostle's dying testimony, and it is a glorious one.

Shortly or Quickly? (4:9)

"Do thy diligence to come shortly unto me" is literally, "Make haste to come to me quickly." Winter was coming on. In his damp, dingy dungeon, the apostle was already beginning to suffer from the cold. And so he urged Timothy to come as quickly as possible, bringing Paul's "cloke" (v. 13), his warm outer robe. The Greek is *phailonēs* (only here in NT).

Books . . . Parchments (4:13)

The first word is *biblia,* which probably refers to papyrus rolls or scrolls. These could have been copies of Paul's own Epistles, although the identification is uncertain. Our word *Bible* comes from this.

The second word is *membranas,* "skins" (only here in NT). It refers to scrolls made of the skins of animals. These may have been scrolls containing at least some of the books of the OT.

Answer or Defence? (4:16)

The word is *apologia.* Today an *apology* is generally

a confession that one is sorry for some wrong he has done. But the original meaning of *apology* in English is "defense"—not saying, "I'm sorry; I was wrong," but, "I am innocent." And that is exactly what *apologia* means: "a speech made in defense." So the reference here is not to some obscure "answer" but to Paul's defense at his trial before the emperor. No person stood by him—except the Lord (v. 17), who "strengthened" (Greek, "empowered") him. At Paul's first trial he was delivered out of the lion's mouth (that is, from death). But the previous verses show that he realized his next trial would result in his execution, for which he was ready.

TITUS

࿓◎II◎࿓

That Cannot Lie (1:2)

This is a single word in Greek, *apseudēs,* found only here in the NT. It means "free from all deceit," and so "truthful" or "trustworthy" (AG). As here, it is used as an adjective to describe God in Polycarp's last prayer before his martyrdom. God has promised eternal life, and this promise will not fail even in the face of physical death.

Before the World Began (1:2)

The Greek says "before times eternal" *(pro chronōn aiōniōn).* This evidently means "long ages past, age-long periods ago" (Lock, p. 126). Weymouth translates it "from all eternity."

In Due Times (1:3)

Literally it reads, "In His own appointed times" *(kairois idiois).* Lock comments: "The thought of the Incarnation taking place at the right moment in the world's history is a favourite one with St. Paul (Gal. 4:4; Rom.

5:6; Eph. 1:10; Acts 17:26), springing from apocalyptic expectations, summed up by the Lord (Mk. 1:15) and expanded by himself in his philosophy of history, Rom. 1-3" *(ibid.).* The exact phrase is found only here and in 1 Tim. 2:6; 6:15; but the singular occurs in Gal. 6:9.

Preaching or Proclamation? (1:3)

The word *kērygma* is widely used as a theological term today, signifying the *message* preached by the Early Church.

The term is derived from the noun *kēryx,* "herald," and the verb *kēryssō,* "to herald or proclaim." In classical Greek it signified "that which is promulgated by a herald or public crier, a proclamation by herald." In the NT it means "the message or proclamation by the heralds of God or Christ" (Thayer, p. 346). In the papyri it is used for "a public announcement" (VGT, p. 343). C. H. Dodd writes that the word "signifies not the action of the preacher, but that which he preaches, his message, as we sometimes say" (*The Apostolic Preaching,* p. 7).

This is in agreement with the earlier declaration of J. B. Lightfoot. He says that *kērygma* means "'the thing preached,' 'the proclamation.' . . . It refers therefore to the subject, not to the manner of the preaching. There is only the very slightest approach in classical writers to this [latter] sense of the words *kēryssein, kērygma,* etc., as denoting 'instruction,' 'teaching'" (*Notes on the Epistles of St. Paul,* p. 161; commenting on 1 Cor. 1:21). Ellicott equates *kērygma* here with "the Gospel."

This contention of the earlier writers, and popularized by Dodd, that *kērygma* refers to the *content* rather than the *act* of preaching has been challenged of late. Even Thayer says that in 2 Tim. 4:17 (the only other place in the Pastoral Epistles where it occurs) it means "the act of publishing." But in the only two places where it is found in the Synoptic Gospels (Matt. 12:41; Luke 11:32) he says it indicates "the proclamation of the necessity of repentance and reformation made by the prophet Jonah." In 1 Cor. 1:21; 2:4; 15:14; and Rom. 16:25—making eight times the word occurs in the New Testament—Thayer thinks it refers to "the announcement of salvation procured by Christ and to be had through him" (p. 346).

Arndt and Gingrich define *kērygma* in the NT as simply "proclamation, preaching," and they seem by this to mean the *act*. They would translate it here, "The preaching with which I have been entrusted."

Friedrich says that at 1 Cor. 2:4 *"Kērygma* is the act of proclaiming." But of 1 Cor. 1:21 he writes: "The foolish message of Jesus crucified saves those who believe." He continues: "At Rom. 16:25, too, the reference is to the message with a very definite content" (TDNT, 3:716). He thinks, however, that in Titus 1:3 it is the *act* of preaching.

It seems obvious that we are confronted here with a both/and rather than an either/or situation. The noun *kērygma* means *both* the act *and* the content of preaching.

This statement is illustrated in the usage of various versions today. Whereas the KJV translates *kērygma* in all seven places by "preaching," the ASV (1901) has "message" in the two Pastoral passages. The NASB (1963) has "the message preached" in 1 Cor. 1:21 and "the proclamation" in the Pastoral Epistles. The NEB (1961) also has "proclamation" in these two passages. This can mean the act, but probably its primary emphasis is on what is proclaimed. Certainly too much emphasis should not be put on the idea that preaching is God's only way of getting the gospel to a lost world. The printed page and personal witnessing are both powerful methods of evangelism.

Committed or Entrusted? (1:3)

A comparison with 1 Tim. 1:11 favors definitely the idea that "preaching" in this verse means the message rather than the act. In the earlier passage we read: "According to the glorious gospel of the blessed God, which was committed to my trust." It appears evident that "preaching" in Titus 1:3 is parallel to "gospel" in 1 Tim. 1:11.

The phrase "which was committed to my trust" (1 Tim. 1:11) is exactly the same as "which is committed unto me" (Titus 1:3)—*ho episteuthēn egō.* It is correctly translated in the RSV: "With which I have been entrusted." Commenting on the Timothy passage, E. K. Simpson writes: *"Egō* is emphatic. Paul thrills with joy at the thought of his high commission of proclaiming a gospel so ablaze with the divine perfections" (p. 32). Here the *egō* may point up more especially his heavy sense of responsibility.

Mercy? (1:4)

All 13 Epistles of Paul have the twofold greeting, "Grace and peace." In the two letters to Timothy "mercy" is added. It appears here also in the KJV. But the oldest and best Greek manuscripts do not have it in Titus, and so it must be rejected as a later scribal addition.

Perhaps "mercy" was added by Paul in the letters to Timothy because the apostle's younger colleague was overly gentle and timid by nature. Simpson makes this comment about "mercy": "That sounds a tender chord, suggested possibly by Timothy's fragile health" (p. 26). The additional "mercy" is found also in 2 John 3.

Set in Order (1:5)

The verb *epidiorthoō* (only here in NT) is compounded of *orthos,* "straight"; *dia,* "through"; and *epi,* "upon" or "further." (In analyzing a compound verb, we begin with the simple root and work backwards through the prepositional prefixes.) So it means *"set right or correct in addition* (to what has already been corrected)" (AG, p. 292).

Paul writes to Titus that he had left him on the island of Crete to complete the organization of the churches there. It is interesting to note that on this very island a second-century inscription has been found that contains this compound verb.

Wanting or Remaining? (1:5)

Titus was to set in order "the things that are wanting" *(ta leiponta).* The best translation is "what remains" (to be done) or "what was left unfinished" (NIV).

Ordain or Appoint? (1:5)

Titus was to "ordain elders in every city." This was the simplest form of church government. It was patterned after the Jewish synagogues, each of which was controlled by a group of elders. It was the method Paul and Barnabas used in establishing the Gentile churches on their first missionary journey—"when they had ordained them elders in every church" (Acts 14:23).

Today is ecclesiastical circles "ordain" has a specific technical meaning. It is used for installing a person in the office of elder. How this is done depends on the kind of church government involved. In the Episcopal church it is done only by the bishop. In Presbyterian churches it is the responsibility of the presbytery. In churches with a congregational from of government, as the Baptists, a person is ordained by a group of his fellow ministers.

Was Titus assigned the authority to ordain elders? Because the answer to that question is a bit uncertain, it might be well to use "appoint" (NIV) instead. It does not carry the ecclesiastical overtones inherent in "ordain." Beyer prefers the word "appoint" here (TDNT, 2:617).

Bishop = Elder (1:5-7)

In verses 5 and 6 we find the qualifications of elders in the church; verse 7 says, "For a bishop must be blameless." This seems to indicate rather clearly that the same church officials were called bishops *(episcopoi)* and elders *(presbyteroi)*. The name "elders" emphasizes the fact that the leaders of the church were to be older men, as was the case with the elders of Israel. The word *episcopos* (bishop) literally means "overseer." So it refers to the function and office of an overseer of the church.

That "bishop" and "elder" are used for the same person is even asserted by Bishop Lightfoot of the Church of England. In his commentary on the Greek text of the Epistle to the Philippians he writes: "It is a fact now generally recognized by theologians of all shades of opinion, that in the language of the New Testament the same officer in the Church is called indifferently 'bishop' *(episcopos)* and 'elder' or 'presbyter' *(presbyteros)*" (p. 95).

He goes on to show that not only was *episcopos* used in classical Greek for various officials, but it is common in the Septuagint. There it signifies "inspectors, superintendents, taskmasters" (e.g., 2 Kings 11:19; 2 Chron. 34:12, 17; Isa. 60:17). He comments: "Thus beyond the fundamental idea of *inspection,* which lies at the root of the word 'bishop,' its usage suggests two subsidiary notions also: (1)

Responsibility to a superior power; (2) The introduction of a new order of things" (p. 96).

Lightfoot gives six evidences that bishop and elder are the same: (1) In Phil. 1:1, Paul salutes the bishops and deacons. He could not have omitted mention of the elders unless they were included in the "bishops." (2) In Acts 20:17, Paul summoned to Miletus the elders of the church at Ephesus. But then he calls them "overseers" *(episcopoi)* of the flock. (3) Peter does a similar thing (1 Pet. 5:1-2). (4) In 1 Timothy, Paul describes the qualifications of bishops (3:1-7) and deacons (3:8-13). The fact that he omits elders here would argue that they were the same as bishops. (5) Titus 1:5-7). (6) Clement of Rome's First Epistle (*ca.* A.D. 95) clearly uses "bishops" and "elders" interchangeably.

It is not without significance that Jerome, writing near the end of the fourth century, recognizes this identity of the two. He says: "Among the ancients, bishops and presbyters are the same, for the one is a term of dignity, the other of age." Again he writes: "The Apostle plainly shows that presbyters are the same as bishops." In a third passage he says: "If any one thinks the opinion that the bishops and presbyters are the same, to be not the view of the Scriptures, but my own, let him study the words of the apostle to the Philippians." Other Church Fathers, such as Chrysostom, asserted the same thing. Lightfoot goes so far as to say: "Thus in every one of the extant commentaries on the epistles containing the crucial passages, whether Greek or Latin, before the close of the fifth century, this identity is affirmed" (p. 99).

Blameless (1:6)

Five different Greek words are translated "blameless"

in the NT. They all begin with *a*-negative, but have little else in common. *Amemptos* (five times) is rendered "faultless" in Heb. 8:7. It literally means "free from fault." *Amōmētos* occurs only once in the best Greek text (2 Pet. 3:14). *Anaitios*, "guiltless," is found only in Matt. 12:5, 7. *Anepilēmptos* (1 Tim. 3:2; 5:7; 6:14) means "without reproach." The word here, *anengklētos* (five times in NT), literally means "not called to account," and so "unreproveable" (Col. 1:22). It is obvious that the idea of blamelessness bulks large in Paul's thinking about church officials.

The apostle proceeds to designate some ways in which a bishop or elder must be blameless. He must not be:

Selfwilled or Arrogant? (1:7)

Authadēs (only here and 2 Pet. 2:10) literally means "self-pleasing." It carries the idea of "stubborn" or "arrogant." Bauernfeind says that in the NT "the reference is to human impulse violating obedience to the divine command" (TDNT, 1:509).

Soon Angry or Quick-tempered? (1:7)

Orgilos is found only here in the NT. It is based on *orgē*, "anger," and so means "inclined to anger." Probably "quick-tempered" (NIV) is the way we would say it now.

Not Given to Wine (1:7)

The word *paroinos* (only here and 1 Tim. 3:3) is compounded of *para*, "beside," and *oinos*, "wine." It describes one who stays by the wine. This was obviously a common fault in that day. *Plēktēs*, "striker" or brawler, is also found only here and in 1 Tim. 3:3. *Aischrokerdēs* (greedy of base gain, "given to filthy lucre") occurs only here and in 1 Tim. 3:8. It is a sad commentary on those times that bishops would have to be warned against such conduct!

Good Men or Good? (1:8)

In verse 8 there are two compounds of *philos,* "lover." The first, *philoxenon,* literally means "a lover of strangers," and so "hospitable." The second is *philagathon* (only here in NT). It means "lover of good"—not "good men," but a lover of what is good. It denotes high moral character, not just an affection for good people (cf. NIV).

Temperate or Self-controlled? (1:8)

The word *enkratēs* is found only here in the NT. Basically it means, "strong, powerful." Then it came to mean "self-controlled" (NIV). Someone has defined gentleness as "strength under control." That is what real gentleness is. Meekness isn't weakness. It is power in the control of divine love.

Self-deceivers (1:10)

In verse 10 there are two *hapax legomena*—words found only once in the NT. The first is *mataiologoi,* "vain talkers," those who talk idly. The second is *phrenapatai,* "deceivers." Literally it means "a deceiver of his own mind" (A-S). Goodspeed translates the whole phrase, "who deceive themselves with their empty talk."

Abominable or Detestable? (1:16)

The word *bdelyktos* is found only here in the NT. It is a strong term, meaning "abominable" or "detestable" (NIV). Probably the second term is more contemporary.

As Becometh Holiness (2:3)

This phrase is one word in Greek, *hieroprepēs* (only here in NT). It means "suited to a sacred character." Every Christian is set apart to God, and so is sacred. We should suit our daily lives to that exalted and exalting concept.

Given or Slaves?

The apostle warns that the "aged women" (*presbytidas*, only here in NT) should not be "given" to much wine. This is the perfect passive participle of *douloō*, which means "to enslave." So the best translation here is "not slaves to much wine."

Keepers at Home (2:5)

This rendering does not catch the exact emphasis of the original. The term *oikourgos* (only here in NT) means a "worker at home." The young women are urged to take care of the home as their first responsibility.

That Cannot Be Condemned (2:8)

This phrase is one word in Greek, the adjective *akatagnōstos* (only here in NT). It literally means "not open to just rebuke." We can hardly hope in this life to escape all condemnation from men. But we should seek to live in such a way as to avoid any justifiable criticism.

Peculiar or Precious? (2:14)

There is perhaps no word in the KJV that is more misleading today than the term "peculiar." That English term now means "odd" or "eccentric." The Greek word has nothing to do with such a caricature of Christianity.

The word *periousios* simply means "one's own, of one's own possession" (A-S). Cremer notes that the term signifies "more than a mere possession"; it is rather "a treasure." He adds: "Accordingly *periousios* is what constitutes *a costly possession, a specially chosen good, that which is a costly possession*" (p. 242). Arndt and Gingrich suggest that the real meaning is "chosen." They note that a married man is called *periousios*, "the chosen one."

Preisker writes: "By Jesus' work of redemption God has created for Himself a people which is for Him a costly possession" (TDNT, 6:58). He also quotes Debrunner as saying that *periousios* is "the people which constitutes the crown jewel of God" (p. 57).

The time was when one would occasionally hear somebody testify, "I praise the Lord that I am one of God's *peculiar* people." The person who talked that way had a sad misconception of what this passage means. When we say today that a certain person is "peculiar," we mean that he is queer, that he's an oddball. It doesn't bring any glory to God or the church when we try to be odd in order to prove that we are holy.

The best advertising of holiness of life is not done by those who dress, act, or talk in a "peculiar" way. It is done by those who are Christlike in their attitudes and who are "zealous of good works." One can be so absorbed—if not actually obsessed—with being "peculiar" that he fails to emphasize as he should the last phrase of this verse. If he were as zealous about doing kind deeds to others as he was about trying to prove that he was "different" from them, he might win many more people to the Lord. Fortunately there are those who have caught this truth and by their kind, friendly attitude are winning new converts.

Despise (2:15)

In 1 Tim. 4:12, Paul says to his younger colleague, "Let no man despise thy youth." There the word is *kataphroneō*, "think down on." Here it is *periphroneō*, "think around" (on all sides). That is, don't let anyone think around you. A. T. Robertson says that the term in 1 Tim. 4:12 is a stronger word of scorn, "but this one implies the possibility of one making circles around one and so 'out-thinking' him." Then he adds this pertinent observation: "The best way for the modern minister to command respect for his 'authority' is to do thinking that will deserve it" (WP, 4:605).

Put Them in Mind (3:1)

The verb *hypomimnēskō* occurs seven times in the NT. It means "cause to remember." In three passages (2 Tim. 2:14; 2 Pet. 1:12; Jude 5) it is translated "put in remembrance." In John 14:26 it is "bring to remembrance." The simplest translation in all cases is "remind" (NIV).

Principalities and Powers (3:1)

The Greek simply says that we are to be in subjection "to rulers *(archais)*, to authorities *(exousiais)*." Today "principality" refers to a territory ruled by a prince.

To Obey Magistrates (3:1)

The Greek has only one word, *peitharchein*, "to be obedient." Polybius said that the Cretans were notorious for a revolutionary spirit. Paul urges here, as in Rom. 13:1, that Christians must be in subjection to governmental authorities. We should be "ready to every good work," so that we won't get in trouble with the authorities, for "rulers are not a terror to good works, but to evil" (Rom. 13:3).

Speak Evil or Slander? (3:2)

The verb is *blasphēmeō* from which we get "blaspheme." That is what it means when directed toward God. When directed to man, it means "to revile, to rail at, slander" (A-S). There is another verb, *kakologeō,* that means "speak evil of." The one here is better translated "slander" (NIV).

No Brawlers or Peaceable? (3:2)

The adjective *amachos* occurs only here and in 1 Tim. 3:3. It literally means "not fighting." Probably the best translation is "not contentious," or simply "peaceable" (NIV). A quarrelsome Christian is a troublemaker in the church and a disgrace to the cause of Christ. One who likes to fight with people should shut himself up alone with God until divine grace has changed his disposition.

Serving or Slaves to? (3:3)

Again it is the verb *douleuō,* which means to be a slave to someone or something. People are not just serving sin; they are enslaved to it. This has been vividly and horribly illustrated in the last few years by those who are addicted to drugs.

Hateful or Hated? (3:3)

The adjective *stygētos* is found only here in the NT.

It is a strong word. The cognate adjective *stygeros* means *"hated, abominated, loathed,* or *hateful, abominable, loathsome"* (LSJ, p. 1657). So *stygētos* means "hated, abominated, hateful" *(ibid.).*

Speaking of the train of "lusts and pleasures" mentioned earlier in this verse, E. K. Simpson refers to "the malice and jealousy it breeds and the seething cauldron of hatred it foments" (p. 114). This is in startling contrast to the beautiful picture of God's grace in the next verse.

It will be noted in the definitions given above that the first meaning of *stygētos* is "hated." This is adopted in many recent versions. The TCNT has, "Detested ourselves and hating one another." Weymouth reads, "Deserving hatred ourselves and hating one another." The NEB has, "We were odious ourselves and we hated one another." Similar is Goodspeed: "Men hated us and we hated one another." It may well be that this is the preferable translation, since "hateful, and hating one another" would be repetitious. The NIV has "being hated."

Kindness Toward Men (3:4)

The kindness of God toward men is put in striking contrast to the unkindness of men to each other (v. 3). The adjective *chrēstotēs* is used only by Paul in the NT (10 times). In the KJV it is translated "goodness" (or "good") five times, all in Romans. Elsewhere it is "kindness," except "gentleness" as a fruit of the Spirit (Gal. 5:22).

Its original meaning was "goodness" or "uprightness," and it probably has that sense in Rom. 3:12. Then it came to mean "kindness" or "generosity." Trench speaks of it as "a beautiful word, as it is the expression of a beautiful grace" (p. 232). Jerome (fourth century) speaks of it as a spontaneous disposition to bless. Bernard says that it "signifies the *graciousness* of the Divine love for man" (p. 177). It has also been said that John 3:16 indicates what it really means.

Love . . . Toward Man (3:4)

This is one word in Greek, *philanthrōpia*, from which comes *philanthropy*. Compounded of *philia*, "love," and *anthrōpos*, "man," it literally means "love for man." In the NT it is found only here and in Acts 28:2.

In Hastings' *Dictionary of Christ and the Gospels*, W. W. Holdsworth has a helpful article on "Philanthropy." In it he makes this significant observation: "Philanthropy is the immediate product of the Incarnation" (2:357). He shows how Christ took the instinct of human pity for human suffering and transformed it into "love unto the uttermost" (p. 356). The article closes with this beautiful statement: "Philanthropy is love without limit, and love is of God, for God is LOVE" (p. 359).

Washing (3:5)

Two verbs are translated "wash" in the NT. *Niptō* means to wash a part of the body, as the hands or face. But *louō* means to bathe the whole body. The noun here, *loutron*, is derived from the second. It occurs (in NT) only here and in Eph. 5:26, where we find the expression "washing of water by the word." That apparently means the same as "the washing of regeneration" here—what Weymouth calls "the bath of regeneration." This underscores the fact that in the experience of regeneration all our sins are washed away and the stain of them is gone.

Regeneration (3:5)

The word *palingenesia* is compounded of *palin,*

"again," and *genesis,* "birth." So it literally means a new birth—an expression we use today for conversion. In the NT it occurs only here and in Matt. 19:28, where it is used for the regeneration of the earth. Here, of course, it describes the new birth of the individual.

Renewing or Renewal? (3:5)

The noun *anakainōsis* (only here and Rom. 12:2) comes from the verb meaning "to make new." Since it is a noun, probably "renewal" (NIV) is a better rendering than "renewing." It refers to the work of the Holy Spirit in the new birth, making us new creatures in Christ Jesus.

Heretic or Factious? (3:10)

The Greek word is *haireticos* (only here in NT), from which we get "heretic." An adjective, it comes from the verb meaning "to choose." So it literally means "capable of choosing" and then (as in Plato) "causing division." While Arndt and Gingrich allow that it may "perhaps" mean "heretical," they prefer "factious, causing divisions." That is probably its correct meaning here, rather than doctrinal deviation.

In secular Greek *hairesis* was used for a doctrine and for a school which held this particular teaching. Josephus uses it for the three *haireseis*—Pharisees, Sadducees, and Essenes. We would call them "sects" of Judaism. Finally, in Rabbinic Judaism the term was used for groups that were opposed by the rabbis, and so were stigmatized as "heretical." This usage was taken over by Christianity and applied especially to Gnostic sects. (See article by Schlier in TDNT, 1:180-85.)

PHILEMON

❧❀❧

A Prisoner of Christ (1)

Paul could truthfully have said, "I'm a prisoner of the Roman emperor." Instead he identified himself as "a prisoner of Christ Jesus" (NIV). He was a prisoner not of fate, but in the divine will. That made all the difference.

The word for "prisoner" is *desmios,* which comes from the verb *deō,* "bind." So this adjective means "bound" or "captive," and as a substantive, "a prisoner."

We find the same phrase as here in Eph. 3:1 and similar expressions elsewhere in these Prison Epistles. Kittel writes: "There can be no doubt that the actual imprisonment of Paul everywhere underlies the usage. But this real imprisonment is set in relation to Christ and the Gospel" (TDNT, 2:43).

Perhaps we can go a step further and say that Paul was bound to Christ as His prisoner. That made him actually a free man in the Roman prison.

Communication or Sharing? (6)

This is the familiar word *koinōnia,* which means "fellowship" or "communion." But the sense that fits best here is "sharing." Paul wanted his converts to be effective in sharing their faith.

Acknowledging or Knowledge? (6)

Thayer says that *epignōsis* means *"precise and correct knowledge;* used in the N.T. of the knowledge of things ethical and divine" (p. 237). The better translation is "knowledge" (NASB) or "full understanding" (NIV). Lightfoot calls attention to an interesting fact: "In all the epistles of the Roman captivity St. Paul's prayer for his correspondents culminates in this word *epignōsis"* (p. 336). (See Eph. 1:17; Phil. 1:9; Col. 1:9.)

Bowels or Hearts? (7, 12, 20)

We have already discussed the term *splanchnon* in Phil. 1:8 (see comments there). But here it occurs three times in this short Epistle of one chapter. One should avoid reading the KJV of these passages in public worship. The correct translation is "heart," not "bowels."

Enjoin or Order? (8)

The word *epitassō* is a strong compound verb meaning "order, command" (AG, p. 302). Occurring 10 times in the NT, it is translated (in KJV) "command" 8 times and "charge" once. Only here is the weak rendering "enjoin" found. The best translation is "order" (NASB, NIV).

Convenient or Proper? (8)

The verb *anēkō* is used here in an impersonal way with an ethical sense: "it is fitting (or, proper)." The KJV "convenient" is completely misleading today. In the seventeenth century "convenient" did mean "fitting" (OED, 2:935). But now "what is convenient" may be exactly the opposite of "what is proper." The latter, of course, is the correct meaning here (cf. NASB, NIV). Doing "what is convenient" rather than what is right is bad ethics.

The Aged or An Ambassador? (9)

The Greek word is *presbytēs* (only here and in Luke 1:18; Titus 2:2). In the other two passages it clearly means "an old man," the translation adopted here in the NIV (cf. "the aged," NASB). But in the Septuagint it is just as clearly used as an alternative form for *presbeutes,* "an ambassador." Lightfoot argues strongly for that meaning here (pp. 338-39). But Vincent says, "'Ambassador' does not seem quite appropriate to a private letter, and does not suit Paul's attitude of entreaty" (ICC, p. 184).

Unprofitable . . . Profitable (11)

It is well known that the name Onesimus (v. 10) means "profitable." But a different root is used here. In verse 11 the Greek has *achrēston . . . euchrēston.* The first of these two words begins with *a*-negative, followed by *chrēston,* "useful"—so "useless" (NASB, NIV). The second has the prefix *eu,* which means "good" or "well."

Mind or Consent? (14)

The Greek word *gnōmē* did have the meaning "mind" in classical Greek (A-S). But Bultmann shows that it is used in the sense of "consent" in 2 Maccabees and Josephus (TDNT, 1:717). Thayer suggests that translation for this passage (p. 119), as do also Arndt and Gingrich

(p. 162). It seems that the best rendering is, "without your consent" (NASB, NIV).

Joy or Benefit? (20)

The verb is *oninēmi* (only here in NT). Arndt and Gingrich translate this passage, "Let me have some benefit from you in the Lord" (p. 573).

Wrote or Write? (20)

The KJV uses the past tense in verse 12 ("I have sent"), in verse 19 ("I have written"), and in verse 21 ("I wrote"). The NIV gives the correct (present tense) translation: verse 12, "I am sending"; verse 19, "I am writing"; verse 21, "I write." It is true that the Greek has in each case the aorist indicative, which ordinarily indicates past time. But we have here what is called "the epistolary aorist." From the standpoint of the reader of the letter the action was past. But from the standpoint of the writer it was just taking place. Paul was at that very moment "writing," and he was getting ready to send Onesimus back to his master Philemon with this personal letter. So from the standpoint of our usage today the past tense in English is incorrect.

Lodging (22)

Paul writes to Philemon, "Prepare me also a lodging: for I trust"—the Greek says "hope"—"that through your prayers I shall be given unto you." The Greek word for "lodging" is *xenia* (now sometimes the name for a city). Literally it means "hospitality." Then it came to mean "a guest room" (AG; cf. NIV). The word occurs only here and in Acts 28:23.